MYSTERIES
OF THE
UNIVERSE
- UNVEILED

MYSTERIES
OF THE
UNIVERSE
- UNVEILED

An Entirely Different Perspective- On The Laws
That Govern The Universe and its Functioning

SATYA PRAKASH VERMA
SATYENDRA

PARTRIDGE
A Penguin Random House Company

Print information available on the last page

To order additional copies of this book, contact
Partridge India
000 800 10062 62
orders.india@partridgepublishing.com

www.partridgepublishing.com/india

To

My Late Parents…

Janki Rani and Dr. Shivnarayan

"Oh God, Kindly give us the power
to realize the truth, and
accept it as well"

"From Darkness to Light
Kindly lead us Oh Lord"

CONTENTS

ABOUT THIS BOOK AND ITS MOTIVE

For almost last sixty years, I have pondered, from time to time, on different subjects with an entirely different angle that is far too different from that of the rest of the world. However, all through these years I never thought of writing down my ideas. I had to pay the price of this lethargy and indifference; most of my thoughts have been lost forever.

Now, when I have almost outlived my life, I have realized that it's important to preserve remaining thoughts to protect them from being buried along with me and letting my entire line of thinking to vanish. I have now decided not to bear the burden of some bizarre, queer or puzzling thoughts alone for the rest of my life; I want to put this burden on the heads of those who would willingly accept the same. I hope that at least a few, out of all the readers, would examine these puzzling thoughts and try to find out their answers. Aforesaid hope has taken the shape of this book, which is on the subject that is related to Cosmology and Astrophysics. *Although numerous books have been written on these subjects till to date,* **but this book is much different from all of them; had there been nothing new to write on the subject, I wouldn't have written this book, wherein I have revealed a different and unique angle on the subject, which nobody might have even imagined so far.**

This book has been written especially for the nonspecialist readers who avert racking their minds to analyze and understand complicated scientific theories; they simply take it for granted that these theories are absolutely correct. In this book some of the well-established theories have been analyzed using simple logics and arguments enabling the prospective readers to verify these theories themselves, side by side, according to their own wisdom and viewpoint, and to find out what could be right and acceptable. The main objective of this book is to induce readers to develop a habit of not to accept even complicated looking matters without analyzing and understanding them properly.

I would like to make it clear that I'm not an expert on these subjects. Higher physics, higher math, or cosmological sciences, etc. have never been my subjects. I really do not have any deep, and crystal-clear knowledge required to write such a book; this is in fact my bold and unauthorized effort to take up this subject. In order to compensate my inadequacy disclosed above, I had to contemplate a lot about various aspects of the subject matter. *This book has purely resulted from the said contemplation of mine.*

There is only one justification for writing this book that is, **"some of the solutions deduced by our scientists didn't appear to be feasible, to me at least."** Hence, I want to spread a general awareness, of such problems, amid as many as I can. In other words, I want to spread this curiosity and disapproval, among as many people as I can, by putting my efforts out there, for consumption by others too. **If, this dream of mine comes true, then this would be a great achievement and a huge reward to me.**

In order to achieve this goal, I have, by means of this book, tried to raise questions on some of the apparent anomalies in the prevailing theories that have been bothering me since long. I hope that these questions might arouse reader's interest in this subject and compel them too, to contemplate over them. **For me this book is the tool not only to search the truth myself alone, but to induce others too, to do the same.**

In this book I have, by going beyond my limits, also suggested solutions to some of the problems. Such suggestions might not be based on conventional scientific theories. However, if these suggestions are rejected without being examined, then this would be unjust not only to me, but probably unfortunate for science as well. **I can only hope that my thinking is not regarded as negative or reverse thinking or as an unnecessary effort to "split the hair." In fact, neither I have opposed any theory just for the sake of opposition, and nor my thoughts have gone aberrant in any way; I have, after long deliberations at my level, brought out only that what appeared correct to me.** I would request the readers, who would disagree with me, to evaluate various logics put forth in this book minutely, before forming any opinion on such points.

The circumstances, under which errors are prone to unknowingly creep into any theory, are especially described in chapter-1 of this book. Under such circumstances, it becomes almost impossible to identify that when and where the error was committed. **Therefore, I have not hesitated to put questions on some prevailing conceptions without caring that how great were the scientists who put forth such theories, or how low is my status as compared to them?** I have questioned only those theories that didn't appear justified to me. That simple it is; raising questions is the easiest of all things in the world, isn't it? **You would agree that questions, with a definite aim, are the best tools for deducing correct answers; science seeks answer to each and every question.**

Very few of the readers might agree with the points raised by me, whereas, others will disagree. I feel that if any probable error, which comes into the notice of anybody, is not highlighted, then, such an error, if it actually exists, could never be eliminated. **My aim, in pointing out probable errors, is only to enable the scientists, if they feel like, to identify and eliminate these errors; my intention is not to condemn anybody.** In this world of uncertainties, **anybody is likely to commit errors** under the circumstances described in chapter-1 of this book, **may he be an eminent scientist, or a layman.**

I would like to make it clear that English not being my language, this book was written originally in "Hindi," the National Language of India. Since my aim is to reach out to as many readers as I can, I have translated this book in English. And, since the sentences in Hindi differ vastly from those made in English, the language of this book might appear a little odd to the readers. I, therefore, request the readers not to judge this book, simply by the language, please evaluate my work by the ideas included in this book, and the alternate angle with which I have viewed various theories.

I don't know whether I have presented my thoughts properly, and to what extent I would be able to achieve my aim. I believe that I have completed my job to the best of my ability; now your turn has begun, you have to decide the fate of this book. I am sure if the book has any substance, then it would certainly establish its place, else it would be lost in the darkness of anonymity. The book will meet the same fate if the readers would not pay any attention on the stuff of this book, or they would negate the arguments made in this book without even trying to understand and analyze them. *However, I feel that this book is like a bomb that has capability to shatter a few misconceptions at least, and bring drastic changes in the world of science, but this bomb is bound to fail to click or explode, because nobody would be willing to accept the alternate ideas brought-out in this book. I would therefore, advice the curious readers who are really interested in this subject, that they shall read this book with patience and without any bias towards the scientific theories prevailing in the present era, so that they can understand the substance of this book; if they do so then, and only then they would understand the spirit of this book and enjoy it; they will start to view our scientific theories with a different and unique angle.*

— **Satya Prakash Verma**

PART – 1

EVOLUTION
OF SCIENCE
&
ITS FUNDAMENTAL LAWS

1: THE JOURNEY OF SCIENCE.

Science and primitive-man both evolved and flourished side by side; this will continue in the future as well. Monkey-type ancestors of human-being, such as "Ardipithecus Kadabba," "Pan Prior" and some other similar species came into existence as early as five to eight million years in the past. Species named "Australopithecus," having mixed features of the Apes and the Humankind, existed about two million years ago or even earlier. As the time passed on, above species either became extinct or due to natural selection and transmutation, they evolved into different kinds of primitive manlike creatures. The modern human species were supposed to have evolved about two to three hundred thousand years ago. Of late, stone tools as old as 2.3 million years have been discovered. 300-thousand years old hearth has also been found in Israel. These discoveries indicate that the human species might have evolved much earlier. In the beginning, the humankind used to live like wild animals. The only difference, between them and other animals, was that the humankind had much bigger brains. The primitive man was more curious; he used to observe each and everything with great curiosity, and also tried to understand such happenings. This extra curiosity and his lust to know the "unknown," separated the mankind, very slowly, from other animals.

Primitive man, according to the capacity of his mind, tried to understand all the strange-looking events that used to happen all-around, and tried to solve different problems faced by him in the day-to-day life. Continuous pondering, over these problems, resulted in the gradual development of his mind. Very slowly his knowledge and the ambit of his curiosity also kept on increasing. From thence perhaps, some bizarre, some strange and curious questions might have started to bother him, such as "what is the difference between live and dead bodies, what is life, what is death; how the death could be skipped, etc.?" Probably some other problems that might have bothered him were "what the stellar objects like the Sun, Moon and various stars, etc., are? Where they come from and where do they disappear in the night, etc.?" Such complicated questions have been bothering the human race since the eternal times; similar questions still bother him even in the present era, with the same severity.

Almost since last 200-thousand years, various tribesmen, depending upon the capacity of their undeveloped minds, have fabricated some weird stories that our world was created merely according to the wishes of some Divine-self; such propositions were probably the easiest and most acceptable solutions at those times and in the present era too. Commoners always look for the easiest solutions, for which they don't need to exert their brains, even by a bit. However, such religious beliefs couldn't deter some curious people from traveling, Far-East and West, in search of the homes of the sun, moon and stars, etc. In spite of such unfruitful efforts, mankind never accepted defeat, or gave-up his efforts. His curiosity persistently compelled him to think-over again and again. Consistent racking of the brain resulted in the gradual enhancement of the ambit of his quest. In this effort the mankind established relation between some constellations of stars and the cycle of different seasons; later on, such observations helped them a lot in cultivation.

Never-ending necessities of the human beings always got preference over his unquenchable curiosities. No matter whether we fail to understand any complicated and strange-looking phenomenon, or could not find the answers to any quaint questions, the world, anyhow, goes on with its own ways, keeping its own pace. The everlasting issues of "hunger" and "security" always keep bothering the man persistently. Fulfilling these necessities always gets priority over all other things. The man, according to his necessities, made weapons, started to rear cattle, started cultivation and built huts. Very soon the hutments developed into villages and then into cities. With such changes his necessities persisted to grow. In spite of the intensity of the necessities, his lust to explore the unknown, kept on bothering a handful of curious people. The degree of complicacy of those eternal questions that existed in the prehistoric times couldn't yet be diluted a bit. Although such questions were neglected or ignored by the masses, some curious people, who were considered eccentric, obsessed or even crazy, and who were not concerned with the worldly problems, continued their efforts to find solutions to these enigmatic questions. From time to time different people, in accordance with the capacity of their undeveloped minds, immature contemplations and limited observations, etc., put-forth different speculative solutions. During each era, such solutions would have been able to satisfy the curiosity of the masses for short periods only. However, shortcomings of such solutions would have become evident after some time, which would have led to new questions. As a result, new solutions would have been thought of, repeatedly, and accordingly the old speculations would have been modified again-and-again, or even abandoned.

Right from the very beginning, only the witch-doctors, chiefs of the tribe, those elders who were considered most wise among all, or any other influential man having a superior position in the society, enjoyed authority to give speculative explanations of any natural phenomenon. The speculations of such influential people must have been considered very wise and knowledgeable thoughts, which would have been transferred from one generation to the next. Only some other powerful man, or witch-doctor, could dare to give another explanation of such phenomena. Any attempt by a common man to do so was sure to attract death penalty. The self-pride and arrogance of the people occupying top positions in the society, and their "mental inertia," that is, dogged-belief in their own conceptions, always thwarted development of any new thought. Such people never allow any new thought, other than the prevailing ones, to flourish. On looking back into the history we find that Socrates was forced to take poison; discoveries published by Copernicus, just before his death, were ignored; Giordano (Filippo) Bruno* was burned alive in the year 1600, and later on, Galileo was put under house arrest; death penalty awarded to him was revoked only on the condition that he shall agree that the sun orbits the earth. Many times in the past, such obdurateness, of the powerful people, resulted in the thriving of wrong concepts for several generations. As a result, journey of science was, several times, diverted to negative direction. Such obstructions resulted in slowing down the rate of progress of science, but they couldn't stop its progress forever. Even under these circumstances the ambit of knowledge has always kept on growing, however, with much slower rate. In fact, knowledge continued to March onward, and the same was enriched step by step, that is, the knowledge gathered by earlier generations was refined and further improved by new generations, by way of some additions and also by the elimination of some of the mis-concepts. A sequence of such improvements and misconceptions has continued since the beginning; the same is going-on even in the present era too.

Preliminary scientific concepts are always based on imaginations, guesswork and hypotheses, which are later-on, tested on the criterion of truth. However, complete truth could never be discovered in one go; truth in several small parts only, could be unveiled at a time, that too each of such part-truths could be discovered after a long gap of time in between each of such discoveries. ***It is an irony that in spite of the fact that each part-truth is also a truth in itself, the same is not a comprehensive truth, and therefore, the same may differ from the complete truth.*** At times when a rat couldn't find a way to escape, it launches counterattack on the cat. If, on the basis of this partial fact, one

---

* Bruno was the first man who proposed that the stars are distant Suns, which are surrounded by their own planets.

concludes that *"rats are capable to trounce the cats,"* then it will be a wrong conclusion based on an incomplete-truth. *This is evident from the example given below that a very clear, but incomplete-truth can differ from the absolute truth.* And, for this reason sometimes even eminent scientists, based on any incomplete fact, may unknowingly deduce wrong conclusions.

An old story may further clarify above point: once some blind students were given the opportunity to practically feel what an elephant looks like? In order to have a real feel, different student touched or groped different body parts of the elephant; and, accordingly, they developed different conceptions. The student, who touched the leg, speculated that elephant looks like a column. The one, who touched the tail, thought that it is like a rope. Likewise, another student conceptualized that elephants are like walls and yet another student thought that elephants are like pythons. *All of the above concepts, being based on incomplete and part-truths, were totally wrong. In spite of the fact that the story of "Blind Students and the Elephant," is merely a story, the same has been repeated several times in the history of the mankind, right from the primordial times until to-date*; in fact, *this is the way science has gradually grown on its journey of evolution.* Scientists have to face similar situations on many occasions; they never get full information before devising any theory. Instead, they discover part-truths in several steps, each of which is discovered after long periods of time. *This is analogous to a concept developed by a blind man who forms an idea about the elephant by touching only one of its body-parts.* Scientists can, therefore, consider only one aspect of a problem at a time; they encounter with other aspects of the same problem, at a much later point in time. *At times, the incomplete-truth, so discovered, might lead to misconceptions.* Sometimes such misconceptions conceived by some renowned personalities, are even considered very brilliant ideas and valuable achievements. As a result *the heritage of falsified knowledge had been transferred, several times in the past, to at least, next 3-4 generations.* This becomes possible, because the common man blindly follows renowned people who are considered extremely wise; normally, no one even bothers to verify the truth; this is the greatest misfortune of the humankind. *Misjudging any fact or assuming such misconceptions as valuable discoveries, might cause science to divagate from its path of finding out the absolute truth*; a very long and valuable time might also be lost in elimination of such misconceptions.

In the present era, new and more comprehensive information may be generated every now and then, at different sources. As a result, new finding might replace the old ones. However, the bank of knowledge can never get filled-up completely; of course, it keeps on growing bit by bit, and accordingly old conclusions may have to be modified in quick successions. *Whenever any new mystery could be unveiled, it points to another, and then yet another mystery. In fact, the face of truth is covered by infinite layers of veils, if one tries to unveil the truth, then new veils come-up one after another;* **the truth, therefore, remains yet as mysterious as it was in the beginning.** Under this situation, new questions come up one after another; *curiosity of mankind could never be quenched, instead the same is enhanced on every such occasion.* This growing curiosity helps science to keep progressing gradually in various steps. Analogous to the phrase "necessity is the mother of inventions," it is also true that "Curiosity is the mother of science." Till the time, curiosity of mankind remains un-quenched, the onward march of science will continue.

×   ×   ×

Till the mankind was living the life of a wild beast, the pace of development of science, was very-very slow. After the end of last Ice-age, when life of human-being became a little easier, he might have gotten more time and chances to explore the unknown. As a result, new ways to improve agriculture, and better methods of construction were invented; new and improved weapons were also made. Some of the oldest civilizations like "Egyptian," "Maya" and "Inca," etc. had made various discoveries; however, the knowledge earned by them was lost after their fall. Probably full details of the discoveries made by Chinese scholars, during prehistoric ages, are also not available. The ancient Aryans are supposed to have migrated to India sometime around three thousand years BC, probably from the Middle or North-East Europe, where the swamps formed after the end of the last ice-age by melting of ice, facilitated abundant natural springing-up of the legendary "Vedic Soma plant." The Aryans also did remarkable discoveries in the fields of mathematics and cosmology; credit to invent the concept of "zero" goes to them. The value of "Pi" (π) and the "Pythagoras" theorem, etc. were also known to them since the ages un-known. The concept of ***atoms*** was also developed by them during the era of "Rig-Veda." Later-on, one of the Aryan scholars Aryabhata deduced, on the basis of the westward movement of the stars, that the Earth spins on its axis. He also very accurately calculated the speed of Earth's spin and the time taken by the earth to go round the sun, and also the distance between the sun and the earth. He also very accurately predicted the time of eclipses of the moon and the sun and very accurately calculated the circumference of the earth. Another scholar Vishnugupt was the first astrologer to describe the property of the earth to attract everything. Besides above, the ancient Aryans also made various other discoveries also. However, invasions by various outsiders resulted in loss of most of the discoveries made by them, especially after the destruction of "Nalanda" and "Taksh-Shila" universities of the ancient India.

The thoughts and books of the ancient Greek scholars like Aristotle, Socrates, Pluto, Ptolemy and Archimedes, etc. are still safe and well preserved, which could be considered to be authentic. Before the era of above scholars, it was believed that the Earth is like a flat plate or disk. Different beliefs related to our Earth, were prevailing at that point in time; according to some of these beliefs, it was thought that our Earth is poised either over the head of a giant snake, or on the back of a tortoise. In some other countries, it was believed that the Earth is held up by a titanic giant named Atlas, over his shoulders. Such beliefs kept lingering-on for very-very long periods of time, and the same were also accepted and adopted by various religions. During that era, it was also believed that the sun, the moon and all the stars, etc. revolve around the earth, which is the center of the entire universe. Around 300 B.C., Greek philosopher **Aristarchus** predicted that the Earth goes around the Sun but nobody took him seriously. For the next one and a half to two thousand years, the ancient belief remained unchanged. In the year 1514, **Nicolas Copernicus** said that the Sun does not orbit the earth instead the earth goes round the Sun. However, for a period of further 100 years, nobody believed him. **Galileo** in 1609, after the invention of the telescope, proved that the earth and other planets orbit the sun. He was punished for above discovery, instead of grant of any reward.

We thus see that most of the predictions, not all, made by the prehistoric philosophers were, afterward, found to be wrong. Based on this fact, we shall not infer that their wisdom, their brains were underdeveloped or inferior. In fact, instead of their brain, their means were inferior; those philosophers were, indeed, owners of very sharp minds, very sharp wit and were wisest thinkers of that era. No database of knowledge or details of the observations made by their ancestors, etc. were available to them. They also didn't possess proper facilities or sensitive and sophisticated instruments that the present-day inventors enjoy; there was nothing to guide them, or shape the line of their thinking. In the absence of any clue, guidelines or systematic strategy, they had to depend only on their imaginations and deliberations. ***Such unsubstantiated imaginations are always susceptible to aberration, especially if the very basis of such speculations is wrong.*** This point could be well understood by the example that ***if someone's calculator malfunctions or else he has pressed the wrong button then, he is certainly going to get a wrong result.*** Likewise, ***if an effort is made to solve a problem without identifying its root cause, then possibility increases manifold that he will get a wrong solution.*** This could be best understood by the story, about two wisest professors, which I read in my childhood. The same is narrated below in brief:

Once, two very learned professors, while walking down a street, saw a ball made of some alloy unknown to them. One of them, out of curiosity, touched the ball and was astonished to note that in spite of bright sunlight and smoldering heat, the ball was much cooler at the top. The other professor also examined the ball and he was also astonished to find that it much warmer at the bottom. ***Both the professors, who knew everything except for the root cause of this problem,*** instantaneously formulated two different theories and they started to discuss their theories about the abnormal behavior of that unknown material. Just at that moment a laborer came there and turned that ball upside down. When inquired the cause, the laborer said that he turns the ball, from time to time, so that it might not get overheated from any single side. ***It is clear, from this story that, it is not possible to solve any problem without establishing and properly analyzing its root cause; any solution based on wrong inputs, is sure to go wrong. If a theory is based on incomplete facts and without establishing the root cause of the problem, it won't survive for much longer periods. If a doctor makes wrong diagnosis, then he is sure to give wrong treatment, he would not be able to find the true cure of the disease.***

×   ×   ×

It is true that some of the predictions made by our ancestors were afterward found to be erroneous. But this doesn't mean that they were unwise people with underdeveloped minds. ***Such mistakes were not resulted due to the limitation of their minds; instead, it was due to limitations of their means.*** In the absence of any database ***they couldn't have established the root causes of the problems they encountered with;*** no one is supposed to establish the root cause of any complicated issue in his first attempt. ***The line of their thinking might also have been obsessed by wrong speculations made by their ancestors. Even, if a wise of the wisest man is obsessed by a misconception and prejudice, he is bound to commit mistakes.*** Looking to the fact that our ancestors were not blessed by proper means or, heritage of knowledge, the credit of their achievements goes purely to their **wisdom and efforts**. ***It is the initiative that is important; anybody can commit mistakes but very few people put efforts or take initiative.*** Efforts, made by our ancestors, roused curiosity in the minds of the next generations, inspired them to use their brains and blessed the next generations with the heritage of rich wealth of hard earned knowledge. They were pioneers of this field; we are only following the path they showed us. We are indebted to them for today's achievements of the mankind.

Brilliance and wisdom of our ancestors could be evaluated from the fact that they made some very remarkable discoveries on the basis of apparently very ordinary observations, and very limited means. The discovery made by the Greek scholar and mathematician Eratosthenes, is a very good example of this fact. About 240 years B.C., he observed that the wooden poles installed in the city of "Swenet" that is located on the Tropic of Cancer and nowadays known as "Aswan," didn't cast any shadow during summer solstice, that is, on the local noon, of June 21-22 when the sun reaches its highest position in the sky, that is, directly above our heads. However, similar poles installed in the city of "Alexandria" which is located about 800 kilometers north, did cast shadow on the same day. On the basis of this very ordinary looking fact, he proved that the earth is spherical in shape and is tilted on its axis at an angle of 27½°. On the basis of the same fact, he hadn't only calculated the circumference of the Earth, he also very accurately calculated the distance between the earth and the sun. ***Even in the present age how many people would make similar discoveries or even take notice of such an ordinary fact?***

Above quoted example brings out the fact that all the work of the ancient scholars, was not wrong; science has progressed, step by step, on the strength of their discoveries. However, at the same time they also conceived numerous miss-conceptions. Their minds might have been prejudiced by the old school of thoughts. Any misconception or prejudice, if infused in anybody's mind, not only influences and shapes the thinking of the next several generations, it also thwarts new thoughts for a long time. Most of the people normally jump to easiest solution without properly analyzing any complicated matter or identifying its root-cause, because such solutions match with their preexisting conceptions. Whenever such easier solutions are selected and accepted by the masses, then thinking of mankind becomes stagnant and keeps revolving around one point only. Analogous to the proverbial "one has to tell hundreds of lies to hide – even just a single lie," it is also true that "if a miss-concept is once formed, then hundreds of misleading pleas may come-up in its support." Results obtained from new experiments would be interpreted and explained in the way that would support the prevailing conceptions, and prove their correctness. ***Whenever a man is bent upon to prove something, then his mind starts to think only on such lines that would enable him to achieve his goal. Only such logics would sparkle in his mind which supports his contentions; he cannot think in any other line.*** It is the nature of the man that he can't visualize his mistakes and if at all he realizes any mistake, then he can't accept it easily; he persistently tries, his level best, to prove that he was correct. Such a doggedness of the mankind, results in stagnation of the progress of science for some time only, not forever. *Under such circumstances anybody's direction of thinking may stray, be he an ordinary man or a specialist. If someone is wearing colored glasses, then he won't be able to see true colors, which is not the fault of his eyes.* And therefore, *faulty preconceptions and incomplete knowledge of the root-cause of any problem, etc., are to be blamed for anybody's mistake, not any particular man in person.*

It may also so happen that, if someone's mind is completely engaged in solving a complicated problem, then he considers only big and difficult solutions, easy solutions, though readily available, either fail to attract his attention, or such solutions might appear worthless to him. The following joke, which I read during my childhood, explains this fact explicitly.

Once the cat of a great scientist gave birth to a few kittens; when the kittens grew-up, the scientist called a carpenter to make two holes in the door, big one for the cat and another smaller one, for the kittens. The scientist didn't believe the carpenter when he pointed-out that two openings are not necessary. However, when the carpenter made one hole in the door, then the cat, along with her kittens, easily passed through that opening. *This can be inferred from this joke that almost everybody normally fails to realize that at times, easier solutions may also resolve enigmatic problems. Apart from above, the roots of prejudices sometimes occupy our brains so deeply that we normally select only those possibilities, out of numerous other possibilities, which match with our preconceptions.* However, such situation doesn't persist forever; at last, new discoveries are bound to be accepted. Preconceptions may deter the progress of science for some time only, not forever.

Although, we are now backed by very sophisticated equipment, and also by very vast knowledge, the direction of our thinking is still based on the old school of thoughts. As against the age of the universe, our modern theories are only 100 to 150 years old. Any theory could be said to be good theory when the predictions made in the same are found to be true over a very long span of time. On the other hand, most of the cosmological phenomena need several millions of years to complete, we therefore didn't get sufficient time to verify and test the truthfulness of our existing theories. It would probably take much longer time, before their truthfulness could be verified properly.

Our ancestors, as early as 5-6 hundred years B.C., made several remarkable discoveries and at the same time they developed some misconceptions as well, the roots of which are still seeded in our minds very deeply. Our history is a witness of the fact that the ideology, which was once considered to be the extremity of wisdom, was, after some time, replaced by new ideas and new thoughts. Science has always made its progress in a similar manner; at times, it had to halt at several places on its way, however, its voyage kept-on cursing, though in small steps. It has happened several times in the past, and, therefore, one shall not wonder in case the history repeats its course of action, sometime in the future too. In fact the journey of science is still in its infancy; we still have a long way to go; ***who knows what will happen in the future, one shall not wonder if the journey of science takes a new turn and it adopts a new direction in the course of its development.***

2: A Broad Introduction To The Most Basic Laws of Science

Our universe is so vast and such a wondrous place that it astonishes the common man and the scientists equally. Since the 15th to 16th century, that is, after the invention of the telescope, thousands of people are gazing the sky, day and night. New discoveries are made almost every day. In order to understand that how big is our universe, it is, first, necessary to know "from how far the light of stars is reaching us and how much time it takes in this process?" The rays of light travel at an unbelievable speed of 299,792.458 kilometers in one second, in one hour it travels one billion and eighty million kilometers, or, about 9.5 trillion kilometers in one year. The distance light covers in one year, is called one light-year. Light, in spite of travelling with such a high speed, takes an unbelievably long time of more than 13 billion years, to reach us from the far distant stars. It is impossible to even imagine such vast distances. Our universe is probably spread over a much larger area. Effort to imagine such vast distances, in kilometers or miles, may bewilder us; such distances cannot even be imagined. Only our own galaxy, the Milky Way, that is, the congregation of billions of stars, of which the solar system is a member, is spread over an area measuring 1 to 1¼ hundred-thousand light-years across. Our nearest star is about 4 light-years apart, from us; light from the Sun takes only 8.3 minutes, to reach us. Light takes a time of about 5 seconds, to travel across the diameter of the Sun, and the Moon is only 1.27 light-seconds apart from us.

On one hand, our universe is so vast, and, on the other hand, it is almost impossible to see the atom, because of its tiny size. The atom, on magnifying its image over several hundred-thousand times, by means of a very powerful microscope, appears like a tiny shimmering point. As of today it is not possible to see the inner construction of the atom. The size, of a Hydrogen-atom, is almost 10 millionth of one millimeter. The nucleus of an atom is comparatively much smaller; it may be about 40 thousandths to 100 thousandths of the atom, in size. The nucleus of an atom is made up of many particles which are even much tinier in size; they are so small that their size cannot even be imagined. Several kinds of such tiny particles exist within the atom, out of which some particles have very short lives; they are destroyed within billionth part of a second. Our scientists, in order to unveil mysteries of the nature, have to keep a vigilant eye round the year on the entire universe and almost all the natural phenomena.

Above extremities might appear to be very hard to believe and beyond the imagination of a common man, but a little knowledge of the basic science might help the common man to understand the working of the universe broadly, and also the achievements of the modern science. This book is totally based on this most-fundamental knowledge of science. This book, with the help of some very simple and fundamental laws of science, points out some possible shortcomings in some of the well-established scientific theories of the modern era. In order to understand my viewpoint, some of the readers might have to abreast themselves with the most-basic lessons of science that they might have learnt during their early childhood.

No! Please don't be panicky, or afraid, of the name of science, no intricate mathematical equations or cumbersome formulae are included in this book. A very simple and basic information and definitions of some of the elementary scientific terms, etc. are given below which could be considered to be general-knowledge, or an introduction to fundamental science, most of the readers might still remember all this stuff. All those, who, very well understand these terms, may directly jump to the next chapter, without wasting their time. However, such readers who have never learnt even the elementary science, or have forgotten the earlier lessons, shall read these definitions carefully, they can easily understand them; all this stuff is very simple and easy to understand. If someone finds it difficult to understand forthcoming chapters, he may repeat these definitions; everything may become easy and clear; ***he would also have to concentrate a little, because this book brings out alternate sides of science, which are much different from the prevailing ideology.*** The readers are requested not to read this book half-heartedly, without proper interest, with indifference, or in haste; otherwise they won't be able to catch-up with the spirit of this book.

Force

Everybody must have heard that somebody is very strong, or, a storm was very powerful, etc. Nobody, by merely looking at any person or storm, can estimate their exact strength, it could only be done on the basis of the fact that how heavy load a person can lift, or how destructive the storm was. The *force* cannot be directly seen or measured, in fact, *"force"* is a quality, capacity or influence, by virtue of which, an object could either be moved or at least a tendency to move the same, could be produced.

Work

Activity, involving physical displacement of an object, is known as work. When any object is displaced from its position, even by a little bit, then, and only then, it could be said that some work has been done; no work could be performed without applying a force. If the object couldn't be moved by applying a force, then no work would be performed; only a tendency would be produced to move the object in the direction of the applied force. The amount of work done is measured by multiplying the mass of the object by the distance it was moved. However, it is not, at all, possible to move an object, in the direction opposite of the applied force; this means that *"practically, it is not possible to perform negative work."*

Energy

Energy is an indirect capacity of an object, body or machine, by virtue of which, it can perform any work or at least produce tendency to do work. In other words, energy is that indirect property or capacity, of an object, by virtue of which, it exerts a force on other objects. The energy, of any object, could also not be measured directly. The energy of any object, a machine or a person, could be measured only on the basis of the fact that how much work they are able to perform.

It is believed that energy could neither be produced nor destroyed; it could only be transformed from one form of energy to another, for example, vehicles are driven by converting heat energy into mechanical energy.

Power

In the colloquial language, it is hard to differentiate between *power* and *energy*; any one of these two words could probably be used for the same purpose. However, in the scientific sense, power means, "How much work any object, natural phenomenon or a person can perform in any given span of time." In other words, at what rate they expend or consume energy, or, simply at what rate they can do the work. Machines, in a given amount of time, can perform many times more work in comparison to any man or animal. Machines are, therefore, considered to be more powerful, because they can perform more work than the living beings, in much smaller time periods.

Inertia

The property of matter, by virtue of which it tends to continue, or maintain its existing state of rest or uniform motion, or it resists any change in any one of above two states, it is called **"inertia."** Any matter or object because of its inertia, continues to remain in its existing position of rest till any force is not applied to displace it. Likewise, a moving object will continue to move with steady speed, until it is not stopped by applying a force, for example, the brakes have to be, necessarily, applied to stop a moving vehicle.

Since heavier objects have more inertia, which is directly proportional to their respective masses, the weight of an object, or more accurately its mass, is also sometimes considered to be its inertia. Greater force is, therefore, required to induce motion in heavier objects, that is, to break their inertia. Likewise, greater force, proportionate to the mass of moving bodies, is required to stop them. On the earth, all the moving objects come to halt without applying any direct force, due to friction, however, the celestial bodies like our Earth, the moon and all the stars, etc. are moving on their respective paths since eternity, because the space doesn't offer any resistance, or friction, they, therefore, keep moving due to their inertia.

Speed and velocity

Speed means "how much distance an object, person or energy wave such as light (photon), etc. travels in a unit time, for example, one second, one minute or one hour, etc." Similarly, speed in any particular direction, is called velocity. Difference between speed and velocity can be understood by the example of a car negotiating curvature of the road, with a steady speed. In spite of the fact that the car maintains unchanged speed its velocity would still undergo continuous change due to continuous change of direction.

In case, the force causing an object to move, is removed after imparting certain speed to that object, even then, that object, will continue to move with a steady speed in the same direction, due to its inertia, subject to the condition that no force causes it to accelerate or retard its speed. The bullet fired from a gun is the best example of this fact. The bullet after leaving the gun is stopped by friction of the air and the gravitational force of the Earth.

Acceleration

If the force, causing any object to move, is not withdrawn, then the speed, rather, velocity of such an object would continue to increase under the influence of that force. This increasing speed, rather the rate of increase of speed, is called acceleration. For example the velocity of falling objects continues to increase because the gravitational force keeps acting on them, continuously.

Momentum

Momentum, in the language of physics, represents energy stored in any moving object; such stored energy is proportional to the product of its mass and velocity. Everybody might have noticed that heavier hammers are more effective while driving nails into the wall. This suggests that any moving body possesses some energy, which is stored within it. The heavier is the body, or faster is the rate at which the same is moving, proportionately more is its stored-energy. Such energy, stored in moving masses, is called momentum, and the same is proportional to the driving force that causes it to move.

Angular Momentum

Similar to the property of momentum of the moving bodies, energy is also stored in the rotating objects; such energy is also proportional to the mass of rotating bodies and their rotational speeds. Angular momentum is an important property of rotating bodies because it resists any change in the rotational axis or in other words, it gives stability to the axis of rotation of such rotating objects. Bikes or motorcycles, etc. have become inseparable part of our day-to-day life; the angular momentum of their rotating wheels and the engines provides balance to the moving bikes.

Centrifugal Force

Everybody might have observed that when an object, tied to a rope, is swung in a circular path, by swinging the rope, than some tension is produced in the rope which depends on the rotational speed of that object. The faster the rope is swung, the higher is the tension produced. The force applied by the hand, acts on the object through the rope, and tries to throw it away, whereas, the rope doesn't allow it to go anywhere. A velocity in a straight line, and perpendicular to the rope, is produced in that object, and accordingly, the object, because of its inertia, tends to move in a straight line; the rope, however, pulls it back. In this way the direction of its velocity keeps on changing continuously; the object tries to move in a straight path, but the rope forces it to go round in a curved path. Tension in the rope is produced due to this reason, which goes on increasing with the increase in the rotational speed. If the rope is released, then the object flies-off in a straight path and falls at a far-off distance. The force that causes such object moving in a circular path, to move away from the center, is called **"Centrifugal Force."** As a reaction to the tension produced in the rope, another force is also produced in the rope, which acts in the opposite direction, i.e., toward the center. Such force is called **"Centripetal Force."** In fact the centrifugal force produced in any object, due to its circular motion, results due to its inertia; the object tries to move in a straight path but the centripetal force acting toward the center, causes it to move in a circular path.

Matter and its construction

Almost everyone might be conversant with the fact that matter is made of very tiny particles like molecules and atoms. Normally matter is found in three forms, that is, elements, compounds and mixtures. Matter in the form of elements consists of only one type of atoms. The molecules of compounds are made of two or more types of atoms, which chemically combine with each other, due to which, an entirely different substance is formed; properties of compounds, so formed, differ entirely from the parent elements. In any mixture, molecules or atoms, of different compounds or elements, could be mixed in any ratio, without being coalesced chemically. Due to this reason each and every ingredient of a mixture, retains its original properties.

Almost everybody also knows that atoms are also not indivisible; they are also made of much tinier particles. It is believed that construction of atom is somewhat similar to our solar-system. The atom has a heavy core or "Nucleus," which are made of positively charged particles "Protons" and electrically neutral particles known as "Neutrons." Almost the whole of the mass, or weight, of the atom, is centered in its nucleus. Similar to the solar system, "Electrons," which are negatively charged particles, and which are supposed to be almost weightless, revolve around the nucleus. The charge of the electrons and the protons are equal in value, but are opposite in direction. Different elements are made of different numbers of electrons and protons, but atoms of each element contain equal numbers of electrons and protons, because of which their electrical charges apparently neutralize each other. And therefore, atoms of each and every element are normally found in neutral or charge-less condition. In short, the matter is made of different kinds of particles and different kinds of electrical charges; it means **"energy is intrinsic to the matter."** The matter, which may appear to be a still, motionless and single-solid-body, is in fact, a collection of particles which are not at all still; the electrons within, move perpetually, in a violent flurry or in a swirling motion, but, this fact couldn't be noticed easily.

Atoms, of most of the elements, are normally not found alone; they normally combine either with other atoms of their own kinds, or with atoms, or group of atoms, of different elements. Such combinations produce molecules of either the same element or of entirely different matter. Molecules, or atoms of any matter, under normal conditions, could never come very close to each other; they always maintain a minimum distance between them. They may sometimes collide, but thereafter, they are pushed away immediately; under normal condition they can't merge with each other to form a new element. However, in the core of the stars where pressure and temperature is infinitely high, two atoms of Hydrogen merge into each other to form one atom of Helium. But even during such merger, positive charge remains in the nucleus, and the negative charge continues to orbit the nucleus. It is believed that matter and energy, both, could neither be created and nor destroyed.

The plasma state of matter

Everybody knows that water has three different states at different temperatures, that is, ice, water and steam. Not only water, almost all elements and many other substances have all of the above three states. If heated to a proper temperature, steel and all other metals first melt to become liquid, and then, they are transformed into the gaseous state. Likewise, when any gas is cooled, then first it liquefies, and then; solidifies. The entire universe is made of matter and its different states.

Apart from the above three states, the fourth state of matter also exists, that is, the plasma state. At very high temperatures, electrons start to break out from the molecules or atoms. If an electron is liberated from any atom, then such atom becomes positively charged, on the other hand, if one extra electron is added to it, then such atom becomes negatively charged. Such charged atoms or molecules are called "Ions" and this process is called "Ionization." Such intensively heated and ionized gas turns into a plasma state of matter. Electric bolt, an electrical spark, or a flame, etc. are some of the examples of the plasma state of the matter.

Besides high temperature, ionization could also be achieved by very high voltages and strong radiation. The glittering flash of light, seen during thunder bolt, is caused due to ionization of air molecules. Deep inside the space, where the temperature drops to almost absolute zero, or very near to it, that is, at near -273.15°C or 0°K, clouds of hydrogen gas, found in the interstellar space, also get ionized due to very powerful radiation of powerful energy waves such as gamma-rays, X-rays, cosmic rays or ultraviolet rays, etc.

In this state, the properties of matter undergo a lot of changes; matter becomes a good conductor of electricity, and it is also affected by the magnetic field. The matter in the plasma state, because of its magnetic properties, could be controlled by magnetic field and it could be confined in any desired place. Apart from gases, the Stardust, which is available in abundance in the space, is also found in ionized condition.

The Mass or quantity of matter

In scientific terms, "Mass" means the quantity of matter contained in any object or body. Most of the people could not properly differentiate between mass and weight; they think that mass and weight, both, are one and the same entities. The unit of both of them is also the same, that is, "Kilogram." But both are much different from each other. The weight of any object is, actually, the force by which, the earth pulls it towards its center. In the space, where the gravitational force is almost zero, all objects become weightless. If weight of any object is measured at different planets, by the same spring balance, then the same object would register different weights on different planets, whereas, its mass would remain unchanged. It is clear from this example that every time, different amount of pull was exerted on the same mass, by different planets, due to which different readings were obtained. It could thus, be concluded that weight and mass differ from each other.

Difference, between the quantity of matter, i.e., its mass and its weight, can also be understood in an another way: if one kilogram of corded or puffed cotton is compressed and compacted thoroughly, then, in spite of the reduction in volume, its weight would not reduce at all, because, quantity of cotton would remain unaltered, only its compactness, or density, would be increased. This means that more is the density more would be the mass, per unit volume, of a substance. It could thus, be concluded that the mass of a body, that is, the quantity of matter stored within it, probably depends on total number of atoms or more accurately on total number of protons, neutrons, etc. contained in that object.

Einstein envisaged that energy and matter, both, could be interchanged in to each other. Accordingly, mass is also defined as the total *energy* of all such particles contained in any piece of matter. Therefore, the mass is also expressed in term of *"electron-volt"* which is the unit of *energy,* as well. *"Electron-volt"* is the energy, which an electron gains from an electric field of one volt. It is also believed that the mass of tiny particles, existing within atoms, is produced by their energies; that's why both of them have the same unit of measure. Scientists also believe that a force-carrying particle named "Higgs-Boson" imparts mass to different matter particles. A brief overview of this belief is given in chapter-4 of this book.

Inertia of an object, that is, is its property to resist any change in its velocity or state of rest, directly depends on its mass. In fact, inertia of any object is produced due to its mass or quantity of matter contained in that object. In other words, more mass an object would possesses, greater would be its inertia, and similarly, lesser is the mass, lesser would be its inertia. This is the reason, perhaps, why scientists consider both of them one and the same entity.

Magnetism and Ferro Magnets

Almost everyone must be conversant with the property of "magnetism." Everybody must have observed the magnets attracting pieces of iron, or repelling other magnets. Everybody might also be conversant with magnetic effect produced by the electric current that flows in a closed circuit. Electrons, revolving around the nuclei of different atoms, create their own magnetic fields. Electrons, orbiting the nucleus, normally form pairs, which cancel magnetic fields created by each other. However, all the electrons do not form such pairs; different substances, in which atoms or molecules comprise some unpaired electrons, exhibit magnetic properties, for example, Manganese, Cobalt, and Iron, etc. The magnets made of such materials are known as **"Ferro-magnets."**

Besides ferromagnetic materials, some other materials also exhibit magnetic properties, though, in a different manner. A brief description of different types of magnetism is given below.

Ferri-Magnetism and Antiferromagnetism

Magnetisms of both the above types, though similar in nature, are different kinds of magnetism. Ferrimagnetic materials comprise two different magnetic substances. In this type of magnets, the magnetic field created by the electrons of the atoms of one of the substances, align with the external magnetic field, whereas, the magnetic field, produced by the electrons of the other substance, opposes the same. The magnetic fields created by the neighboring electrons of both of these different types of magnetic materials, point in opposite directions. However, in the Ferrimagnetic materials the field strength, in one of the directions, is comparatively stronger. Whereas in the Antiferromagnetic materials, the magnetic fields created in both the directions cancel each other, being equal in strength.

Para Magnetism

Any magnet, under normal temperature, attracts a piece of iron, or exerts a repulsive force on the other magnets. However, when magnets are heated up-to 800°C or above, they normally lose their magnetic property. Weak magnetic fields normally couldn't affect any magnetic material at such a high-temperature. Only very strong magnetic force is able to attract different magnetic materials at such a high-temperature. This kind of magnetism is called "Paramagnetism."

Diamagnetism

Almost all the nonmagnetic and carbonaceous materials possess the property of diamagnetism. Contrary to all other sorts of magnetic materials, magnetic fields always repel the diamagnetic materials. However, this repulsive force is so weak that it couldn't be even noticed. At a very low-temperature that normally exists in the space, magnetic fields exert very powerful repulsive force on all sorts of diamagnetic materials.

The magnetic properties are sometimes also found in some of the gases also; the molecules of Carbon-di-oxide gas rotate in the direction perpendicular to the magnetic field. Oxygen and Lithium have paramagnetic properties, whereas water molecules possess diamagnetic properties. Solutions of some chemicals, made with water or alcohol, also react to magnetic forces. Almost all the carbonic substances exhibit diamagnetic properties.

Superconductivity

Probably almost everyone knows that the electrical resistance of different good conductors of electricity increases at high temperatures, whereas, at lower temperatures the same decreases. In other words, conductivity increases at lower temperatures. Electric current is, in fact, a flow of free electrons through any conductor. The speed of electrons, orbiting within the atoms of any conductor, increases at elevated temperatures, and as a result, the flow of free electrons, flowing through that conductor, is obstructed; this in turn results in the increase of the resistance of that conductor. Opposite of this is also true; the resistance of a conductor decreases at low temperatures.

Scientists have observed that when some alloys or nonmetallic substances are cooled to almost absolute zero (0°K), then their conductivity increases to such an extent that once an electric current is established in a circuit, then the same continues to flow even when the source of current is removed. Such extreme conductivity is called *"Superconductivity."* Such a low temperature doesn't naturally exist on the earth. However, this is a most common feature in the space.

Superconductivity and Magnetism

Generally, super-conductive materials don't exhibit magnetic properties at normal temperatures; magnets neither attract nor repel them. When a superconductive material, having especial composition such as "Yttrium-Barium-Copper-Oxide" alloy ($YBa_2Cu_3O_7$), which comes under the category, type 2 of the superconductors, is cooled below a critical temperature by dipping it into liquid Nitrogen, then it exhibits a very strong diamagnetic property. If a very strong permanent magnet is placed over the superconductor and then cooled by liquid Nitrogen, then as soon as the temperature of superconductor drops below a critical temperature, the permanent magnet, placed on the super-conductor, suddenly levitates in the air. The reason is, as soon as the super conductor cools down below the critical temperature, the magnetic field of the permanent magnet causes the free electrons within the superconductor, to flow in a circular path, in an unrestricted manner. As a result, a magnetic field of the same polarity and strength, as that of the said permanent magnet, is induced in the superconductor. In other words, a "mirror image," of the permanent magnet, is created in the superconductor. This mirror image repels the said permanent magnet, and thereby causes it to levitate freely in the air.

Effect of the Magnetic field on the Nonmagnetic Materials

Apparently a magnetic field doesn't affect nonmagnetic materials. However, since all the nonmagnetic materials are, in fact, diamagnetic in nature, all magnets repel them with very feeble force. However, it is very hard to notice this force. This picture completely changes in very strong magnetic fields, which repeal all the carbonaceous materials such as wood, fruits, and even the living beings such as mice and frogs, etc., with such a strong force that they are forced to levitate against gravitation. Both, gravitation and magnetic forces act on such materials independently; however, effect of only the stronger force could be noticed. This fact suggests that in the space, where the temperature remains closer to absolute zero, all natural phenomena might be governed by the combined effect of these two forces.

London Moment

Sometime, during the period 1930 to 1934, scientists observed that the spinning superconductors generate magnetic fields, polarities of which, exactly line up with their axis of spin. This phenomenon is called **"London-moment."** Very low temperature to support superconductivity is a common feature out in the space, and as such combination of **superconductivity, magnetic force and gravitation, which rule the outer space, may play an important role in some of the cosmic events**. It is also believed that rotating mass may induce a weak gravitational field too; however, to the best of my knowledge, such a phenomenon could not yet be detected.

Accretion

Accretion, in general, means growth or accumulation of wealth or people. In cosmology or astrophysics, accretion means gathering of particles at any place, which results in the gradual growth of additional layers of matter. In 2003-04, astronaut Donald R. Pettit, and his college Stanley G. Love, during their stay on the space-station, performed an important experiment in almost zero gravity conditions. They shook a transparent plastic bag containing some granules of grounded coffee, salt and sugar, etc. They noticed after a few minutes that the granules, contained in that bag, started sticking together to form small clumps. *It is believed that, the formation of such clumps was caused by static electricity that was generated due to mutual rubbing of the granules.* This property of matter is of great importance in astrophysics. It is believed that during the process of formation of stars and planets, this property, as a first step, helped matter particles, which were scattered all over in the universe after the big-bang, to congregate and clump into compact clusters. With time, such clusters persisted to grow gradually, and in a period of next few million years, they formed compact cores of stars and planets, etc.

I, at the age of 11-12 years, observed that small pieces of paper those were floating, here and there, on the surface of water, clumped together, within a period of half an hour or so, in different groups. At that time, I thought that this was caused by surface tension of the water, but such grouping might have been caused, perhaps, by accretion as well. I am not sure about this phenomenon, but, if, accretion can cause small objects floating on the water surface to congregate, then the static electricity could have no role in this phenomenon. It seems to me that some sort of very feeble force of attraction, which becomes effective only in the absence of any other force, might be behind such congregation.

The Fourth Dimension

Almost everybody might be conversant with three dimensions namely length, breadth and height. Maps can show only two out of three dimensions, these two dimensions are: length and breadth; third dimension is, necessarily, required to determine the height of any object. Sometimes you might have seen that any particular article was kept at a particular place, and after some time, some other article is seen at the same place. This fact reveals that the place, though, remains the same, different articles might be kept at that particular place, at different points in time. If we can go back in time, then we can find an article, which was kept at that place, at any particular point in time. This fact indicates that dimension of time is also required to locate that article. Meaning of fourth dimension of "Time" is not limited to this extent only; in this continuously changing, rather expanding universe, fourth dimension, which is the combination of "space and time" (distances and time) is required to establish the location of celestial bodies. This continuum of space-time is also said to be expanding with a very high speed, almost with the speed of light. The system of four dimensions determines the location of any celestial object, at any particular point in time. This system includes the location of any particular event as well as the time when that event did actually happen.

The vastness of the universe is beyond imagination; a new unit of "light-year" is required to measure very large distances existing within the ambit of the universe. Light rays travel at a speed of 300,000 Km per second - even then the rays that were emitted from the furthest stars, about 13 to 14 billion years in the past, are reaching us in the present time. It is not sure whether such distant stars still exist; if they do still exist, then, by now they would have moved far-away from the place where they appear to exist. In fact, we are presently watching past of all the stars; no means are available to determine their present locations. In case a star, from which light takes more than 10 billion years to reach us, dies today or ceases to shine, even then we would continue to see the same for next 10 billion years or so. If the human species, somehow, survives for the next 10 billion years, only in that case, our future generations would see it dying. Likewise, if a star takes birth today at a location about 10 billion light-years away from us, then the living beings on Earth would see it taking birth only after 10 billion years from hence. This simply means that the star that has died today will continue to exist for us for the next 10 billion years, and similarly, the star, which has already taken birth today, wouldn't have any existence for us for the next 10 billion years. This weird phenomenon is the magic of the fourth dimension of time. What deems to be the existing time of different stars, that is, their "present," is, in fact, their past! The far-away we look back in the sky, that far back in the time we reach out; distances and time, thus appear to have merged and mingled into each other.

Location of any place on Earth could be determined by three dimensional coordinates, because all the places are stationary with respect to each other. This is not possible in the outer space where everything changes continuously with time. Every moment all the planets, all the stars keep on changing their locations; on the other hand, some stars appear to be stationary! How is it possible? Our sun along with all of its planets is orbiting the galactic center (center of the Milky Way galaxy) with an amazing speed of about 250 kilometers per second. Our Sun, moving with this speed, takes about 250 million years to complete its one orbit. Hundreds of billions of stars including our sun, contained in the Milky Way galaxy, orbit the galactic center, in such a way that the Milky Way always retains its spiral shape. Although, different stars might orbit the galactic center with different speeds, the stars located at almost equal radial distances from the center, rotate with almost equal speeds, and thus, their respective locations remain unaltered over billions of years. Such stars, therefore, appear to be almost stationary, for millions of years. At least, no alteration in their respective locations could be noticed during the life period of a man. The locations of the celestial bodies in this four-dimensional universe are therefore, determined with respect to the line joining our Sun and the nearest star named "Alfa Century." The locations of different Stars, so determined, denote the location of their past, not the present ones; which include an element of time also. Although all the stars exist in their present time, but their present locations could neither be seen, nor be determined.

Higher Science and the Mathematics of the Negative Numbers

The concept of negative numbers might have developed due to borrowing and lending of money, or other articles. Up to a certain extent, the mathematics of the negative numbers is similar to the normal or positive numbers; however, multiplication and division of the negative numbers is somewhat different. The repetitive addition of the same number is called multiplication, and likewise, the process of dividing something repeatedly into equal parts, is called Division. The negative numbers are opposite to their positive counterparts; therefore, multiplication and division of the negative numbers is a process reverse in nature to what applies to the positive numbers. If a negative number is reversed once, then it becomes positive, and if reversed yet another time, it again becomes negative. Analogous to the above phenomenon, if two negative numbers are multiplied once, then their product becomes positive. However, on multiplying them by yet another time, their product again becomes negative. Same also happens during the division of negative numbers, ***but the nature or sign of the charge of an electron in any of its multiples, whether in odd or even number, never changes.***

One should always keep in mind that everything that we find in the nature is real; nothing is imaginary or lesser than a unit number, i.e. negative. Therefore, only the real things, which exist physically, could only be borrowed or given back in the actual life; imaginary or nonexistent things couldn't be given or taken back. It is not at all possible that while in necessity you take out some money from your empty wallet and at a later point in time, when you put some money in the same wallet, then an equal amount of money, borrowed earlier, goes back in the wallet automatically and vanishes. However, numerical problems, based on similar imagination, can be solved by mathematics.

In spite of the fact that product of two numbers having similar signs, that is, both the numbers having positive signs or both having negative values, can never become negative, even then the imaginary and nonexistent numbers are in vogue in mathematics. The square root of the digit "-1" ($\sqrt{-1}$) is denoted by an imaginary and a nonexistent number "i," which is a mathematical term. Although any such number does not exist, in reality, even then, mathematicians and scientists have found a solution to this problem also. In higher science, math becomes still more complicated and difficult. Most of the equations might contain imaginary and nonexistent numbers. Apart from the use of imaginary and nonexistent numbers, some more nonexistent entities such as negative energy and imaginary time, etc., are at times assumed in modern science, to solve some of the complicated problems. This means that even as of today we still have to depend on imaginations and assumptions. Unlike the primitive ages, the imaginations of our scientists and physicists are not so baseless, but assumptions are, after all, only assumptions. There are still some possibilities that the imaginary factors, things or quantities might not exist at all. This implies that if any of our assumptions go wrong during any stage, then it couldn't be detected immediately. Normally when the results obtained

3: The Puzzle of Whirlpool

This is a well-known fact that the electrons revolve around the atomic nucleus. The Moon orbits our Earth, the earth, in turn, orbits the sun. The sun, with the family of all of its planets, asteroids, and comets, etc. revolves around the Galactic Centre of the Milky Way, which is our home Galaxy. This series of whirling motion doesn't end here; probably a few people might be aware of the fact that the Milky Way accompanied with a few other nearby galaxies, orbits a bigger galaxy named Andromeda, thereby a local group of galaxies is formed. Such groups are also known as local clusters of galaxies. The local clusters of galaxies, with other nearby local groups of galaxies, normally orbit a much bigger local cluster. As a result countless super-clusters of galaxies, consisting of hundreds of local groups of galaxies, are formed. This series of whirls, formed within one after another whirl, is an enigma, which probably conceals a very complicated and deep mystery of the universe. This puzzle of many whirls swirling within one after another whirl is an open challenge for everybody to solve this enigma of formation of whirls. As far as I know, this puzzle could not yet be resolved.

The whirlpool formed within a wash basin, is the best-known example of such whirls. Washbasins generally have a plug or lid by which the opening of its drain-pipe can be closed or opened at will. If the drain-plug of a washbasin is removed, then the water stored within the basin, flows out in a spiral path; a whirlpool is thus created. The whirlpool, so formed, resembles, a little, with the spiral galaxies of stars. It might mean that the whirlpool can enable us to solve the puzzle of the formation of the spiral galaxies. However, it seems to me that no serious effort has been made to unveil this mystery.

If we study the whirlpool formed in the washbasin, then it would become obvious that the quantity of the water flowing out of the drain, and its speed, both depend on the size of the drain and the height of the water surface above the drain, that is, the head of water. If we observe above phenomenon carefully, and think over this process a little, then it would be evident that the whirlpool isn't created instantaneously on opening of the drain; it is formed after a very small time-gap. The higher is the water head and bigger is the size of drain opening, vigorous is the whirl. In case the size of the drain is very small, then the size of the whirlpool, so formed, is also very small. In such a case the water though continues to flow from even beyond the outer edges of the whirlpool, the surface of water beyond the outer edges of the whirlpool might appear to be stationary. It may thus be concluded that the rate of flow of water has a direct relation to the formation of the whirl and its size. On the other hand, when the size of drain is so big that the whole of the water flows out in one gush, then the whirl is not at all created. On the basis of this observation, it could be concluded that the vigor of the whirl depends on the head of water and the size of the drain as well; whirlpool could only be created when water flows with a speed above a certain minimum value, but if the quantity of water flowing out increases abruptly, that is, the entire water flows out suddenly with speed beyond a certain limit, then the whirlpool is not formed. Thus it could further be concluded that in addition to the size of the drain, the speed of water flowing toward the drain is also equally important, more precisely the force of gravity is of great importance, because it sucks in the water through the drain. *This fact is contrary to the theory of Relativity wherein it is believed that the celestial bodies and planets, etc., orbit the massive stars because of the curvature of space-time instead of the force of gravitation (please see chapter-6). If this hypothesis is correct then variations in the size of the drain shouldn't have any effect on the size or speed of the whirl, because this won't affect the curvature of the space-time.*

In case some granules of Potassium-Permanganate or granules of any other soluble color are sprinkled in the basin, then the observer would see that the whirl is not immediately created after opening the drain instead the water first starts to flow radially toward the drain, that is, in a straight line from all the corners. A very short while thereafter different water currents coming from all the directions gradually adopt independent but identical curved paths. This observation signifies that the whirl is not formed immediately; formation of whirl takes some time. It could also be observed that the curvature of different currents also increases gradually before the whirlpool stabilizes. Likewise, if water contains some suspended particles, alternatively, if any fine powder is spread over its surface, then it could also be observed that when almost all the water is drained out or when a very thin film of water is left in the basin, then the whirl ceases its flurry, and the remaining water, coming from all the directions, flows out radially in straight lines. Above observations suggest that very weak water currents having quantities and speeds lesser than a minimum limit, couldn't support the formation of the whirlpool.

It could also be observed that the whirl, so formed, never rotate in any arbitrary direction; it always rotates in the same direction. Had the direction of its rotation been controlled by the Earth's rotation, then the whirl shall always rotate with constant speed and this speed shouldn't be affected by the size of the drain-opening or the head of water, this, however, never happens. The Earth on its axis always spins from west to east; if the whirl is created due to spin of the Earth, then in the Northern-hemisphere the whirl shall rotate counter-clockwise, and in the Southern-hemisphere, in clockwise direction. But what actually happens is contrary to the above conjecture; in the North Hemisphere the whirl rotates in clockwise direction, and in the Southern Hemisphere it rotates in the opposite direction, that is, the direction of rotation of the whirlpool, in both the hemispheres, is opposite to the above prediction. It could thus be concluded that the direction of its rotation is not at all affected by the direction and speed of the earth's spin.

I understand that the scientists believe that whirls are probably created by the gravity waves. Here, a question arises that if above belief is correct, then why the whirl is not created immediately after the drain is opened and why it dies off during the last moments when the flow becomes very weak? Had this belief been true, then creation of the whirl and its rotational speed shall have no relation with either the size of the drain, or the quantity and speed of water flowing out. The question also arises that how these waves were produced, did the opening of the drain produce these waves? If the gravity waves are capable to swirl the water so vigorously, then it shall also be possible to measure the energy of these waves. However, till to date it has not become possible to feel or detect the gravity waves. Then, what is the cause of creation of the whirl? A speculative explanation of the same is given below, which is based on the most fundamental rules of science.

The flow of water is produced by the gravitational-force that pulls down all the water molecules through the drain, not directly; therefore, the suction created by the drain would go on reducing gradually with the increase in the surface area. This means that further away the water molecules are located from the drain, lesser is the pull acting on them. Accordingly, the water molecules located just above the drain are immediately sucked-in by the gravitational force, but inertia prevents the rest of the water molecules to flow instantaneously; they start to flow after a little time-lag. During the initial instants, only that much water from all around rushes toward the drain that could flow out at a time through its opening. Since the water flows from bigger area toward gradually reducing area, its speed also increases gradually in the inverse proportion of the reducing area. As a result, the speed of water molecules flowing downstream, that is, the molecules flowing toward the lower part of the stream, heading towards the drain, would increase at a much faster rate than that of the upstream molecules, i.e., the molecules coming from behind, or from the higher part of the stream. Therefore, during a very small initial moment, water molecules from all the directions, would rush toward the drain without any restriction, in a straight line, that is, in the radial direction.

Above scene won't last much longer; acceleration caused by gravitational force would gradually increase the speed of this flow, however, till the quantity of water flowing out would remain lesser than the capacity of the drain, the radial flow will continue. When this quantity tends to surpass the capacity of the drain, then both, the speed and the quantity of the water flowing out, would become saturated. Thereafter, different water currents rushing toward the drain, from all the possible directions, would congest the drain and obstruct the free flow of each other. As a result the pull of gravity would fail to increase the speed as well as the quantity of the out-flowing water any further. But this limitation won't apply at the banks of the basin, where the speed of water-molecules would *continue to increase under the influence of the gravitational force*. On the other hand, congestion at the drain would reverse the pattern of the *rate of increase of acceleration* of all the water-currents rushing toward the drain, their acceleration would, now, start to *gradually reduce instead of increasing, as if a brake has been applied at the drain. As a result of this congestion the molecules coming from behind, in spite of their higher accelerations, would not be able to flow freely, because molecules flowing ahead of them are gradually slowing-down; the molecules coming from behind would not get any room to keep flowing radially, i.e., straight toward the drain.*

Under this scenario every individual molecule coming from behind, because of its momentum and comparatively higher rate of acceleration, would develop a tendency to move ahead of the downstream molecule, which is flowing just ahead of it with a gradually reducing rate of acceleration. Since the molecules coming from behind with higher accelerations, won't get any room to move straight toward the drain, they, in their endeavor to keep moving with higher acceleration, would move sideways, i.e., perpendicular to the line of their final goal. The congestion at the drain would thus split the gravitational-acceleration into two different components; one of the components would act *radially,* i.e., directly toward the drain, whereas the second one would act in the *tangential* direction, that is, in the *transverse* direction to the former.

All the molecules that would start to flow from all around the bank, would start with zero speeds, therefore, the rate of increase of speeds of different streams starting to flow from the banks, would be infinite times higher compared to their initial "zero" speeds. Since the acceleration of water molecules flowing in the transvers direction is generated due to the difference between two consecutive molecules flowing one after another, the rate of increase of their accelerations, and accordingly the value of the said transverse component of acceleration would also be the highest at this point. Now, as the water molecules would be drawn ahead by the gravitational force, their accelerations would though gradually increase, the difference between the ratios of the speeds of two molecules flowing one after the other, would go on reducing; this would be true even for the particles/objects flowing in an unrestricted manner. Congestion at the drain would further reduce the rate of increase of this transverse acceleration, and therefore, the value of the transverse acceleration would also gradually reduce. Contrarily, as the flow would move ahead toward the drain, its radial acceleration would continuously increase due to the increasing suction at the drain. The radial speed of the flow would reach its peak value at the end of its journey. As a result of the varying values of these two components of acceleration, different water-molecules would flow in the direction of the resultant acceleration of these two components. Therefore as explained below, they would adopt a *spiral path*.

The whirlpool consists of countless streams of water molecules rushing toward the drain. The coordinate "0-0" in the Fig-1 depicts the point of origin of a single stream that originates at the banks of the washbasin. The initial stream of water that started to flow radially toward the drain is depicted by a solid straight line that joins the starting point "0-0" to the mouth of the drain, which is depicted by the letter "D." As the suction produced at the drain would suck the water-molecules a little in the radial direction, the molecules located at the banks would be simultaneously dragged away in a perpendicular direction to a much greater distance, the transverse acceleration being comparatively much stronger than the force of suction acting at this point. As this stream would move further ahead, the transverse speed of the water- molecules would go on decreasing, whereas their speed in the radial direction would go on increasing gradually. As a result displacement of water-molecules toward the drain would gradually go on increasing. Almost after the halfway to the drain, when the suction created by the drain becomes stronger than the transverse acceleration, the stream would gradually bend toward the drain, instead of moving further away from the drain.

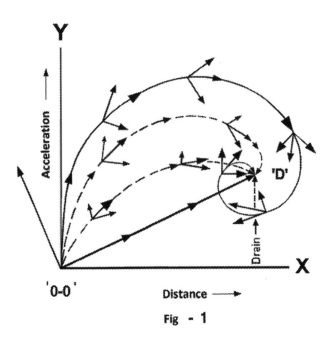

Fig - 1

In the aforesaid drawing, different curved streams generated during the transient period, that is, before the whirl could grow to its full size, are shown by different dotted lines. Approximate magnitudes and directions of both the aforesaid components of accelerations, acting simultaneously on different molecules, are also shown in the aforesaid figure 1. Following the resultant of these two accelerations the flow would approach the drain through a curved path; as the curvature of these transient streams increases the centrifugal force generated in different water molecules also goes on increasing. This increasing centrifugal-force tries to counterbalance the suction of the drain but couldn't succeed in its effort; as the molecules are drawn closer to the drain the force that sucks them, increases at a much higher rate. As a result different water streams would persist to bend toward the drain, and finally, when they come very close to the drain, they would be sucked-in abruptly by the drain; ***this can be seen in most of the barred-galaxies.***

Clearly, the suction created by gravitational force is a must for the creation of such a whirlpool instead of the gravitational waves. Since the maximum transverse acceleration is generated at the outer edges of the whirl, maximum rotational speed is also generated there. As the flow advances, toward the drain, the congestion produced at the drain would cause its transverse acceleration to reduce gradually. As a result, rotational speed of the whirl might also reduce gradually until the flow reaches the drain where the water is sucked in abruptly. Spiral galaxies, too, exhibit the similar pattern of rotational speeds, that is, the stars located further away from their respective galactic centers have slightly higher rotational speeds. *This fact indicates that the galaxies are formed by the gravitational force acting toward their galactic centers.*

Above phenomenon may also be understood in another way. Although gravitational force causes the speed of all the water streams to increase persistently, congestion created at the drain causes these streams to take a longer time to reach the drain. Therefore, all the streams have to travel through much longer distances than the shortest (radial) distance between the bank of the basin and the drain. Analogous to the fact that a much longer rod has to be coiled to accommodate the same into a smaller space, said longer streams also have to adopt different but identical spiral paths to reach the drain.

The mystery of whirlpool doesn't end here; this riddle has one more unresolved twist, which is, "the whirl never rotates in an arbitrary direction." As discussed earlier, the whirlpool always rotates in opposite directions in both the hemispheres of the Earth. This behavior of the whirlpool, suggests that probably, a natural force that acts in opposite directions in the different hemispheres of the earth, decides the direction of the rotation of the whirlpool. Out of all the natural forces, only one natural force acts in opposite directions in both the hemisphere, which is the direction of the magnetic field of the Earth's magnet. As per the prevailing conventions the lines of magnetic force, in the Northern Hemisphere, come out of Earth's surface, whereas, in the Southern Hemisphere they enter into the earth's surface. Since the whirlpool in different hemispheres, rotates in opposite directions, the direction of the magnetic field remains unaltered with respect of the rotation of the whirl. This could be understood by observing a timepiece or wall-clock from both the sides; though the clock always runs in a clockwise direction, it appears to run in an opposite direction when the same is seen from behind.

At a glance it might appear that magnetic force should have no influence on the nonmagnetic fluid like water. However, all substances contain some free electrons; moreover, water possesses the property of diamagnetism too. Therefore, while the water molecules flow toward the drain, the magnetic force might cause them to rotate in a pre-fixed direction. The speculation that magnetic field can influence the direction of rotation of the whirl, might be tested by reversing the direction of the magnetic field around the washbasin before opening the drain plug. This can be done by placing a very strong magnet below the washbasin.

It may also be noticed that the gases that damage the Ozonosphere are mostly produced in the Northern Hemisphere - even then damage to the same is prominently seen in the Southern Hemisphere. This is a matter to ponder that whether this could be linked to the direction of the earth's magnetic field? This appears to be a matter of research.

As brought out in the next chapter "Quantum Mechanics," under the subheading "Some Least-known Properties of Light," magnetic force can arrest even the photons or light waves. Lately, I gathered that light coming from distant galaxies exhibits a red-shift in the Northern Hemisphere of the Earth, whereas, light coming from distant objects, when viewed from the southern hemisphere, exhibits a blue-shift. I am not very sure of this phenomenon, but I have learnt that some of the scientists have inferred from the above fact that light can travel at different speeds in different places. In case above information is correct, then it might also be possible that instead of the speed of light its frequency might also be affected by the polarity of Earth's magnetic field; it might decrease in the Northern Hemisphere and the same might increase in the Southern Hemisphere. At least some possibilities of such an effect might exist. This phenomenon also appears to be a matter of research.

What the scientists think on the aforesaid matter is not known. Anyhow, magnetic field certainly affects subatomic particles very prominently. During 1956, American physicist Chien Shiung Wu, who was of the Chinese origin, noticed that whenever nuclei of a radioactive substance "Cobalt-60" were lined up in a magnetic field, they start spinning. On changing the polarity of the magnetic field the direction of rotation of above nuclei was also reversed. This experiment suggests that the direction of rotation of charged particles can be controlled by the polarity of the magnetic field. In other words the nature knows that under what circumstance a particle would rotate in what direction or in what direction the same should be permitted to rotate. This fact indicates that the direction of the magnetic field might have some relation to the direction of spin of the water-whirl. The direction of rotation of galaxies, stars and planets, etc. might also be decided by the Magnetic Force. This might also be a subject of research.

As brought out earlier, whirling motion is not alone formed in water; a number of examples of the whirling motion can be seen in the nature, such as electrons orbiting the atomic nucleus, stars whirling within any galaxy and galaxies whirling within a local group of galaxies, etc. This fact indicates that this series of whirls, forming within bigger whirls, might hold a key of some deep mystery of the universe. This appears to be a matter of research that whether there is or isn't any relation between the directions of rotation of the celestial bodies with the magnetic fields of the more massive bodies like nearby stars? In the present era, Mars doesn't have any magnetic field, but a few billion years ago it certainly had one. This fact suggests that the riddle of the fixed direction of rotation of the whirl must necessarily be solved. If this could be done, then we might be able to understand various unresolved mysteries of the universe in a much better way. This problem should not be taken lightly.

In the above context one more question bothers me persistently. Considering a case that any single object or a tiny particle, under the influence of a force exerted by any massive body, starts moving from rest, that is, from "zero" initial speed. In such a case, the ratio of the rate of increase of its speed at the starting point would be infinite. As this object would move ahead, though its speed would continuously increase, the ratio of the rate of increase of its acceleration would continuously fall. This pattern of increase in the acceleration of such an object resembles to that of the water molecules moving in a whirlpool. In this scene, the question arises that "what path, such an object would adopt, particularly if it has to cover a very big distance when compared to its size?" This also appears to be a subject for research.

PART – 2

EMINENT
SCIENTIFIC THEORIES
-
AN ALTERNATE ANGLE

4: QUANTUM MECHANICS-
THE WORLD OF SUBATOMIC PARTICLES

The universe generally comprises an infinite quantity of matter in different forms, varying from very fine and minute particles to the very big and massive stellar bodies. Matter in all these forms is spread all over in the space. The space is believed to be filled with infinite energy also. This energy is not only stored in the space, it also propagates throughout the space in all the directions. As per the recent scientific theories energy propagates in waves as well as in the form of particles; it has dual properties. It is also believed that at a far-remote point in time, matter, and subsequently the entire universe was created by an abrupt explosion of energy, which was, initially, contained in an infinitesimally small point. To me it appears necessary that in order to understand these hypotheses to at least some extent, we shall acquire, at least, some basic knowledge of the science related to energy and very tiny particles.

The discipline of science, related to the study of tiny particles, is known as "Quantum Mechanics." This is an entirely different branch of science that was developed sometime during the period 1920-26. The word *"quanta,"* which is plural of quantum, was first used by Max Planck, in the year 1900. Earlier, it was believed that the hot bodies give off energy waves at an equal rate at all the frequencies. This means that at very high frequencies the rate of emission of energy would increase manifold. In 1900, Planck suggested that rays of light can't be emitted at an infinite rate; they are emitted in certain packets or "quanta" of energy. The amount of energy contained in each of such quanta bears a direct proportion to the frequency of the waves emitted. He also suggested that the emission of a single quantum of energy would require more energy at higher frequencies. As a result, radiation at higher energies would be reduced; this would also limit the rate of the energy radiation.

In the quantum mechanics, which is based on the "Uncertainty Principle," no definite or specific solution of the complex scientific problems is predicted; instead, the most likely solution out of a number of different possible solutions is selected. Unfortunately, I never systematically studied this discipline of science. Whatever broken and incomplete information I could gather from different unauthentic sources, is the limit of my knowledge in this field; I don't know anything beyond that. And, therefore, I wouldn't be able to give here more or accurate details. However, much deeper knowledge of this branch of science does not appear to be necessary at the level of a common man.

Uncertainty and Unpredictability

The principle of uncertainty is of great importance in the world of very tiny particles; therefore, a very brief introduction of this principle is given here.

Sometime, during the 18th-19th century, some scientists were trying to establish a theory that would allow prediction of everything including the human behavior and even the future. Prediction of future necessitated exact determination of the present positions and also the speeds of different particles so that the future positions and speeds of those particles could be determined. For this purpose the particles had to be exposed to powerful light. Soon scientists noticed that if particles are exposed to intense light, then their speed starts to increase. Thus it was found that the exact speed and exact position of any particle at any particular instant can't be measured. Thus the idea to formulate such a theory had to be abandoned. However, uncertainty in the positions and velocities of the tiny particles led to the formulation of the famous **"Uncertainty Principle."** According to this principle, *"uncertainty is an inescapable property of all entities of the world; nothing in the world is exempted from this property. However, the uncertainty, in the velocities and positions of particles, can never be lesser than a certain value."* In order to honor Max Planck, this "certain value or limit" is named as **"Planck's Constant."** This principle enjoys a profound status in particle physics and quantum mechanics; most of the complicated issues are solved by this principle. These days, speed and position of the subatomic particles are not considered separately; these have been replaced by their combination, which is, now, known as **"quantum state"** of the particles.

One may wonder that if at present it is not possible to measure the exact positions and speeds of particles separately, then would it not become possible to take accurate and separate measurements of these entities in the future also. And whether the same is impossible for the Nature too? Many things, which are apparently uncertain, are several times repeated in the nature, but it appears impossible to predict them in advance, for example: through which path the thunder bolt would pass? This might appear to be uncertain to us; however, the nature practically chooses the correct and the only possible path for this purpose. Of course, the next time it may choose any other path that would be the only possible and practicable path under the changed circumstances.

Many such uncertain things often happen in the nature, which are seemingly not governed by any rule, for example: when and how the clouds would form? When a cracker or a bomb is exploded, then in how many pieces would it be shattered and in what manner its pieces would scatter? And how its smoke would spread? Mankind might not solve such problems by any rule; however, it is not, at all, difficult for the nature, which instantaneously finds out the only possible solution. There being no means available to the mankind to determine such events in advance, the same seems uncertain to him, however, nothing is uncertain for the nature, it can solve any situation in its own ways.

In case some dust particles are sprinkled in the blowing wind then it is not possible for the mankind to find out that in what manner different dust particles would be blown away, and at what different places would they deposit? Hundreds of datum, which are very difficult to collect, would be required necessarily to predict a possible solution to this problem. If somehow the entire datum could be collected and fed in a supercomputer, even then it is possible that direction and speed of the wind might change several times before pressing the "enter" button. What I mean to say, the man can predict such things to some extent only not exactly. On the other hand, the nature finds out the only possible solution, instantaneously. Einstein had very rightly said "God does not play dice." Accordingly, nature always carries out its work to suit the situations prevailing at any particular moment of time. It could, therefore, be said that all the deeds of the nature are "unpredictable," instead of being "uncertain." Although natural phenomena may appear uncertain, but in fact, they are not, at least for the nature. The entire universe, the entire lot of atoms and subatomic particles, etc., in the universe, always follows the rules of nature. Since the circumstances prevailing at different times and places, keep changing persistently, the nature accordingly keep modifying these solutions persistently to match with the changes that have taken place; it is, therefore, not possible for us to predict such solutions in advance.

The man-made rules are mostly framed on the basis of imaginations, presumptions and observations, etc. that are made over limited periods of time. As a result the rules made by the mankind, might give correct result within certain limits only; not always. These rules, beyond such limits, might sometime give erratic results. Everything, therefore, might seem to be uncertain. When a direct and exact solution of any complicated problem cannot be deduced, then probable solutions, based on the uncertainty principle, are worked out. Such solutions can be revised if necessity is felt. But the nature always functions according to its own rules, whether mankind has or hasn't set-out any rule to explain any natural phenomenon or the rules framed by them differ from the nature's rules; nature is not bound to abide by man-made laws. This doesn't mean that whatever happens in the universe is always right and good, or similar solution would always be formulated under similar circumstances. At times, such circumstances may arise in which more than one solution might be possible. Under such circumstances the nature chooses the most practicable and a straightforward solution. Such solutions cannot be changed - even if they are not the best solution; nature does not have the option to change or discard its decisions. Such decisions, instead of uncertain, shall be said to be nature's ***choice***. Since the laws of nature always remain unchanged, whatever has happened in the past or what would happen in the future, shall happen according to the laws of the nature, which are well-set. Therefore, if the laws of nature could be understood properly, then we might be able to predict future happenings to at least some extent, subject to exactly predicting the circumstances that might prevail in the future. Therefore, it appears to me that nothing is uncertain in the nature; instead the same is ***unpredictable***.

Development of the Atomic Theory

During the ancient times it was believed that all the things of our world are made of five elements, that is, the earth, water, air, fire and sky (Aether). But, in fact, none of the above entities is an element. Different kinds of matter, whose molecules comprise atoms of the same kind, are known as elements. Even the smallest particle of an element, known as atom, possesses the properties of the same matter. The idea of the atom was first developed in India, about 600 BC, or even much earlier. Similar concept was also developed by the Greek philosophers, about 500 BC. In the Greek language, the word ***atom*** means "indivisible."

In the modern era almost everybody is aware of the fact that even the atom is also made of subatomic particles; some of them possess intrinsic electrical charge. Electric charge was probably known to mankind since the prehistoric ages, but the Greek philosopher, named ***Thales***, was the first man who in 600 BC, mentioned in writing about electrification of "Amber rod" by rubbing it with fur. Different names such as "electric," "electricity" and "electron," etc., were derived from the Greek name of Amber. First machine to generate the static electricity was made as early as 1660. Later, in the year 1733, it was assumed that the flow of two different kinds of liquids produces two different types of electricity. In the year 1750, American scientist Benjamin Franklin, proved that there is only one kind of electricity, not two. Subsequently, Michael Faraday also proved in 1839, that though the electricity is only of one kind, but it has two different poles. These poles, being opposite in nature, were named as positive and negative poles. About 210 years in the past, that is, in the year 1805, John Dalton introduced the concept of atoms. Later on, the concept of two opposite poles, or opposite charges of electricity, was also adopted in the atomic theory. This concept of two opposite kinds of electric charges is still in vogue.

In 1897, J. J. Thomson observed that the Cathode Rays are, in fact, a shower of extremely minute and almost mass-less tiny particles, each having a negative charge. He suggested that these particles are part of the atoms and must be coming from within the atoms. The name "electron" was given to these particles. A little time thereafter, that is, in 1909, some scientists observed that when positively charged "alpha" (α) particles are fired on extremely thin gold foil, then most of these particles passed through it without much deflection, but a very few particles were found to deflect by very large amounts. Scientist Rutherford, on the basis of the aforesaid observation, concluded that the atom must have a positively charged nucleus surrounded by electrons. He further predicted that electrons orbit the nucleus due to their mutual attraction. Since atoms don't have electric charge, it was assumed that the electrical charges of the nucleus and the electrons must be equal in value but opposite to each other in nature, that is, the charge of the nucleus must be positive.

Scientists didn't have to think much, while deciding the nature of the charges of the nucleus and the electron, because their properties had been decided much earlier. Now, since the negative sign represent values lesser than zero, any common man might think that if some positive charge could be taken out of a neutral particle then the same would develop negative charge. Likewise, if double the quantity of positive charge is added to a particle having unit negative charge, then it should become positively charged. Everybody is probably aware that when two insulated materials are rubbed together, then some electrons, from one of these materials, are transferred to the other one. The material, which gains extra electrons, becomes negatively charged, whereas, the other one, which loses some electrons, becomes positively charged. However, the charge of any subatomic particle can't be transferred to another one, by any means. Neither it is possible to add extra positive charge to the electrons to convert them into positively charged particles or even make them neutral, and nor the protons or positrons could be converted into electrons by removing two units of positive charge from them. The electron, in the hydrogen atom, orbits the nucleus from a very-very small distance of 20 millionth part of a millimeter, but the electrical charge, of any of these two particles, is not able to jump from one particle to the other - even from such a small distance.

It could be inferred from the aforesaid facts that different kinds of charges are inseparable and intrinsic properties of these charged particles; in any case theirs charges could neither be separated from them nor be converted into the charge of opposite nature, that is, the values of their respective charges can neither be increased nor be decreased. Both kinds of these charges exert similar attractive forces on all the neutral substances. These two charges can only nullify the effect of each other, they do not annihilate the charge of each other; they always maintain their independent and unique identities.

In the above prospective it doesn't seem justified to say that charge of any one of these two particles is really negative, having value lesser than unitary charge. The charge of the electron is in itself an independent property, which is not, at all, produced by deficiency of any other kind of charge; the same is only opposite in nature to that of the charge of the proton. In fact, both kinds of charges are two different, independent, unique and real properties, certainly having definite values above zero. The aforesaid perception might appear weird and impossible; in case the charges of both of these particles are equal in magnitude and opposite in nature, then how is it possible that both of them be real, having values above zero, that is, pointing in the same direction? Although this seems impossible, but the same might still be possible in the Nature. For the sake of example, if a man travels northward from a point and another person travels southward relative to the same point, then it cannot be said that one of them would travel through a negative distance. Similarly, the distance measured from the center of a circle or sphere, would always be positive, in whatsoever direction it is measured. If, from any point situated on the periphery of a circle, the distance is measured backward, toward the center, we can never go in a negative direction, as soon as we cross its center, we will again move in the positive direction with reference to the center. Likewise, two opposite walls of a balloon can't be said to be positive and negative with reference to each other. The pole strength of any magnet, irrespective of the fact that they exert force in opposite directions of each other, is not considered positive or negative. It, thus, appears to me that the electrical charge of the electron shouldn't be treated to be negative in nature, because the same is neither the deficiency of positive charge and nor its value is lesser than zero; moreover, it exerts a positive force on all the neutral objects.

The atomic theories, made during the last 100-125 years, must have been made on the basis of results obtained from different experiments and complicated mathematical calculations. These theories must have been made after long deliberations and, therefore, there is not even a slightest chance of any error being crept into these theories. If, the charge of the electron is called negative, for the namesake only, then it makes no difference whatsoever, however, this will be only a relative term, without having any relation to its absolute value. We all know that modern science depends on very complicated mathematics. This fact gives rise to a possibility that in case any equation is formulated depending on the negative value of the charge of the electron, then most likely the solution of such equation would contain a negative, imaginary or non-existent number. However, it appears to me that all the physical and material things, found in the Nature, are real; for example, mirror images, dreams and thoughts, etc. are, though nonphysical or nonmaterial entities, but they surely do exist, either in the form of light rays, or electrical signals. Therefore, such results in imaginary or nonexistent numbers might be misleading, and in turn they might make the things even more complicated. However, it is up to the scientists, not an ordinary person like me, to decide whether the existing system of negative charge or imaginary and nonexistent numbers, etc., need to be reviewed or the same shall be continued as it is.

The Atom and its Construction

Few models of the structure of the atom were, first, proposed in 1902 to 1904. However, at that time nobody had any idea that the atom possesses a nucleus too. During the period 1909 to 1910, it was established by the experiments performed by Rutherford that atoms comprise of positively charged nucleus, which is surrounded by negatively charged electrons. In view of this conception, Rutherford in 1911, proposed a model of an atom that was similar to the solar system, in which, the electrons, instead of gravitational force, orbit the nucleus due to the force of attraction acting between these two particles. However, there was one limitation in the above model; During 1860s, James Clerk Maxwell proposed in his theory of electromagnetic radiation that whenever any charged particle, such as an electron, is subjected to acceleration or change of direction, it shall lose some of its energy in the form of some kind of radiation. This theory implies that, the electrons, due to the persistent change in their directions, should gradually lose their energy, and as a result, spiral inward until they fall into the nucleus. Scientist Niels Henrik David Bohr, in 1913, came up with a partial solution to this problem. He suggested that the electrons don't orbit the nucleus in any arbitrary orbit; instead, they orbit the nucleus from certain specified distances, which have certain fixed levels of energies. The electrons, orbiting in the fixed energy levels, won't lose any energy, and therefore, their energy levels would remain constant. The Rutherford-Bohr model of the atom was further refined, sometime during the period 1925-26, that is, after the formulation of the theory of "quantum mechanics."

The quantum mechanics predicts that the subatomic particles have the properties of both, waves as well as particles. The electrons in the form of waves can orbit the nucleus only from such distances, which possess a certain level of energy, and which would correspond to a whole number of waves. The paths, at which electrons orbit the nucleus, are known as "orbitals," "shells" or "energy levels." Closer the electrons orbit the nucleus, the stronger is the force exerted on them, therefore, proportionately more force is required to move them away from the nucleus. The scientists, due to the aforesaid reason, believe that greater is the radius of any arbitral, more is the energy stored in the electron orbiting the nucleus. Accordingly, if any electron gains some extra energy or absorbs some energy from any other source, then it would jump out from an inner orbital to the outer orbital, which have more energy. Similarly, if any electron loses some energy, then it would jump from an outer orbital into an inner orbital. The flash of light generated due to release of energy, can be noticed by very sensitive instruments.

I somehow, feel that above theory does not explain **"wherefrom the electron gets energy to move continuously, or how the electron in the form of a wave can move in a circle around the nucleus, because waves normally move in straight lines or they spread out radially from their sources."** Further, the concept that mass of a particle is thought to represent the energy of any particle, gives rise to another question that is, **"does the electrons occupying higher energy levels, possess higher masses?"** However, this seems almost impossible.

The Electron and its images

Since 1900 or even earlier, scientists had been trying to understand the inner structure of the atom. In that era it wasn't possible to see the atom. In spite of this limitation the scientists, by Oil Drop Experiment, succeeded in 1909, to establish the relation between the mass and charge of the electrons. Almost during the same period, scientist Rutherford established that a cloud of negative charge envelops a tiny but dense core from all around. Thereafter, further properties of subatomic particles were studied by very simple equipment such as cloud chamber; in that era no other means were available to see any of these particles. Later, during 1925-26, that is, after formation of quantum theory, scientists developed a concept that electron and other subatomic particles behave like waves. It was also predicted that even molecules too, behave as waves. Therefore, the term "matter wave" was tossed by the scientists of that era.

During 1956, atoms could be seen for the first time by very powerful "electron microscope." The image of atom, after enlarging by several hundred-thousand times, appeared like a bunch of very small shimmering points. A single atom could be seen, for the first time, during 1981, by "Scanning Emission Microscope," but even by that time the inner structure of the atom couldn't be seen. In 2005-06, that is, about 8 to 9 years ago, glimpses of an electron could be seen by very advanced equipment like "Field Emission Microscope" and "Atomic Force Microscope." The image of the electron observed through above equipment, looks like a mist or fog that envelopes the nucleus from all around. This envelop appeared to be comparatively denser near the nucleus, but as the distance from the nucleus increases, the density of this envelopment go on fading-away gradually. This mist, at the outer edges of said envelop, appears very thin and defused. Such an image might strengthen the idea that electrons are, in fact, like clouds or "waves." ***However, this is also possible that this blurry appearance of the electrons might have resulted because of the speeds at which they orbit the nucleus.***

In 2008, Swiss scientists exposed the atom with a pulse of laser beam for a very-very small instant of one "attosecond," that is, a fraction of one billionth of one billionth second, or 10^{-18} second. This small exposer not only enabled the scientists to see the electron, it also enabled them to make a movie of the electron while the same was in motion on its orbital. In the above experiment, it was found that the electron orbiting the Hydrogen atoms, takes a time period of about 150 "Atto seconds," or 150×10^{-18} seconds, to complete one revolution around the nucleus. Diameter wise the Hydrogen-atom measures about 1.1 Angstrom (Angstrom means 10^{-10} meter, or about 10 millionth part of a millimeter), accordingly, it can be calculated that the electron travels at a speed of about 2300 kilometers per second. The electron, traveling with such a high speed, completes about 6.66×10^{15} revolutions around the Hydrogen-nucleus in one second, that is, it completes 6.66 thousand-trillions ($6.66 \times 10^{3} \times 10^{12}$) orbits, or 6.66 million-billions ($6.66 \times 10^{6} \times 10^{9}$) orbits in a second.

The aforesaid fact suggests that due to the tiny size of electrons, and their very high speeds, it is not possible to focus a camera on them; **this may probably be the reason, why they appear like a blurry fog.** During December 2011, MIT America, exhibited a camera that is capable to shoot one trillion (10^{12}) photo-frames in a second, that is, even faster than the speed of light. This camera is capable not only to take snapshots of moving light beams it can also make a movie of light beams propagating on their way. In such a movie, the light waves could be seen to move like expanding bubbles, expanding at a steady speed; no fluctuations whatsoever are seen in their motion. If the attosecond technology could be combined with the aforesaid camera, then we might also be able to make a movie of the inner structure of the atoms, that is, of the electrons moving in different orbitals within different atoms.

The atomic structure of the elements, whose nucleus comprises a large number of protons, is very-very complicated. The nuclei of elements having atomic number around 100 or above, because of their higher positive charge, must be exerting about 50 times greater attractive force on the electron orbiting in the innermost orbit, when compared to the force exerted by the nucleus of the Hydrogen atom. And at the same time, all the outer electrons must be pushing the inner most electron toward the nucleus, with equally strong force. It is very difficult to imagine the inner structure of such complicated atoms. In case the inner structure of such complicated atoms could be studied by combining the attosecond technology and the above mentioned camera, and a movie of the electrons orbiting the nucleus of such complicated elements can be made, then we might be able to understand the inner structure of atoms in a much better way. In that case, we might also be able to determine that, whether or not, our present conception of atomic structure fully matches with the actual atomic structure. If, at all, any difference between the theoretical and actual atomic structures is found, then all the work done so-far in this field would require a thorough review. In that case our existing theories might also need some modifications.

Spin of the Tiny Particles

During 1920-22, scientists ***Otto Stern and Walther Gerlach***, observed that when a beam of neutral particles, such as silver atoms, is sent through an inhomogeneous magnetic field, which is produced between two magnetic poles of uneven strengths, then some of the particles are deflected either in the direction of the stronger pole, or away from it, that is, some of the atoms were attracted by the stronger pole and some of them were repelled by the same pole. The scientists also noted that the particles were deflected by an equal amount in both the directions. Based on this observation, they concluded that the tiny particles must have their own magnetic fields, which in analogous to the field of a spinning bar magnet that has the capacity to maintain a fixed direction of its polarity. This could be the only reason that the tiny magnets were either attracted or repelled by the stronger magnetic pole.

The aforesaid conclusion could be understood by the example of very simple toys such as the top or the gyroscope. Such toys, while spinning, have the capacity to remain steady and erect on their axes of spin. This property of the spinning objects, to maintain balance on the axis of rotation, is called "angular momentum." In analogy to this property, it was concluded that tiny particles too, must have similar property by the virtue of which they retained the direction of their magnetic fields. Later on, scientists also noticed that though the direction of the magnetic fields of these tiny particles could be changed, it is not possible to change the value of their magnetic fields. Looking into the intrinsic electric charges of the subatomic particles, such as, electrons and protons, etc. scientists, at first, thought that spinning of these particles around their axes, generates their magnetic fields, therefore, their magnetic fields have stable directions. On the basis of this assumption, this property of the subatomic particles was given the name of *"spin."* However, soon the scientists realized that such a strong magnetic field could be created only if these particles were rotating at faster-than-light speeds. Such high speeds of rotation of the atoms being impossible, scientists had to drop this idea, anyhow, even as of today this property of the subatomic particles is known as "spin."

If an object having regular shape is rotated slowly, then after some time it again starts to look similar to what it was looking at the beginning. Analogous to above phenomenon, it is believed that the property of particle "spin" tells us how they would look like from different angles. Since it is not possible to see the subatomic particles, their similarity is judged by the similarity of their properties. These particles have different kinds of properties such as different types and amount of electrical charges, masses, spins, energies and speeds, etc. some of these properties, such as spin, charge and speed, etc., have definite directions also. Out of all these properties, some properties are variable in nature and others have fixed and finite values. The system formed by the combined effect of all these properties of the subatomic particles, decides that how any particle would behave in a field of force. After the applied field of force is removed, this system, which is known as "Quantum State," comes back to its initial state. Coming back to the same quantum state, is analogous to the "Symmetry" of the subatomic particles. The number of turns required to maintain symmetry of any particle, determines the value of its spin. If, turning a particle by 180°, brings it back into its initial state, then after completing one full circle, that is, turning it by 360°, it would come back twice to its initial state. Such particles are called "spin 2" category of particles. Likewise, if a particle, by turning it through one full circle, comes back to its initial state only once, then it would be called "spin 1" particle. If, any particle comes back to its initial state only once, after rotating it through 2 full circles, then after completing only one circle, the same would be halfway to return into its initial state. Such particles are called "spin ½" type particles. And, if, the quantum

Internal Structure of the Atomic Nucleus

When neutrons and protons are made to collide head on with each other, at a very high energy, then they break up into yet smaller particles of different kinds. This fact reveals that they are composite particles made of even much smaller particles, which are known as "Quarks." It means that quarks are the elementary constituents of the nucleus. As per the latest information there are total six (6) kinds of quarks, which have different amounts of masses and charges. Different kinds of quarks for the namesake are called "flavors." All the 6 kinds of quarks have electric charges in fractional numbers, instead of whole numbers. Three of these flavors of quarks have positive charge; these quarks, in the ascending order of their masses, are respectively named as "up," "charm" and "top" quarks; each of these quarks has $2/3^{rd.}$ of the unit positive charge. The remaining three types of quarks have negative charge, which, in the ascending order of their masses, are respectively known as "down," "strange" and "bottom" quarks; each of which has $1/3^{rd.}$ of the unit negative charge. Only two out of these six kinds of quarks, namely "up" and "down," are the stable varieties of quarks, both of which possess the least mass. Remaining types of quarks are unstable and are found at very high energies that is produced either in the particle accelerators, or when cosmic rays or gamma (γ) rays enter the Earth's atmosphere and collides with any atomic nucleus. Quarks with higher masses decay very rapidly into lighter varieties of quarks. Scientists believe that, a very compact and heavy substance (known as *strange matter**), is made of strange quarks. A new type of quark was also discovered in December'11, which has been named as "Beauty;" much details of this variety of quark are not available.

Besides the electric charges, quarks also possess another kind of charge, which, for the namesake, is called "Color Charge." This charge, in fact, has nothing to do with colors. Color charge has three varieties which are named after different colors, that is, "red," "blue" and "green." Each flavor or type of quarks, according to their color charges, has three different sub-types, one each in above colors. Quarks of one color don't attract other quarks of the same color, but they have a great affinity for the quarks of other colors, due to which they are never found alone, they are normally found in the combination of one each of these three colors to form colorless particles. Sometimes quark of one color, combine with another quirk of anticolor; as a result an unstable pair of quarks, called "meson," is produced. Only three quarks of different colors

---

*   See chapter -11, under "quark Nova"

can form stable combinations. Protons and neutrons are made by different combinations of quarks. The protons are made up of two "up" and one "down" type quarks; total of their electric charges, therefore, becomes {(+⅔) ×2} + (-⅓) = 1. Whereas, neutron is made of one "up" quark and two "down" type quarks; the summed up value of their total electric charge becomes mathematically zero, that is, [{(-⅓)×2} + ⅔] = 0.

The "Standard Model" of Particle Physics

Scientists believe that every function of the universe, is carried-out through a few basic building blocks, which are called fundamental particles and four natural forces, that is, the **"strong nuclear force" (strong interaction), "electromagnetic force," "weak nuclear force" (weak-interaction) and "gravitational force." Matter is supposed to have been created by the first three forces and few elementary particles; gravitational force is not supposed to play any role in the construction of the atoms.** Scientists further believe that all the natural forces perform their work through the exchange of different kinds of force-carrier particles. Understanding about how matter particles and the remaining three forces are related to each other, is encapsulated in **"The Standard Model of particle physics"** that was developed in the early 1970s. A broad introduction to various kinds of particles, excluding the mathematical framework of this theory, is given below.

Different kinds of the matter-particles are known as *"Fermions,"* to honor the scientist *"Enrico Fermi,"* and the Force-Carrier-Particles, on the name of Indian scientist *"Satyendra Nath Bose,"* are known as *"Bosons."* The Fermions, which cannot be split any further, are called fundamental, or elementary particles, such as, electron and quark, etc. And the particles, which are made of two or more elementary particles, are called composite particles or "Hadrons;" protons, neutrons and atomic nuclei, etc. come under this category. Hadrons are further divided into two subcategories, that is, "Baryons" and "Mesons." Out of these, "Baryons" are stable or long-lived particles made of three quarks, whereas, "Mesons" are the short-lived hadrons made of the pairs of quarks and antiquarks.

Elementary Fermions are further divided into two subcategories, that is, *"Quarks"* and *"Leptons."* Introduction of six types of quarks has already been given previously. The remaining elementary fermions, which normally do not constitute the atomic-nucleus, are placed under the second category of "Leptons," which also have six sub-varieties. Leptons react only with weak interaction; strong interaction doesn't affect them in any way. Out of this lot, three leptons have unit negative electric charge; *"electron"* is the lightest one out of them. Remaining two charged leptons are known as *"Muon"* and *"Tau,"* each of which also have a unit negative charge, however, these two particles are several times heavier (more massive) than the electron, therefore, they are unstable and short-lived ones. Remaining three leptons are neutral particles having no electric charge. These leptons, according to their ascending values of the masses, are, respectively, known as *"Electron Neutrino," "Muon Neutrino"* and *"Tau Neutrino."*

It could thus be seen that in-all there are only 12 types of matter particles known as *"fermions."* Each of these matter particles has one antiparticle too; accordingly, there are, in all, 24 matter particles. Everything in the universe is created of different combinations, of these 24 particles. On the other hand, if the particles and antiparticles come in contact with each other, then they will annihilate each other; they can even destroy everything in the world. It is understood, that almost similar description of creation and destruction of the world, is given in *"Bhagavad Gita"* too, which was written as far-back as several thousands of years BC. This appears to be incredible, rather unbelievable.

All the matter particles, classified under the category "fermions," possess a very special property, which, on the name of scientist *"Wolfgang Joseph Pauli,"* is known as *"Pauli's exclusion principle."* According to this principle, *"identical fermions can never occupy similar quantum state at the same time and place. In the case two fermions occupy similar state at the same time and place, then, at least, one of their properties, such as spin, charge or velocity, etc., shall differ from that of the others." This is a very important property of all the matter particles; they acquire their shape and stiffness, only because of this property.*

The standard theory predicts that natural forces, such as, "strong," "weak" and "electromagnetic" forces, affect subatomic particles by exchange of very tiny and mass-less particles. These particles are known as *force carrier particles*, or *mediators of different forces*. Each force has its own force-carrying particle, or in other words, different forces act through different kinds of carrier particles. These force carriers, or mediators, are thought to be mass-less, but some of them have different amounts of masses, which decide their range of effectiveness; however, none of them has any sort of electric charge. All the force-carrying particles are, for the namesake, called *"Gauge Bosons,"* or, simply *"Bosons,"* to honor the Indian scientist *"Satyendra Nath Bose."* All the Bosons have spin in integer numbers, such as, 0, 1 or 2, etc., that make them different from the "Fermions," because all the fermions are "spin ½" type particles. Moreover, the bosons don't follow "exclusion principle." It is believed that because of this property, there is no limit to the number in which Bosons can be exchanged between different matter particles.

The Bosons or force-carrying particles are believed to be virtual particles. They couldn't be detected directly, or seen like real photons (which are emitted by any glowing object). This could be clarified with the example of a magnetic field. The force acting between two magnetic poles is resulted due to the exchange of virtual photons between them. Although, emission of these particles can't be detected - even in a particle detector, but the effect of this emission can be felt and measured conspicuously. In spite of the fact that it is not possible to detect virtual particles, scientists have adequate proof of their existence.

Force carriers are, in fact, not particles; instead they are resulted due to the interaction of two or more energy fields. Real and virtual particles are thought to be waves; scientists believe that an electron is a disturbance in the electron field and a photon is a disturbance in the electromagnetic field. Real particles can be sent to other places as beams of electrons or light (photons), this is however not possible with the, so-called force carrier particles. The energy fields of the real particles never die-off, therefore, they have long lives. On the other hand, virtual particles don't have their own energy fields; when the energy fields of two or more Fermions interact with each other, then disturbance is produced in their fields; this disturbance is thought to be the virtual particles. These disturbances die-off immediately after the cause of creation of these disturbances is gone or removed; therefore, they don't have long lives.

A series of questions arise on this concept- "how a disturbance (real particle) is created in a field of force and how such disturbance may persist to exist in that field at a small location for billions of years, why doesn't it die-off, or permeates the entire field; how the matter-particles remain unchanged over these years, do these fields always maintain uniform strengths? How these disturbances, in the form of photons, travel through the distances of billions of light-years? Why don't they subside?"

Pluto Experiment

Scientists, before conducting this experiment, knew that when electrons and positrons (antielectrons) are made to collide, then jets of quark and antiquark are produced. During the middle of 1979, experiment similar to the earlier ones, but with much higher energy, was repeated at Pluto Collider, which is installed at DESY laboratories, Hamburg, Germany. In this experiment another jet of gluons was also produced in addition to the aforesaid jets of quarks and antiquarks. The end result of the above series of experiments, known as "Pluto Experiments," puts a question mark on the conception "particles and their antiparticles can completely annihilate each-other, and as a result only pure energy is emitted in the form of photons." These series, of experiments, attract yet another question that is, "where do these quarks and *gluons* have come from?" There appear to be two possibilities for this (1) the energy of the collision had transformed the original particles into quarks or gluons & (2) quarks and gluons were produced as debris that was left over after the destruction of the electrons and their antiparticles. Presence of quarks and gluons gives rise to one more question that is, "does the so-called elementary particles are made of even much tinier particles, which were held together by the gluons?" Possibilities of this can't be ruled out completely because the smallest unit of the negative charge is $^1/_3{}^{rd}$ of that of the electron's charge.

"Higgs Boson" The Particle that Bestows the *Mass*

Almost the whole of the mass of the atom is concentrated in the neutrons and protons, that is, within its nucleus. The more is the number of neutrons and protons contained in the nucleus, the heavier it becomes. The mass of proton and neutrons are respectively 1836 times, and 1839 times greater in comparison to that of the electron. Proton and Neutron are made of a combination of three quarks, but the combined mass of these three quarks, when taken together, is much lesser than the mass of either the proton or the neutron. The question therefore arises "this extra mass has come where from?" Alternatively, "whether this increase in the mass has resulted due to the coalescing of the quarks?" Scientists believe that quarks combine with each other by exchange of the force carrying particles named "gluons." Gluons are not supposed to have any mass, but probably, protons and neutrons gain extra mass due to the energies of the gluons; only the scientists are capable to clarify this point.

Scientists earlier believed that all kinds of force carriers, namely "bosons," are mass-less particles. However, contrary to this belief, it was found later on that the force carriers of the *"weak interaction"* have higher masses. Now if the bosons were fundamentally mass-less, then how and where from some of them have acquired high masses? The solution to this problem was suggested by **Peter Higgs**, in 1964. He suggested that an invisible energy field exists in a vacuum or interstellar space, and which permeates throughout the universe; this field interacts with different particles in different ways. Whenever, any matter particle or boson enters or passes through this field, then the force carrier particles of this field, which are known as ***"Higgs Bosons,"*** interacts with the particle entering this field, and transfers energy or "mass" to them. In honor of Peter Higgs, this energy field is known as ***"Higgs Field."*** The amount of energy or mass transferred to any particle depends on the property or capacity of that particle to absorb mass, that is, the mass gained by any particle is proportionate to the amount of energy absorbed by it. This is analogous to a swab of cotton or any other porous matter, which, while passing through water, depending on its porosity, absorbs some water. The additional weight gained by that material, due to the ingress of water, depends on the porosity, that is, the capacity of that material to absorb water. It is clear from the above description that the "Higgs Field" doesn't create or generate mass, it simply transfers mass to different particles, and this weight-gain depends on the capacity of different particles to absorb mass.

Looking into the properties of this particle, that is, its capability to permeate throughout the universe and also the key role it plays to bestow mass upon various particles, physicist Leon Lederman probably inadvertently called this particle as "God Particle." But, in fact, this particle has no relation with the God; it is merely a particle having some special properties, and of course, it too, is one of the creations of the "God" or the Nature.

Although, the existence of "Higgs-Boson," was predicted as early as 1964, but it has been eluding the scientists almost up till now. During Dec'2011, when the nuclei of a heavy metal were collided head on, at very high energies, a new kind of fundamental particle was observed, which had an extremely short life. Properties, of this newly discovered particle, bear some similarities with the theoretical "Higgs Boson." Later on, scientists, on 14th March, 2013, tentatively confirmed that the newly found particle is, in fact, "Higgs Boson."

The so-called Higgs-Boson has extremely short lifespan of about 1.56×10^{-22} seconds. This fact attracts a series of questions. The prospective Higgs-Boson particle is produced at a very high energy of 126 GeV and above that would have been produced a little after the big bang. Thereafter, before completing its life, i.e., within an extremely short period of time, it should have bestowed mass upon the entire lot of particles. This, however, seems impossible, because the Higgs-Field, during such a short time period, could have spread over a very short sphere having a radius of 4.68×10^{-11} millimeters, which is several thousand times smaller than the atom. This particle would have vanished immediately after the energy level fell below the required level; its energy field would also have been extinct thereafter. In case the matter particles were created a little earlier, then the said Higgs-Field would not have even reached-out to them.

However, the matter particles were created at much lower energy of 1.88 MeV or so, therefore, the said Higgs-Field might have died-off before the creation of the matter particles. In that case mass could not have been transferred to the newly created matter particles. And in case the matter particles and the Higgs-Boson both were created simultaneously, then the entire universe would have been squeezed in to an atom-sized point. Another point, which goes against this ideology, is "since, matter particles, at the time of their creation, were moving at faster-than-light speeds, Higgs Field couldn't have reached out to them." The fact that the force carrier particles of weak-interaction are also supposed to possess mass, gives rise to many questions, those are: 1) how the force carrier particles of the weak nuclear force, which are merely a disturbances in the energy fields of other particles, could absorb mass? 2) The electromagnetic force and the weak-interaction become one and the same at high energies, this means that the Bosons of the E&M force acquire some mass, and that of the weak-interaction lose some mass, but how the mass once absorbed by any particle, can desert it? 3) How the matter as wave can acquire mass, because the waves are not supposed to have mass? These questions suggest that the concept of the Higgs-Boson might need a thorough review.

Matter as "Matter Wave"

Scientists, over a long time period, have observed that sometimes subatomic particles behave like particles and sometimes like waves; even atoms and molecules also have been observed to behave like waves. It is even felt that the atoms do not exist at fixed locations, they are sometimes observed at one point and the next moment they appear to be located at some other point. In other words, it couldn't be said that subatomic particles have fixed locations; they appear to be spread over all places. Solid objects, though, appear to be still, motionless and placid, but at the atomic level, the matter particles are full of a vigorous and violent flurry; electrons, not only orbit the atomic nuclei, they also jump from one atom to the other. Matter particles, because of the periodic motion of electrons, might always appear to fluctuate like waves. Probably, for this reason, the atoms, since 1920, are considered to be "matter-waves." But unlike matter, two waves can neither be made to collide nor could they rebound after any such collision. Waves cannot be picked up and shifted like matter, moreover, it is not possible to either break the waves into pieces, or melt them; however, the individual atoms, in all of these cases, would continue to fluctuate. *In view of these facts it appears to me that by nature the energy waves are somewhat different from the matter-particles.*

Matter particles such as atoms, electrons and protons, etc., though, thought to be waves, but such waves, if at all they are waves, must vastly differ from waves of light or other energy waves, because the energy waves, after emanating out of their sources, continuously propagate outward. On the other hand, various objects made of matter, normally remain stationary at their fixed places. Therefore, particles of different objects would remain confined at definite limited places or regions. Probably, this is the reason that matter particles are considered to be "three dimensional standing waves" or simply "stationary waves."

The "standing waves" are the waves, which are formed by the interference of two different waves, traveling in opposite directions. These standing waves fluctuate between two points of zero displacement, which are known as nodes, and whose locations remain fixed; due to the up-and-down undulation of these waves, their crests and troughs, which are also known as antinodes, are created between the fixed nodes after regular intervals.

In case, matter waves are created by interference of two waves, then the nucleus of any hydrogen atom should consist of three stationary waves representing the quarks. And similarly, another stationary wave shall orbit the nucleus in place of the electron. Now, in order to create standing waves representing three quarks, there shall be at least 3 or maximum 6 sources of waves, which should emit waves propagating in the direction opposite of each other, so that three standing waves could be formed in place of three quarks. Likewise, two separate sources of waves would also be required to produce one standing wave representing a single electron. In order to fulfill this condition, it is necessary that two separate sources of waves shall orbit the nucleus, at different radii. But this appears impossible; no such sources, of waves, have ever been seen within the atom. In case, proton is one source of waves and electron the other one, then the waves emitted by these two sources could never meet each other exactly at the electron, instead, they would cut each other somewhere at the midway. Numbers of questions arise out of this possibility (1) wherefrom the waves that create the electron, are generated and how, especially for the creation of the free electrons that break out from the atoms? (2) Do the sources of these waves also travel in any electric circuit along with the electrons flowing through that circuit? (3) Is it possible to produce an explosion like an atom bomb by simply breaking any wave? (4) How any wave can possess "mass," or absorb the same from the "Higgs field?" (5) What is that *"thing or medium,"* which vibrates to form the matter waves?"

The only possibility, which emerges out of these questions, is that the subatomic particles are not formed by the interference of any sorts of waves;

instead, they simply fluctuate, or vibrate, in their respective places. This fact is supported by the **String Theory,**[*] which envisages that the subatomic particles are made of vibrating strings; they are not solid and placid as they appear to be. During the year 2011, scientists have taken a photograph of the shadow of the Yttrium (Yb) atom; different photographs of electrons were also taken at different laboratories. I feel that neither photograph of a wave can be taken and nor it can cast a shadow; this fact suggests that, in fact, particles are not waves; they exhibit properties of waves because they keep fluctuating within themselves. This could be the probable reason that particles have dual properties of waves as well as particles. Alternatively, the so-called elementary particles too, might have some kind of inner construction.

Duality of Particles and Waves

Ancient philosophers believed that light rays travel in particles. James Clerk Maxwell, contrary to this belief, proved in 1861, that *"light rays are actually electromagnetic waves or disturbances, in the electromagnetic field."* Probably after this finding the property of particles found in the light rays, became secondary. In 1900, Max Plank suggested that light and other rays could not be emitted in arbitrary quantities and in an arbitrary rate, instead they are emitted in packets or quanta, as they are called, containing certain amounts of energies; these packets have proportionately higher energies at high frequencies. In other words, the higher is the energy or frequency of the wave higher is the amount of energy contained in each of its quanta.

After the decade of the 1920's, that is, after the formation of the theory of quantum mechanics, scientists started to believe that radiation of energy has properties of both: waves as well as of particles too, that is, there is duality of waves and particles in the radiated energy. Any incident light ray, when falls on any surface or collides with it, then it exerts a very feeble pressure on that surface. This pressure is known as radiation pressure and the same is a proof that light rays have the properties of particles. Scientists, by utilizing this property, are planning to make spaceships, which would be able to travel through the interstellar space, at a very high speed; that too without using any fuel. Looking at the similarity to the sailboats, such future spaceships are called "solar sail," "photon sail," or "light sail."

---

[*]   Please refer chapter-9, for a broad overview of this theory.

Besides above property, light rays have some other properties too; anybody can observe that while looking at the shadow of any object; the shadow cast by the edges of that object, doesn't appear as clear and distinct as that of the object itself. Likewise, a beam of light, after coming out of a small hole, goes on diverging. Above property of light is known as diffraction." Scientists, on the basis above property, have concluded that light moves in waves.

The conclusion that matter particles also behave like waves, can be deduced from another phenomenon. Analogous to magnets, the molecules and atoms also attract other molecules or atoms, but this property somewhat differs from the magnetic attraction. Magnetic force draws magnetic materials till they collide with the magnets that attract them, whereas, atoms when reach very close to each other, say at a distance of about the atomic diameter, then they are pushed away or repelled by each other. This phenomenon is known as "quantum deflection." Scientists, on the basis of this phenomenon, have concluded that particles have properties similar to waves.

When two sets of waves move together, and if all the crests and troughs of these waves are created at the same place, at the same instant of time, that is, they coincide with each other, then it can be seen that their energies get added up. Such waves are said to be moving in one and the same phase of time. In contradiction to this, if crests of one set of waves are formed along with the troughs of the other set of waves, that is, if both the sets of waves are in opposite phases, then their energies would cancel each other. This property of light rays can very easily be tested with the help of a very simple experiment, which is known as "two-slit experiment." The equipment to carry out above experiment comprises a partition board made of any material having two narrow and parallel slits. A source of light of only one color is placed on one of the sides of this board to ensure that only a particular wavelength of light is emitted from its source. When a screen is placed on the other side of this partition, then a series of bands of bright and dark strips, which are also known as "fringes," are seen on the screen. The reason is that different light beams passing through different slits, have to cover different distances to reach the screen, therefore both the beams of light having the same frequency, go out of phase. Accordingly, bright bands of light are formed at the places where strength of two beams adds up, and dark bands are formed at the places where the strength of beams cancels each other. This is known as "interference of waves," which is considered as proof that light travels in waves.

In the above experiment, if the source of light is replaced by a source of the beam of electrons, or any other kind of particles, even then we get exactly the same result. On the basis of above experiment it is concluded that sometimes particles also behave like waves. It is, however, amazing to see that if only one electron is fired at a time, even then similar fringes are formed on the screen. This could only be possible when the same electron could simultaneously pass through both the slits. This may appear to be odd and weird! When only one electron is fired, then it should pass through only one slit at a time, not through both the slits! Probably on the basis of above phenomenon, scientists say that there is no place for the common sense or general knowledge, in the world of the quantum science. This field is so strange, amazing and mysterious that the things that appear to be extremely impossible, may come true or may really be found to happen practically.

Analogous to above, it is also said that even a single electron, fired from an electron gun, may hit three or even more targets at the same time. Scientists might have seen this happening practically, but a common man fails to understand that how it could be ascertained that only one electron was fired at a time? In case only one electron was fired, then did it hit all the three targets, simultaneously, or it jumped from one target to the next and so on. In case the path of such an electron could be monitored by a "particle detector," the "attosecond technology," or by the camera* capable of taking one trillion photo-frames in one second, then could it not be possible to verify that how a single electron can pass through two slits simultaneously. This should also be verified that can an electron, travel on three different paths simultaneously, so that it may hit three targets at a single instant of time? If this could be done, then it could also be seen that whether a single electron while marching onwards on its path, travels like a wave, undulating up and down, or it travels on a straight path.

Unification of the Natural Forces

Scientists believe that there was only one force at the time of creation of the universe, which is known as "Super-Force." Immediately after the big-bang, this super-force divided into four natural forces, namely "the gravitational force," "electromagnetic force," "strong interaction" and the "weak interaction."

These forces have different properties and strengths, and they are believed to interact with matter particles through different kinds of force carrying particles. Scientists have observed that the properties of the forces-carrying particles of all the three nuclear forces changes gradually with the increasing

---

*   Please refer "Image of the Atom"

temperatures. Accordingly, strengths of these forces are also affected. All the force-carrying particles are not mass-less; the carriers of the weak interaction, which are of *"spin 1" type* bosons, have a much greater mass than that of the carrier particles of the other forces, this is the reason that their range of effectiveness, that is, their reach, is much shorter in comparison to the other forces. In 1967, Steven Weinberg and Abdus Salam suggested that the force carrier particles, which at normal energies behave differently, shall, on much higher energy, behave in a similar manner. During that era, it was not possible to achieve very high energies. However, this prediction was found to be true in the next 10-12 years. Weak interaction and electromagnetic forces, at very high energies, became one and the same force. On the basis of this finding, it is also believed that these two forces shall unite with the strong interaction at much higher energies. Generation of, the required level of energies, is not possible in the present era; therefore, it is not possible to verify this prediction in the near future.

The phenomenon of unifications of the weak interaction and the electromagnetic force, at high energies, poses a question mark on the relation of mass and the energies of the subatomic particles. Such unification means that at a much higher energy, the range of effectiveness of the carrier particles of the weak interaction increases and becomes equal to that of the electromagnetic force. In view of the fact that the carrier particles of the electromagnetic force, reach out to far-off distances, it might mean that the force carrier particles of the weak interaction lose their mass at high energies instead of gaining it. ***This fact contradicts the prevailing convention that mass is the measure of energy and therefore, it should increase with the increase of energy.***

<u>Antimatter and Antiparticles</u>

Almost 99% of the entire visible matter of the universe is concentrated in very hot stars like our Sun. Most extreme conditions of temperature and pressure do exist within the cores of all the stars, where simpler atoms merge into each other; as a result heavier atoms are formed. Even at such high energies, atoms of all the elements retain their normal structures, due to which positively charged particles remain in the nucleus, and the negatively charged particles orbit them from outside. This means that even at such high energies, the strong interaction continues to perform its work properly. It is clear from the above fact that such high energies are normal for the matter; however, the properties of all the elementary particles, including that of the force carrier particles, start to change at these extreme conditions. Scientists have observed that strength of the *weak interaction* as well as that of the *electromagnetic force,* *gradually* increases at high temperatures whereas, the strength of *the strong-interaction* decreases. Scientists believe that all these three forces should become equally strong, at much higher temperatures. Accordingly, these three forces would get united at a certain very high energy by merging into each other; thereby they would become one and the same force. At the energies higher than this limit, speed of the elementary particles increase to such an extent that they break-open the bonds of all these atomic forces. Quarks and gluons form a soup of plasma at energies higher than this limit, whereas, other particles move in an uncontrolled and erratic manner. Such extremely high energy might have existed at the time of creation of the universe. In the present era, such high energy is found either in gamma rays, cosmos rays, or it is created in different particle-colliders, where antiparticles and antimatter, etc. are created in very small quantities.

Antiparticles, corresponding to any kind of normal particle, have normal masses, but their electric charge and the color charge, both become opposite in nature. Similar to the normal matter, the antiprotons and antineutrons, etc., are formed as a result of different combinations of the antiquarks. The antineutrons also have no electric charge, which is similar to normal neutrons; whereas, the antiprotons possess negative electric charge. The atoms of antimatter are formed by negatively charged nucleus surrounded by the antielectrons, which have positive charge; the antielectrons are also known as "*positrons.*" Antimatter is supposed to have the same properties as that of normal matter, but because of their opposite electric charges, they may annihilate normal matter. We are very fortunate that at the time of creation of the universe the normal matter and antimatter were not produced in exactly equal quantities, otherwise, the universe would have been annihilated or destroyed completely. Abundance of normal matter gives rise to a question that is, "whether this is merely a matter of chance, a mistake of the Nature, or is it resulted due to a very well planned Natural-selection?"

As we have already seen that the matter retains its normal structure, even at very high energies and temperatures found in the cores of the stars. This means that atomic structure remains unaltered till the natural forces that govern the structure of the atom, perform their work in a normal way. If the energies of the particles increase further, beyond a critical limit, then properties of these forces change to such an extent that they cease to function properly; structure of matter breaks-down beyond this limit of energy. When the energy of particles reduces a little, but remains just around this critical limit, then these forces try to reactivate and regain their normal properties, but might not succeed fully; at this limiting value of the energy, they may act erratically. Antimatter is probably created at such critically high energies. But the question remains that why only normal matter is created in abundance, that is, in excess to the antimatter?

The answer to this question is probably hidden in a very old discovery. Scientists knew it beforehand that electrons are emitted during the decay of the radioactive substance 'Cobalt-60'; this emission is called Beta-Decay (β-decay). During 1956, American physicist Chien Shiung Wu, of Chinese origin, observed that when the nuclei of cobalt-60 are lined up in a magnetic field, they start to spin on their axes. She also observed that, if the nuclei are made to spin in a direction opposite to their natural spin, then the emission of the electrons due to beta-decay increases, that is, the rate of their decay, in comparison to that of the normal particles, increases. This experiment shattered the belief that the laws of physics always obey *symmetry "P,"* that is, *"laws are same for any situation and its mirror image." **Besides this, it also indicated that the Nature knows that what it should do in adverse situations.*** Probably, because of this property the antiparticles, after their creations, would decay at faster rates; this might be the reason that they are rarely found in the Nature. Whenever the mill of nature spins in the reverse direction, for whatsoever reason, then antiparticles are, probably, produced not only at a much slower rates, they decay at much higher rates too. ***The production of the antiparticles is, probably, controlled in accordance with the well-set laws of the nature, not by any coincidence, or by the mercy of the Nature.***

Scientists have probably seen that sometimes when the quarks are made to collide with each other at sufficiently higher energies, then they sometimes transform into the antielectrons and sometimes into electrons. But the biggest question about this fact is that "quarks possess fractional electric charges, whereas, electrons and antielectrons both possess unit electric charge, that is, charge in whole numbers." Had the electron been made of quarks or any other tinier particle, then such conversion could have been possible, but electrons are thought to be elementary particles without any internal structure. This fact raises several questions on convertibility of the quarks into electron or positron; these questions are: 1) "How a particle with fractional charge can be converted into another particle having unit charge?" 2) "Wherefrom this extra charge did come?" The fact that quarks, because of their color-charge, are never found to exist alone, poses yet another question, "how can a single quark sometimes be converted into electron or antielectron? Whether these particles are also made of quarks?" The fact that "the quarks possess many times more mass in comparison to any electron or antielectron," poses yet another question, that is, "if the quark was converted into electron/antielectron, then where its extra mass is disposed-off; does such collisions cause particles to lose energy instead of gaining more energy?" This question gives rise to yet another question on the disposal of the strong nuclear force associated with the quarks? These unresolved questions point toward a deep mystery that is yet to be explored.

Some Least-known Properties of The Light

Light rays always travel in a straight line, but ignoring this property of light, the mankind, since past several thousands of years, has been pursuing an ambitious dream of becoming invisible by wearing an invisibility cloak. Although this seems to be impossible, but efforts are, perhaps, being made to divert the light rays similar to the water current flowing around the obstacles coming in their way, so that the light rays too, may go round a man or any other object without blocking the vision of others. For the last few decades, scientists, all around the world, have been working in the field of invisibility. Probably, someone might achieve this goal within the next few months or a few years.

During December, 2007, a unique and unprecedented property of the light-waves was discovered by a group of Indian scientists led by Rasbindu Mehta. This team of scientists passed a laser beam through a soup of nano-sized and micro-sized magnetic particles; as soon as a magnetic field was applied on this soup, the laser beam passing through this soup disappeared. Later on, when the magnetic field was switched off, then a flash of light suddenly flashed out from the aforesaid soup. This experiment indicates that light waves can be trapped within an electromagnetic field for a desired period, and these waves can be released whenever desired. It was also proved that the energy of the trapped photons was neither destroyed nor their momentum to keep moving was lost or destroyed. This is the reason, why a flash of light was produced when the magnetic field was switched off.

As early as in 1927, Einstein envisaged that it is possible to trap the photons. In 1999, Lene Hau, a Danish physicist of Harvard University, observed that the speed of light reduces within the super-cool sodium atoms (cooled to almost 0°K) to as slow as 17 meters per second; later, she also succeeded to stop a light beam totally. In the year 2005, she succeeded in transforming light waves into matter waves and thereafter transforming them back into light waves. All such experiments show that light too, can be affected by either the electromagnetic force or by the super-cool conditions. This fact puts the wave-nature of light under a question mark; how the light, in the form of pure waves, could be affected by a force, or by extremely low temperature, etc.? This fact indicates that probably light propagates as particles, because only particles can be affected by such conditions, not the waves.

Positive and Negative Energy

Normally, atoms of all the elements possess equal amounts of positive and negative electric charges, and therefore, the resultant electric charge of an atom appears to be zero. Thus it could be said that at the level of atoms, the zero electric charge is, in fact, the summed up value of equal amounts of positive and negative charges. In yet other words, the *"zero electric charge"* of any neutral atom, can be divided into equal units of positive and negative electric charges. Analogous to above fact it is believed in Quantum Mechanics that pairs of positive and negative energies are continuously formed and destroyed in a vacuum or in the space. It is also believed that matter is formed by such pairs of positive and negative energies. It is also believed that matter is created by positive energy, whereas, the space is filled with infinite negative energy.

Paul Dirac, in the year 1929-30, suggested that, theoretically vacuum is an infinite sea of particles with negative energies. This "sea," in honor of Paul Dirac, is known as "Dirac Sea." According to QFT (Quantum Field Theory), the vacuum is filled with *operators* of *creation* and *annihilation,* out of them the *operators* of *creation* have positive vibrations and the operators of annihilation have negative vibrations. The operators having negative vibrations are thought to reduce the energy of any particle, and on the other hand, the operators having positive vibration, increase the energy of such particles. These operators, of opposite nature, annihilate vibrations of each other. A common man fails to understand such complicated theories; ***two particles vibrating in opposite phases would surely annihilate vibrations of each other, but the question arises on this concept that "how any particle may have negative vibrations?"*** Whenever any real physical object vibrates, then it can vibrate on the both sides of a middle position, which is the position of its rest; only such vibrations about the position of rest of that object can be said to be vibrations of positive nature. Normally, a negative sign is given to a number or any other thing, when its value is supposed to be less than zero. This concept poses a question mark on the ideology of negative vibration; ***the question is, "if any object is vibrating in a negative manner then in what direction would its particles be displaced relative to its position of rest?" Displacing any particle in a direction that is lesser than zero, doesn't seem to be feasible.***

In spite of the above fact, scientists believe that negative vibration and negative energy, both, do exist in the world of very tiny particles. Quantum theory predicts that the vacuum is not simply an empty space; short lived pairs of particles and antiparticles, or the pairs of the virtual electrons and antielectrons, are regularly created and destroyed in the vacuum. Scientists have practically observed that even the vacuum too, can be excited by applying a magnetic field. When a magnetic field is applied across a vacuum, then these pairs reposition or reorganize themselves in such a way that they oppose the applied field. The strength of the said field is thus found to be weaker than what it should have been. Reorganization of these pairs of virtual particles is called *"polarization of the vacuum."* However, it might also be possible that the force carriers of the magnetic field, that is, virtual photons, might encounter resistance due to the permeability of the mediums like air and glass, etc., through which the virtual photons have to pass through. This, in turn, might be the reason that the field-strength was found weaker than what was expected. Therefore, above aspect shall also be considered and evaluated while ascertaining the possibility of formation of such pairs of particles-antiparticles. Whatsoever be the reason of this phenomenon, scientists have reason to believe that such pairs are continuously created in the vacuum at the speed of light, and subsequently they annihilate each other with the same speed. Pairs of real particles and their antiparticles may also sometimes be produced in a vacuum. Probably, because of this reason, Swiss scientists in November, 2011, achieved success to produce light from a vacuum. The success of this experiment is considered to be a proof that particle-antiparticle pairs are sometimes produced in the vacuum.

We all know that some energy is required to break the solids into smaller pieces. This simple fact indicates that the molecules of different kinds of matter are bound together with a very strong force; they have a great affinity towards each other. On the other hand, matter particles, at the subatomic level, repel each other. It appears from this fact that two different kinds of forces do exist within the matter, which act in opposite directions of each other. These forces, though, act in opposite directions, they do not nullify each other; they perform their work independently. One of these forces holds all the particles together, whereas, the 2nd force prevents them from merging into each other; individual particles thus maintain their independent existence. The state of balance between these two forces gives shape, size and other properties to different kinds of materials. The forces acting within the atom also perform different duties; the strong force and electromagnetic forces bind different subatomic particles with each other, whereas, the weak force breaks the unstable combinations of particles. However, these forces don't oppose or nullify each other. Both of these facts indicate that the forces acting within the matter, though act in opposite directions, do coexist without nullifying each other.

Photons, the carrier particles of light, are considered to be the pairs of one unit each of positive and negative energies. Sometime, during 2007, I saw news that Australian scientists have succeeded in storing an entire image on a single photon. This news poses a question mark on the above mentioned concept. In case photons are really pairs of positive and negative energies, then it shouldn't be possible to store images on such an unstable pair of the energies of opposite nature, these opposite energies whenever come in contact, shall annihilate each other. Whereas, such pairs instead of instantly annihilating their constituents, continue to travel through space for billions of years. This fact suggests that photon shall not be a simple pair of opposite kinds of energies; different constituents of such pair might never come into physical contact with each other; the lighter one of them might orbit its heavier counterpart with a very high speed.

×   ×   ×

Scientists believe that "one has to expend some energy to separate two particles or objects against their mutual attraction of gravitation;" therefore, the energy spent to separate them, is stored in those objects. Accordingly, it is also believed that the particles located far-apart from each other have more energy than those located closer to each other. Based on the aforesaid ideology, it is interpreted that gravitation is a negative energy. On the other hand, Quantum Mechanics envisage that matter is made of positive energy.

Somehow, I feel that both of the aforesaid ideologies, about the negativity of the gravitational energy and the positive energy of the matter, contradict each other. If both of the aforesaid concepts are correct, then the total quantity of matter (in any accumulation of matter), which represents its total positive energy, shall annihilate its entire negative energy of gravitation, but this never happens practically. *In case both the opposite kinds of energies do not annihilate each other, then they shall, at least, nullify the effect of each other. This means that such an accumulation of the matter shall become a body having zeroed summed up energy, i.e., any accumulation of matter, regardless of its mass, shall not exhibit the property of gravitation, for example: the total summed-up charge of an atom becomes zero.* Contrarily, gravitational force of any accumulation of matter increases proportionately with the increase of its mass. This fact signifies that something, somewhere, is wrong or misconceived; I feel that gravitation is not, at all, a negative energy;

it never performs negative work. It is a well-known fact that a spaceship needs far-more energy to lift off from the earth, as against the energy required by the same spaceship to liftoff from a space-station; obviously earth has a much greater positive energy than the space-station. It is a point to ponder that the far-off planets were never dragged away from the sun, instead they were formed at their respective locations; therefore, no energy was expended to move them away from the sun. Of course, depending on their mass distance from the sun, more work would be required to shift them to the sun; they therefore, have more potential energies, accordingly as the sun tries to draw them closer, then some of their potential energy is converted into kinetic energy. In view of this fact, I feel that the conventional concept about the nature of energy stored in different bodies, needs to be reviewed.

One more fact signifies that Gravitation is not a negative energy. Some liquids, such as Helium-3 and Helium-4, etc., when cooled nearly up to 0° Kelvin, exhibit a unique property of superfluidity. These liquids, at such a low temperature, behave as if they have zero viscosity. Such super-cool liquids exhibit ability to self-propelling, or flowing automatically – even against the gravitational force. This property is not resulted because the gravitational force, being a negative energy, pushes them away; it is resulted due to the capillary forces, i.e., due to mutual attraction of the molecules. Although such super-cool liquids climb up, or creep along the surface of their container, against the force of gravity, they eventually drop down under the influence of gravity. This fact reveals that gravity never repels anything under any condition, it always attracts, and thereby it always performs positive work. Or in other words, gravity is a positive energy; had gravity been negative energy then it should have performed negative work and repel all kinds of materials.

The concept of negative energy totally depends on the *Uncertainty-Principle,* which envisages that field strength of any energy-field can never have zero value, because in that case its value and the rate of change of its strength both would have precise values (zero), which is against this manmade law. According to the *uncertainty principle,* there must be a certain minimum amount of *uncertainty,* or *quantum fluctuations, in the value of the strength of any field.* On the basis of this concept, it is believed that pairs of virtual particles and their antiparticles are always created in the vacuum. These particles, at any particular instant of time, appear together and thereafter they move apart; soon they again come together and annihilate each other. Chain of such action, of creation and destruction of such pairs, always continues. ***This concept again raises a question "where from such particles gain energy to move apart against their mutual attraction?" The energy, to split these pairs can't be*** *created all by itself, which is against the laws. Moreover, the sum of total energy of such pairs would certainly be zero, which is also against the spirit of the Uncertainty Principle.* When everything in the world is uncertain, then how it could be believed that the "uncertainty-principle" certainly applies to each and every thing in the world? How it can be said firmly that pairs of "particle and antiparticles" are "certainly" created and destroyed in the vacuum? Firm belief in this principle is totally against the spirit of this principle.

During the period 1928 to 1930, scientists observed that a few particles sometimes move in a field of force in the direction opposite of that of the others, as if they possess negative energies. However, I feel that the vector direction of energy shall not alone be decided by the direction of the displacement of such particles in any particular direction; the direction, in which the applied force intended to displace such particles, shall also be considered. *Since the capacity to displace any object is called energy; therefore, the "capacity to do negative work" shall only be treated as negative energy.* Any force, because of the different properties of different particles, would act on them in different directions; magnetic poles attract dissimilar poles but repel similar poles. Likewise, same force would respectively act in different directions on the electrons and the antielectrons. In any magnetic or electric field the positrons would always be deflected in the direction opposite of that of the electrons, but both of them would certainly move in the direction of the applied force. *Based on the direction of displacement of these particles, any one of them can be said to have negative energy with respect to the other-one, whereas, none of them moves in the direction opposite of that of the applied force.* This fact suggests that energies of such particles are though opposite of each other, none of them possesses negative energy. Therefore, before deciding the vector direction of the energies of such particles, it should also be examined whether these particles are displaced in the direction of the applied force or opposite of it. *In case any particle, instead of moving in the direction of the force, is displaced in the direction opposite of it, only then the same could be said to possess negative energy, or alternatively, the applied force is of a negative nature. Moreover, mass of any particle is the measure of its energy, therefore, if its energy cannot become negative until its mass also becomes negative, but this is impossible. This fact, if correct, clearly tells that energy can never become negative.*

In case above viewpoint is correct, then possibility of existence of negative energy seems to be very slender rather impossible. Anyhow, particles having energies equal, but opposite to each other, such as, electrical and color charges, etc. do certainly exist. It is also possible that any other charges, which are not known to us till to-date, might also exist. I personally feel, that different sorts of virtual and real particles are probably made of extremely tiny charged particles having charges opposite to each other. If, this is possible, then these particles having opposite energies might never meet each other directly, *instead the lighter particles would orbit the heavier ones with very high speeds. Smaller would be the distance between them faster would be the speed of such particles which orbit the heavier one, due to that their energy fields would fluctuate very rapidly. Probably, the quality of spin is produced in the particles because of this reason only. Although these speculations of mine have no base whatsoever, no decision shall be taken without thoroughly examining these speculations; every available data shall be very minutely analyzed without ignoring even the trivial facts.*

5: Propagation of Energy Waves

It is a well-known fact that the heat energy of any hot substance could be felt from a little distance without even touching it. Scientists believe that some of the heat energy of any hot substance reaches us as energy waves. Such transfer of energy, in the form of waves, is called radiation. When energy of any substance increases, then the speed of the electrons, orbiting its atoms, also increases proportionately. Therefore, such substances start to emit energy waves. The frequency of the waves emitted from such substance, probably, depends on the speed of the electrons. This means that higher would be the energy of a substance, more powerful energy waves would be emitted from it. Energy waves are not necessarily emitted only from hot substances - even very cool substances too, emit waves of low energies. However, the intensity of such waves is so weak that we fail to take notice of them. Only very sensitive instruments can detect such weak energy waves.

Scientists, till the end of the eighteenth century, believed that energy waves propagate in the interstellar space through a medium called "Aether or Ether" This belief continued for hundreds of years. Einstein's theory of "Relativity" ended this belief in the year 1905. Since then, scientists believe that ***the energy waves, while on their voyage, travel undulating through the fabric of space-time.*** The quantum theory that was developed over a couple of decades thereafter, introduced the concept of duality of particles and waves. Scientists generally believe that light waves are analogous to the two-dimensional water ripples. In contradiction to this conception, light waves, after they are emitted from a source of light, propagate like a three-dimensional bubble which goes on continuously expanding steadily. Light or any other energy wave can never travel in one or two rays because any single ray couldn't be seen from all the directions. In fact, even the dimmest light can be seen from all the directions. Above fact indicates that at least one spherical wave that could spread in all the directions, must be emitted at a time. Thus, the weakest radiation also spreads equally in all the directions, even though it might not be possible to detect it, for lack of intensity.

The radiation of energy has one more property: waves, immediately after emanating from the source, spread radially outward in all the directions, in straight lines. These waves could be diverted by a prism or mirror or even absorbed by blocking their path, but couldn't be stopped till their path is not obstructed, that is, once the energy rays set on their way, they continue their outward journey to infinite distances until any object doesn't come in their way. As a result the intensity of their energy per unit area goes on diminishing continuously, but the same could never become zero. Even after traveling for several billions of light-years, energy waves maintain their original frequencies, wavelengths and speed, etc. If a wave on its way encounters an obstacle then it exerts a very feeble pressure on the same. This fact signifies that the waves possess the property of particles too.

Propagation of the waves in three dimensions

Despite the fact that all energy waves propagate in three dimensions like continuously expanding spheres or balloons, almost everybody thinks that waves propagate in a fashion similar to ripples undulating on the two-dimensional surface of the water. While such ripples propagate onward, the water surface fluctuates up-and-down in its own place, that is, in the direction transverse to the speeding waves, or in a direction perpendicular to the direction of their propagation. For propagation of a three-dimensional wave, it is necessary that countless two-dimensional ripples should spread, from its centre, in all the possible two-dimensional plains, to constitute a spherical wave. Since all the two-dimensional ripples would vibrate in the direction transverse to the direction of their propagation, the summed-up vibrations of all such ripples, that is, that of the spherical wave, would become zero. Another eminent difference between these two types of waves is, "the water ripples, unlike energy waves, do not exert any pressure on anything coming in their way." It is clear from both of the aforementioned differences that the three-dimensional wave do not vibrate like water ripples, that is, in the direction perpendicular to the direction of their propagation. Thus comparison of light waves with the water ripple, cannot give a correct picture of the fact that "how three-dimensional waves vibrate while they spread in three-dimensions." Above fact explicitly indicates that three-dimensional waves can't undulate like water ripples. An actual video, of an expanding light wave, is available on the Internet, the wave, in this video, is seen to expand steadily, like an expanding balloon; however, this wave doesn't appear to undulate or vibrate at all. It appears to be beyond imagination that how a sphere, while spreading in all the three dimensions, could vibrate?

The sound waves are formed within the medium of atmospheric air and water. Immediately after production of any sound, the medium at the source of the sound, probably starts to vibrate, due to which a fluctuating pressure region is created at the source of such sound. Thereafter, this pressure-region goes on expanding as spherical shell. Such spherical shells might be periodically emitted from the source, one after another. Such waves probably vibrate to and fro, in the line of propagation, not perpendicular to it.

In the quantum-mechanics, it is envisaged that the energy waves have the properties of particles too; this fact makes the matter even more complicated. Although, undulation of the waves is natural, but how the particles, while traveling in a straight line, would vibrate in an "up and down" or "to and fro" motion? In the absence of an alternating force the particles can move only steadily, in the straight lines, not in any wayward motion. This problem suggests that spherical waves shall propagate in a different manner, much different from the water ripples or the sound waves. It seems to me that this matter has slipped the attention of the scientists.

The energy and intensity of waves, propagating through a medium, goes on diminishing gradually and the same dies-off sooner or later; reason for this is probably inertia of the molecules of that medium. This dampening effect doesn't exist in the space, therefore, the intensity of the waves propagating through the space, goes on diminishing because of persistent dilation of these spherical waves, but they never die-off. They maintain their original qualities such as frequency and wavelength, etc., - even after propagating for billions of years. Probably lack of medium facilitates their survival. The light waves, which can travel through billions of light-years in the space, lose their entire energy in the depth of a few hundred feet of the seawater. On the basis of this fact, it could be concluded that any medium suppresses the wave motion by obstructing their movement. Scientists have observed that speed of light increases in a complete vacuum. This fact indicates that waves can propagate better without any sort of medium. The problem with this idea of wave motion is, "how the waves would undulate without medium or what thing would vibrate to sustain the wave motion?" No vibrations could be sustained without a medium. And in case the energy travels in particle mode, then how the particles would move in an up-and-down motion? Until these questions are not resolved, it isn't possible to understand that how the waves propagate through emptiness. Einstein, in 1905, suggested solution to this problem. The limitations of this solution are discussed in the forthcoming Chapters Six and Seven.

Any piece of matter, when heated, emits light in the form of a shower of photons or energy-waves. This emission of photons might be of periodic in nature. Let us consider for a moment that analogous to the sign-waves, this emission might increase gradually, but its rate of increase goes on decreasing smoothly, before reaching to its peak; thereafter, this emission of photons, starts to reduce gradually in a similar pattern as described above, and dies off smoothly. If, periodicity of this emission is continually repeated, maintaining same pattern, then pulses of photons would seem to vary about an average value, like a wave. If such pulses of photons are emitted periodically from any source and spread like expanding spheres, then this emission would not need any medium to propagate in the space, moreover, such emission would exhibit duel properties of waves and particles, as well. However, such emission of photons would not produce the characteristic pattern of *light and dark fringes* that is produced in the two slit experiment. ***Thus it is concluded that such an emission is not a feasible model of energy propagation.*** Now, the question arises that how the energy propagates? And how it exhibits the property of duality?

Atoms are made of many subatomic particles, which are even several thousand times smaller in size, in comparison to the atom itself. Composite particles such as protons and neutrons are made of three quarks, which are bound to each other by the force carrier particles named "Gluons." The bondages developed between the quarks are very flexible and are known as "flux tubes." Scientists believe that photons are actually pairs of positive and negative energies. Probably the constituents of all the composite particles, because of their flexible gluon-like bonds, keep vibrating at their locations. However, this doesn't seem the case with the elementary particles. Although, the smallest unit of negative charge is $\frac{1}{3}^{rd}$ of that of the charge of the electron, even then electrons are not supposed to have any internal structure. Despite this belief, gluons were produced during collision* of the electrons and positrons. In this experiment creation of gluons was unexpected; therefore, the same puts a question mark on the source of their creation. *Did the gluons were simply bound to the electrons and antielectrons, before they were made to collide, or the same were produced due to the destruction of the internal structure of the above, so-called, elementary particles?* Scientists have also observed that *when two composite or elementary particles are made to collide in a particle-collider, then different kinds of new particles having extremely short lifespan are produced; different particles so produced, immediately after their births, start to move on different curved paths.* ***This fact reveals that these tiny particles must have angular (rotational) momentum. This angular momentum further suggests that the so-called elementary particles too, might be made of still tinier particles, which***

---

*   See Chaptar-4, "Pluto Experiment."

revolve around their Havier-companions, which also might be a very small particle having comparatively greater masses.

In the present era, scientists believe that electrons and other elementary particles don't have internal structures. Anyhow, according to the *"String Theory'"* all kinds of the subatomic particles and the energy carriers, etc., are made of vibrating strings. If this theory is correct, then all the particles, including the force carriers, always keep vibrating; *continuous vibrations are intrinsic to them.*

Now, in case a shower of such vibrating particles is emitted from a source of any sort of energy, then these particles would travel in straight lines and would spread in all the directions like an expanding sphere, whereas, the inherent-vibrations of these particles would bestow the property of the wave to such a shower. The waves, so formed, would behave exactly like the "de-Broglie" waves in which the vibrations remain confined within a small region, and this region propagates steadily in a straight line. *Such a shower of particles would possess duel property of the particles as well as the waves; such a wave would not require the medium of even "Space-Time",," to propagate. Properties of "diffraction" and "interference," both, would be produced in such waves, due to their intrinsic vibrations. This mode of propagation of waves would also explain the reason of why the rays, coming out of a pinhole, go on diverging. Various kinds of radiations are, probably, the showers of photons having different frequencies or energies.*

While such a wave would spread spherically, its intensity, that is, the flux of photons per unit area, would persistently go on reducing, however, the same would never die-off or become zeroed, till all the photons are not obstructed and stopped totally. Any obstacle in the path of such waves would block propagation of only a few photons, whereas, the rest of them would continue their onward march; this will cast a shadow. It may be implied from this fact that any kind of radiated energy propagates in the form of a spherical shower of the vibrating photons, not in the form of a continuous spherical structure or a spherical wave.

---

*   A broad overview of this theory is given in Chapter-9.

**   Please see Chapter-7 under "Relativity and Propagation of Waves"

The Doppler Effect

How the speed of a moving light source can affect *the frequency of the light waves, emitted from that source,* was first studied by Christian Doppler, in the year 1842. Doppler, after studying the light coming from a binary star, for a considerable time, discovered that the frequency of light coming from any moving source is *apparently changed* due to the relative velocities of such a source and the observer. This effect, after his name, is known as "Doppler's Effect." The speed of any moving source affects the frequency of light, sound and all other energy waves only apparently; in reality the frequency of these waves is not at all affected.

Whenever a moving source of sound, for example, a car blowing the Horne, moves toward any observer, then he feels as if sharpness of the horn is apparently increasing. Similarly, horn of a car moving away, sounds softer than actual. What actually happens in the former case that though the waves move with their normal speed, but every new sound wave, coming from the car moving toward the observer, is emitted from a shorter distance, consequently the next wave reaches the observer earlier than the previous one. The observer, therefore, feels as if the frequency of the incoming waves, that is, their sharpness is gradually going on increasing. In case the car moves away, then this process would be reversed, and due to which the sound would seem to have become soft.

Everybody probably knows that visible light is made of seven colors. Red color, which has the lowest frequency, always remains at the one end of the rainbow, and the violet color, having the highest frequency, appears at its other end. The light, when split into its constituent colors, is known as "spectrum." Every element has its unique spectrum by which scientists can identify different elements. During 1924-29, Hubble observed that light-spectrum of different galaxies resembles with that of our galaxy the "Milky Way," however, different colors are not seen at their normal places; they are shifted toward red color. This shifting, of colors, is called "Redshift," based on which it was concluded that far-off galaxies are moving away from us, at a very high speed. "Blue shift" was also observed in some of the galaxies, which indicate that they are moving toward us, or alternatively, we are moving toward them.

Emission of Energy from the Moving Sources

Several trillions of celestial bodies exist in this vast universe, and all of them are moving with their own speeds. Since none of these bodies are at rest, speeds of different objects have to be measured with reference to any other moving object. That's why, the velocities of the celestial bodies have to be measured relative to that of the others; absolute velocity of any one of them couldn't be ascertained. Each light-source continuously emits a shower of photons or energy waves. And therefore, every new wave follows the waves emitted from it earlier, all of these waves propagate radially outward with equal speeds, that is, a series of waves keep emanating from these sources from the point of their origin, all of which propagate one after another. Photons are supposed to propagate with uniform, unvarying speeds. Seemingly the reason for this is: the photons are almost entirely mass-less, therefore, their speeds are not, at all, affected by the speeds of their sources, that is, no additional momentum is imparted to them due to the speeds of the sources that emit them; may these sources move with whatever speeds. Subject to the condition that this assumption is correct, they should always move with their natural uniform speeds, be it in the direction of the motion of the source, or opposite of it.

Any wave, after emanating out from a moving source, spreads out spherically from that very point from where it was originated; though the source moves away from this point but this point of origin always remains fixed for that particular wave. Once the waves leave the source, all of their contacts, with their source, are cut off. These waves spread outward from that very point, in all the directions, with their normal speed. Simultaneously the source of these rays also keeps moving on its own path, with its own speed. Each individual wave emitted from such a moving source, at different points of time, appears like an expanding sphere; each, of such spheres, expands from their respective points of origin. Accordingly, whenever we see any wave, maybe after billions of years of its origin, it would appear to come from the point of its origin; its source would also appear at that very point and at that very instant of time, that is, when that wave was originated. That wave would always carry the information about the time when it left the source; it would not give any further information about the source. However, subsequent waves, emanated from their respective new locations, would be seen, one after another, and as a result, such light source would appear to move with the speed at which it was moving at that point of time. And therefore, the source would be seen that far-remote in the past, when those waves were emitted from it. In case the source ceases to shine at a remote point of time in the past - even then this couldn't be noticed in the present time; our future generations would see this event, when the rays emitted from such a source, at the time of its destruction, would reach the earth.

As per the conventions prevailing in the present, speed of the source doesn't add up to the speed of the photons that the source emits while moving. Waves, therefore, always move with a fixed uniform speed and the source also continues to move with its own speed. Therefore, light, compared to the speed of the different moving objects, must move with different relative speeds. The light, however, moves with such a high speed that this fact could only be verified when any moving object is allowed to move through a considerably longer distance. The distance between the sun and the Earth is about 150 million kilometers. Light waves, moving with the speed of approximately 300,000 kilometers/second, take a time-period of about 8.33 minutes, to cover this distance. In the same time-interval, the Earth, moving with a speed of 30 kilometers/second, that is, about 10 thousand times slower as compared to the light, also moves through a distance of about 15 thousand kilometers, that is, about 0.05 light-seconds.

Now, considering a case in which any source of light is moving with an absolute speed of ½ the speed of light. In this case any wave emitted from its point of origin, would, after 100 years, spread as a sphere having a radius of 100 light-years. During the same time-interval, the source would also move, in the direction of its motion, through a distance of 50 light-years. This means, the relative velocity of the light waves, in the reference frame of the moving source, in the same direction, would be only ½ of its normal speed, whereas, in the opposite direction, relative speed of light would appear 1½ times of its normal speed.

Now, in case two light sources are moving independently, in opposite directions, each at ½ the speed of light when measured from any imaginary point, which is at rest in the space. Then, both these sources, relative to each-other, would move at the speed of light. People, in such a scene, generally believe that the light, emitted from such light-sources, would never reach the other source. However, this is, in fact, not correct. Any wave, after emerging out from any one of these sources, would spread spherically, from the point of its origin. On the other hand, the second source, in the reference frame of the same point, would move with only half the speed of light. Now, since the light wave, emitted from the first source, would be moving at double the speed of the second source, it would certainly reach the second source after some time. However, when observed from the second light-source, very large redshift would, certainly, be observed in the said wave. Now, in case one of these sources is at rest, and the other one is moving with the speed of light, then the light rays, emitted from the stationary source, would never be able to reach the other source.

People generally believe that any source of light, which is moving with the absolute speed of light, couldn't be seen because, light rays won't be able to emanate from any such object, which is moving with the speed of light.

However, there could be two possibilities 1) Speed of light would not at all be affected by the speed of the source. & 2) Contrary to the aforementioned accepted conventions, the speed of the source would be added to the speed of the light emanated from it. First we will discuss the earlier possibility; the second possibility would be discussed later.

Let's analyze the former case first. In this case, all the light waves, emanating from such a source, would surely be radiated from their respective points of origins, and spread spherically in all the directions, with their normal speeds; this is depicted in Fig 2, given below.

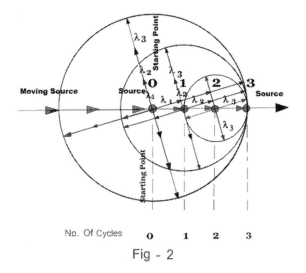

Fig - 2

The point of origin of a wave that emanated from the moving source, moving at an absolute speed of light, is shown in Fig-2, at the point "0." This source, after each frequency of the wave, or one complete cycle, would move ahead by one wavelength. Each and every wave, emanated after each cycle, would also spread spherically, by the same distance, that is, by one wavelength. Consecutive three cycles of waves and corresponding three wavelengths λ_1, λ_2 and λ_3 etc., are respectively shown in Fig-2. After completion of each cycle of the waves, both, the source of light, as well as the waves emanated from it, would move ahead by one wavelength each.

Since the source and the first wave, both, began their journeys together, both of them after completion of the first cycle would travel through the distance of one wavelength each. Accordingly, the source, and the wavefront of the first wave, would arrive at point 1, simultaneously. Immediately thereafter the source would emit the second wave. During the next cycle, the source as well as the wavefronts of both, the first and second waves, would again move through one wavelength each. Accordingly, after completion of the second cycle, the source and both of the wavefronts would simultaneously arrive at the point 2. Similarly, at the end of the third cycle, the source and also the wave fronts of the first, second and third waves, would move to the end of the third wavelength and arrive at the point 3.

Thus, it is clear that all the wavefronts, moving in the direction of the source, would never be able to move ahead of their source; the source and the wavefronts, both, would always move together. In other words the relative speed of the light, in this direction, in the reference frame of its source, would be zero. Although the waves would move with their normal speeds, but in the reference frame of the source, the wavefronts, moving in the direction opposite of their source, would appear to move at double the speed of light. Subject to the condition that the speed of light is not affected by the speed of its source, these waves wood surely travel in the direction opposite of that of the said source. However, it might not be possible to detect them due to very large redshift.

It could be concluded on the basis of all of the above examples that the light shall travel with different relative speeds when viewed in the reference frame of different moving objects, whether moving with very high or very low speeds; the law shall be same in all the cases. However, the speed of light is almost infinite times higher than that of the objects moving with speeds that appear normal to us. The light, therefore, moves past, such objects almost instantaneously. We, therefore, fail to take notice of the important fact that "do the light waves while moving past any moving object really move past that objects with its normal speed, or, does it move with a different relative speed in the reference frame of the said moving object?"

In order to have a better idea of the fact "what is relative speed and how it changes when viewed in the different reference-frames," let us take up a case of a passenger travelling in a train, who is playing with a ball by tossing it up and catching it back, to pass his time. Since, all other passengers are apparently stationary with respect to the train and the said passenger, it would appear to them that the ball, when tossed up, moves vertically upward and after reaching a certain height, it falls back vertically downward, in the hand of the said passenger. Now, this is a matter to ponder that when the said passenger was moving ahead with the train, then had the ball traveled in a true vertical up and down motion, then it should have fallen at the initial location, from where said passenger tossed it upward, not in the hands of the same passenger. Since all the passengers were stationary in the reference-frame of the train, the ball, relative to them, would appear to move up and down in a true vertical line. However, a stationary observer, looking the ball from outside, would see that the ball was traveling in a lob, that is, going upward from the initial location, on a parabolic trajectory and falling back in the hands of the same passenger who moved ahead by a few meters with the moving train. Similarly, in the reference frame of the sun, the ball would move ahead by a few kilometers with the Earth. It could, thus, be seen that different reference-frames give different information, which are only partially correct for any particular reference-frames, not comprehensively correct for all the reference-frames.

In the aforesaid example the ball, in the reference-frame of the train, was moving straight upward and simultaneously, due to its inertia, the said ball was moving with the train, as well, with the same speed. Therefore, its resultant or final speed, in the reference frame of the Earth, would be the sum of both these two speeds. However, this picture changes when we talk about light, whose speed is almost, repeat almost not actually, infinite times higher than all the known things that move on the Earth. Therefore, light moves past all the other things within almost negligible time-interval, so that we fail to realize that such moving things, during the same time interval, also moved through a small distance, though negligible; therefore, we feel that light moves past the moving objects with its normal, unaffected speed.

×   ×   ×

It is a general belief that the speed of the photons is not affected by the speed of their sources. However, nobody knows, what happens when the speed of the source approaches the limit of the speed of light. Therefore, let us examine that what might happen if the speed of the source would get added to the speeds of the photons, though this is totally against the prevailing conventions. In this special case, the photons, moving in the direction of the source, will travel at twice the speed of their normal speed, whereas, in the opposite direction they could not be able to emanate from the source; in this direction, their speed relative to the source, would be zero.

Since no direct means are available to trace or directly observe any particular ray of light right from the point of its origin to its destination point, it is not possible to find out whether the speed of the light is affected by the speed of its source, or not. I, somehow, feel that this fact may possibly be determined by geostatic satellites.

The geostationary satellites orbit the Earth at the height of 35,786 kilometers or 22,236 miles above the Equator, and they orbit the Earth in the direction of its spin, at a speed of 3.07 kilometers (1.91 miles) per second. At this speed, they complete their one orbit, around the earth, in exactly 23.93446 hours, that is, exactly in one day. As a result, they always appear stationary in the reference frame of their footprint formed on the ground. Light-waves take approximately 0.12 seconds to travel from the earth to these satellites. Whereas, the Earth, during this time-interval, moves by 3.6 kilometers on its orbit and the satellite too, moves by approximately 0.36 kilometers on its own orbit around the earth. Therefore, during this time-interval, it moves by a total distance of 3.96 kilometers. Speed of Earth is far-below the speed of light, therefore, its speed might not have any effect on the direction of the light beam sent toward the satellite. However, this fact may be verified roughly by sending a pulse of laser, or radio wave, vertically upward, toward the satellite. Now, in case speed of light is not affected by the earth's speed, then by the time the said beam would reach the required altitude, its target would move ahead by about 3.96 kilometers, therefore, it would miss its aim. In case it is found that the beam missed its target by a distance lesser than 3.96 kilometers, then it may be concluded that the speed of light is also affected by the speed of its source. This can be verified by sending the beam at such an angle that it is reflected back from the satellite, and received back on the earth. In case the distance between the footprint of the satellite, and the point where the beam was receive back, is found greater than the distance between the footprint of the satellite, and the point of origin of the beam, then it can be inferred that the speed and the direction of the light-beam, emanating from a moving source, are certainly affected by the speed of that source.

6: An Introduction to The Theory of Relativity

In the prehistoric ages, it was believed that our Earth is the center of the universe. Besides this belief, roots of numerous other misconceptions had grown very deep into our minds. During the fifteenth and sixteenth centuries, people like Copernicus and Galileo, tried to break some of these mis-concepts. The invention of the **telescope** brought similar revolution in the world of the **cosmological science,** as would have been brought by the stone weapons in the lifestyle of the primitive man. **Galileo** was the first man to tell "all the celestial bodies have **relative m*otion*** with respect to each other; none of them is stationary." Seventy to eighty years thereafter, **Sir Isaac Newton** suggested that the **gravitational force** holds all the celestial bodies together. In that era, people believed that the universe is eternal, endless and it is all the same all over; it always maintains steady-state; all the stars remain in their respective locations due to uniform gravitational force acting from all the directions. It was also believed that the universe is in the steady-state since the eternal times, and the same will remain so, in the endless future too.

In the sixteenth/seventeenth century, it was discovered that the Earth is not the center of the universe; it orbits the sun, which is an ordinary star situated at the inner edges of one of the spiral arms of the Milky Way galaxy. This galaxy is a congregation of nearly two to four hundred-billion stars; the Sun is just an average-sized star out of them. The whole of this congregation of stars, including the sun and its family of planets, is rotating about the center of the Milky Way, which is known as the **"galactic center."** Great chaos was created by this discovery; earlier, people believed that the earth is at rest, but this belief was shattered after the above mentioned discovery. Up till that time, the distances of other celestial bodies were measured with respect to the earth, but now no place in the whole of the universe, could be said to be at rest. As a result, the concepts of the *"position of absolute rest"* and the *"absolute God Time"* were shattered. In that era, it was also believed that light propagates through a substance, named *"Aether" that* is present everywhere in the inter-stellar space. Different scientists of that era made continued efforts to remove such misconceptions; they thereby changed the direction of the development of science entirely.

Background of the Theory of Relativity

James Clerk Maxwell proposed in the year 1864, that light, electricity and magnetism, etc. are the disturbance produced in the same substance. He suggested that light also obeys the laws of electromagnetism. After Maxwell's above discovery, everybody believed that light propagates rippling through a medium named "Aether" or "Ether" that permeates throughout the universe; it was also believed that the universe is stationary with respect to the Aether. Accordingly, Aether, in the reference frame of the moving Earth, should appear to move in the opposite direction of Earth's motion. As far-back as 1887, American scientists Michelson and Morley, in order to verify the truth of the aforesaid belief, compared the speed of light in the direction of the earth's motion, as well as in the direction perpendicular to it.

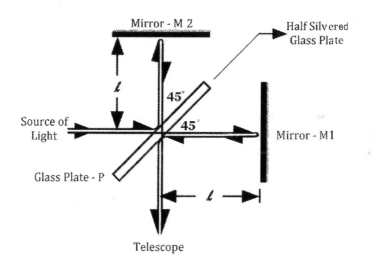

Fig- 3

The equipment used by them, is illustrated in Fig-3. In this experiment a beam of light was first divided by a half-silvered glass plate "P," into two independent beams running at 90° to each other. Thereafter, these beams were reflected back by two mirrors M-1 and M-2, which were placed at an angle of 90° to each other, and at an equal distance "ℓ" from the said half-silvered glass plate "P." Both of these beams were, then seen together through a telescope. Michelson and Morley imagined that light would travel faster when moving in the direction of the moving aether, but the speed of that of the 2nd beam running in the direction perpendicular to it, would not be affected at all. Therefore, different speeds of these two beams would result in the change of their phase. As a result interference fringes would be seen; contrarily, no fringes were produced. ***This experiment utterly failed to prove the existence of the Æther; actually it didn't prove anything.***

Although, this experiment failed to prove the existence of the aether, even then scientists continued to believe that light ripples through aether. This belief of scientists led to the conclusion that light travels with the same speed in both of the above directions. This meant that light, in the reference frame of any moving object, persists to move with its normal speed of 300,000 kilometers/second; it doesn't have any relative speed while moving ahead of such moving objects. Lorentz, with the aim to justify this conclusion, proposed in 1895 that the "null" result obtained by Michelson and Morley, was resulted due to the contraction of their apparatus that was caused by the drag of aether. ***He thus created a misconception to justify a wrong and impossible conclusion.*** Thenceforth, it is believed that the distances do contract and time dilates at the speed of light. ***However, this inference is absolutely fallacious.***

At that time the scientists, probably, because of their belief in the existence of aether, didn't contemplate that though, the light beam, while moving in the direction of Earth's motion, would have to travel some extra distance to reach the mirror M-1, but on its return journey, the plate "P" would also move ahead, therefore, light would have to cover a lesser distance; lesser, by the same amount. The effect of Earth's speed for this beam, moving both ways, would have thus nullified; therefore, the said beam would have covered a total distance of exactly "2ℓ." This means, the null result was received because both the light beams would have traveled through equal distances, not due to contraction of the equipment. In fact, the effect of Earth's speed couldn't be ignored; by the time light moves through a distance of 5 kilometers, the Earth, moving with the speed of 30 kilometers/second, also moves through a distance of ½ meter. In order to cover this extra distance, light takes a time of about 1.66 nanoseconds, which is though very small but still measurable. ***However, nobody ever realized this ordinary but simple fact; instead, the aforesaid experiment was misinterpreted, which resulted in formation of the misconception that distances do contract at the speed of the light.***

Based purely, on the constancy of light's speed that was established by aforesaid experiment, Einstein, in the year 1905, proposed his theory of ***"Special Relativity"*** that rendered both, *"Absolute Time"* and *"Aether,"* unnecessary. This theory is based on very intricate mathematics; however, a very broad introduction to this theory, excluding its mathematical angle, is given below.

The Special Theory of Relativity

This theory is based on the following postulates (unproved speculation): (1) "speed of light is not affected by the speed of its source," (2) "nothing may travel faster than the speed of light" and (3) "laws of science should be the same for all the freely moving observers, no matter, they are moving with whatever speeds in the reference frame of the source of light."

Efforts are still being made to find out proofs of these postulates. Anyhow, based on above assumptions, Einstein suggested that "The speed of light always remain same for all the observers, irrespective of the speeds and directions of the moving sources of light." In other words, different freely moving observers may take different readings of the distance traveled by a light beam and the time taken by that beam to cover those distances. However, when the speed of light would be calculated, on the basis of different measurements, every one of them would get the same result. *This theory led to the conclusion that the objects are measured to be shortened in the directions they are moving.*

As per this theory, nothing except the mass-less energy waves can travel with the speed of light; no massive body can attain this speed. Einstein suggested that matter and energy are interchangeable into each other; he also established the famous equation $E = mc^2$. The Atom bomb was also based on the above equation. Atom bomb if exploded, releases immense energy by converting very little amounts of matter into very large amounts of energy.

Einstein also suggested that space and time are not two different things, independent of each other; instead, they combine to form a single continuum or object called **"Space-Time."** This idea revolutionized the concept of distances. Since the speed of light was widely regarded to be finite and fixed, it became possible to define long distances in the terms of time, for example, light-year or light second, etc. Einstein suggested that the interstellar space is not an ordinary empty space; instead, it is like a fabric woven from, the warp and weft of space and time. Although, the theory of relativity is entirely based on the concept of the continuum of space-time, but the same was not an original idea, its roots are very old. 'Incas', the ancient habitants of the Andes, also believed in the continuum of space-time, which in their language is known as "Pacha" or "Quechua." Arthur Schopenhauer in the year 1813, and Edgar Allen Poe, in 1848, respectively, brought out similar ideas in their books. Famous book, "The Time Machine," written by H. G. Walls, which was published in 1895, was also based on similar idea. ***However, Einstein introduced an entirely new idea that "light waves travel, undulating like water-ripples, through this*** *fabric of space-time."* This idea ended the necessity of the imaginary medium of "Aether," which was earlier thought necessary for propagation of light.

As per this *special theory of relativity*, the time, at the higher speeds, lapses at slower rates. Accordingly, a moving clock shall run at a slower pace in comparison to a stationary clock. And if, by any means, a moving object could be made to move with the speed of light, then the time would totally stop for such an object; the speed of ticking of time for that object, would become zero. This theory also envisages that such variations, in the ticking speed of time, depend on the speed of the moving object, not on its acceleration or direction of its speed; change in the rate of ticking of time would always depend only on its speed, whatsoever its direction may be. Since the rate of lapse of time slows-down for the moving objects, scientists probably, believe that such objects might move a little ahead in the time and enter into the future; this effect, for the slow-moving objects, would be so small that it could even not be noticed. The effect of the speed, on the ticking speed of time, would become eminent only at the speeds that are very close to that of the light.

In view of the interconvertibility of the matter and energy, this theory envisages that at higher speeds, mass of the moving objects would increase at a much higher rate. Accordingly, at higher speeds, much more energy would be needed to increase the speed of the moving objects. As the speed of the object would increase, its mass would increase at a much more rapid rate. As a result, the need of energy to increase its speed would also go on increasing at a comparatively much higher rate. Since the energy requirement, at the near-light-speeds, increases exponentially, the mass of the objects, moving with this speed, would tend to become infinite. Accordingly, infinite energy would be needed to raise their speeds any further. Now, since it is not possible to produce energy at infinite rate, speeds of all the moving objects must be confined to the limit "lesser then the speed of light," except for the mass-less energy waves.

The General Theory of Relativity

In the theory of gravity, Sir Isaac Newton established that all the celestial bodies are held up with each other by the attractive force of the gravitation. It meant that as soon as any of these bodies, moves from its place, the gravitational force acting between all other celestial bodies would change instantaneously without any loss of time. It directly meant that the speed of the gravitational force is infinite*; the effect of the slightest movement, of any celestial body, travels to infinite distances at the very same instance. On the other hand, Einstein, in his ***special theory of relativity,*** had proposed that nothing could move faster than light. The infinite speed of gravity appeared to violate this concept. In order to eliminate this anomaly, Einstein, in 1915, after deliberations over several years, came out with a new theory, which is known as ***"The General Theory of Relativity."*** In his new theory, Einstein made a revolutionary suggestion, which totally changed the concept of the gravitational force. A broad overview of this theory is given below. In this context Chapter- 7 & 8 may also be seen.

As per this new theory, space-time is not truly flat as was believed in his earlier theory the ***"Special theory of relativity."*** The name ***special relativity*** was given to his earlier theory, because it deals only with the special cases, in which the objects and observers move with constant speeds, in straight lines only. When the speed changes or diverts from its straight path, even slightly, then ***special relativity*** ceases to apply; here the ***"General Relativity"*** comes into picture, ***because it can explain the general cases, that is, any sort of motion.***

According to ***special relativity***, all the contents of the intergalactic space, that is, all the planets, stars, galaxies, matter, energy and subatomic particles, etc. collectively, constitute the universe. The universe is actually is constituted of space and time, which are interwoven with each other to form the continuum, or fabric of space-time. All the celestial bodies are supposed to float over this fabric of space-time.

Einstein proposed that space-time is not flat as envisaged in his earlier theory, instead it is distorted and warped in accordance with the distribution of the matter and energy; each and every celestial body, whether big or small, warps or makes the "space-time" to sag under such objects, as a result a curved depression is formed in the fabric of the space-time, whose size and depth depends on the masses of such bodies. ***Einstein envisaged that the objects, in the absence of any force, move as if they are falling freely. As a result, the slope of the indentations, formed due to the warping of the space-time, draws the smaller objects toward the massive ones.*** The smaller objects, while moving ahead toward the bigger ones, push the fabric of space-time because of their masses. With whatever force, these objects, push the space-time while

---

*   Chapter- 8 ***"The Puzzle of Gravitation"*** may also be seen to have a better idea of the speed of gravitation.

moving ahead, the space-time also pushes them back, with the same force. Thereby space-time compels moving bodies to follow its curvature. Einstein further envisaged that smaller bodies move toward the nearest massive body in straight paths, however, due to the curvature of the warped space, they appear to move in circular orbits. These straight-paths made in the warped-space, are called "geodesics." Smaller celestial bodies get trapped within these depressions formed by the massive ones, which continuously compel them to go round-and-round, along the curvatures of these curved depressions.

However, I am unable to find out any proper justification of the above concept. The question that bothers me is, "where from these bodies get energies to move, that too in a particular direction?" In the micro-gravity environment, where no force acts on any object, how merely the slope of these curved indentations, in absence of any force, can cause any celestial body to move toward comparatively heavier or more massive objects? Probably this logic is merely a baseless assumption.

Anyhow, this theory envisages that different celestial bodies like our Earth and other planets, etc., are neither held together by the Gravitational force nor they orbit the sun, or any other star, due to the gravitational force. Instead of gravitational force, they are trapped in the warped space and as described earlier, though they move in straight lines toward any massive star, they appear to move in circular orbits due to the curvature of the space-time. As envisaged by Einstein, gravity is not, at all, a force like other forces, it is **merely a consequence of these curved paths made in the "space-time"; more would be the curvature, more would be the effect of gravity.** All the things, which move through space-time, have to follow these curved paths. Even the rays of light, which happen to pass through any such curved path, also feel such curvatures, due to which, following such curvatures, they are deflected from their straight paths.

We have earlier seen that, **"special theory of relativity"** envisages that time slows-down at high speeds. Similarly, the theory of **"general relativity"** predicts that the speed of ticking of the time should slow down in stronger gravitational fields; the reverse of this is also correct, time should run faster in the weaker gravity fields. Accordingly, the clocks placed at higher altitudes, or in the space, shall run faster than the clocks placed on the Earth's surface. On the other hand, clocks placed on the surface of the massive planets, shall tic at slower rates, because the gravitational force, of such planets, is stronger as compared to that of the earth.

Conception of the Theory of Relativity

This theory is broadly based on the speed, or more accurately, speed of light, however, the concept of this theory differs a little from the general conception of the speed. The passengers, traveling in a train or a car, might have noticed that the speeds of the vehicles, approaching them from the front or rear, appear to have changed. For an example, if one of such vehicle is running with a speed of 40kilometers/hour and the other one is running with a speed of 60kilometers/hour, then while they approach each other, their relative speed would appear to be 100 (60+40) kilometers/hour, whereas, while following each other, their relative speed would be 20 (60-40) kilometers/hour. Now, if their speed is measured relative to the earth's surface, or any other stationary thing, then no change could be observed in their respective speeds. It is clear from the above example, that *the change in the speeds* of those moving vehicles was only *apparent,* relative to each other, which was merely an *illusion,* not a reality. Even then, based on the apparent change noticed in their velocities, their future positions can easily be calculated.

Above mathematics, holds well within the limit of the speed that seems normal to us. However, scientists believe that these rules, at the near-light-speeds, start to change. They believe that light travels past the moving objects, or observers, regardless of their speeds, with its normal speed of 300,000kilometers/hour. This belief that light always travels with a steady and constant speed is though 100% correct, scientists believe that, the speed of light doesn't change in the reference frames of the moving objects too; no apparent change occurs in its speed due to the relative motion of other moving objects. Here the twist comes in, if the speed of light doesn't change, then what changes occur elsewhere, at this speed? Scientists have widely accepted the idea that the very structure of the universe, that is, the scoff and weft of the fabric of the space-time, start to change at the speed of light, or the speeds very close to it. Scientists believe that the lengths (space) and time, measured by different observers, undergo changes at this speed; time dilates and distances or objects contract. This enables different observers to measure distances and time differently. *Contrarily, different examples given in the previous chapter-5, explain how the speed of light is apparently affected by the speeds of other moving objects; readers may refer to these examples again, if they feel it necessary.*

Practical Applications of the Relativity

Relativity has very wide applications in cosmological science. Hundreds of satellites were sent to the space, during the last five decades. We have sent manned rockets to the moon, landed various probes on Mars and the other planets. Our spaceships and probes have reached Jupiter, Saturn, Pluto and even beyond. These rockets, on their way, had not only avoided collision with any planet, they also utilized their gravitational force to obtain power to move ahead. All this could only be achieved by very accurate and precise calculations of time. The slightest mistake in such calculations, amounting to even a smallest fraction of a second, could have resulted in any disaster. Such precise time-calculations could only be achieved by the equations of ***Relativity***.

Besides the space, theory of relativity is practically serving the humankind on the Earth also. GPS or Global Positioning System, which is based on *relativity,* has been found very useful worldwide, for finding correct routes and correct locations on the Earth's surface, as well as in air and sea navigation, etc., also. This equipment works with the help of different satellites orbiting the Earth. Presently, almost 2,500 to 3,000 satellites are orbiting the Earth, out of which, 30 satellites are exclusively used for Global Positioning System. The satellites used for this purpose, are orbiting the Earth at different angles with a speed of 14,000 kilometers/hour, and at the height of 20,200 kilometers or 12,550 miles. With this speed, the satellites complete one orbit in every 12 hours. Angles of the orbits of these satellites are so selected that at least 4 to 6 satellites could always be viewed from any place on the Earth. The atomic clocks, carried by these satellites, continuously send radio signals to the Earth. These signals convey very accurate information about: (1) exact time of the origin of the signal & (2) exact location of the satellite in its orbit, from where the signal was originated. When these signals reach the receiver carried by a moving vehicle, then based on the time taken by the signal to reach the moving vehicle, the receiver, which is mounted on the moving vehicles, calculates the distance between the satellite and the receiver. Likewise, the receiver, by measuring the angle formed at the receiver by at least 3 satellites, calculates the exact location of the vehicle, its speed and the direction in which the vehicle is moving.

As envisaged by the *general relativity,* the atomic clocks, carried by satellites, are supposed to run faster than the clocks placed on the Earth's surface, because the strength of the gravitational field diminishes at such a high altitude. At the same time, the said clocks, as per the provisions of *special relativity,* should click at slower rates because of their very high speeds. Now, in case, above clocks were showing exactly the same time that existed before launching the said satellites, then after establishing these satellites in their respective orbits, they surely would show different times, and as a result the GPS would not be able to function at all. However, in order to decide the locations and speeds of all the receivers exactly, it is necessary that the clock carried by the satellites and the other one, placed on Earth's surface, must always show exactly the same time.

In order to deal with this problem, the clock carried by the satellite is adjusted before launching the satellite, so that after the satellites are established in their respective orbits, the clocks carried by them would show exactly the same time as would be shown by their counterparts placed on the earth's surface. The correction, to be made in these clocks, is decided on the basis of the complicated equations formulated by Einstein. In the present era the GPS has become an essential element of the lifestyle of almost everyone, hundreds of million people are finding their destination places with its help. The proper functioning of this equipment is considered a solid proof that the theory of relativity is absolutely correct; it is not a fake by anyway.

Although success of the GPS is considered to be an undisputable proof of *Relativity,* the effect of *speed* and *varying strength of gravitational field* on the *ticking rate of time,* is discussed in the next chapter, under the sub-heading "Different *Predictions* of the Relativity Theory" (please see - prediction nos. 2, 3 and 4).

In contradiction to the *predictions of Einstein,* the discussion in the above-referred section of this book, suggests that *"though the ticking speed of time remains unaltered, the scale of measurement of time of the atomic clocks, is probably, affected by variations in the speed of moving objects and the strength of the gravitational field around them."* However, the said speculation of mine needs a thorough verification.

7: ANALYSIS OF THE RELATIVITY THEORY

Relativity enjoys utmost importance in the field of the cosmological-science; however, it is too complicated for a common man to understand. In case the distances "contract" at the speed of light, and the time ceases to "lapse," then, at least, the light should not require even a smallest fraction of time, to travel from one place to another, but everybody knows that this is not true. Moreover, the distance of one kilometer, from the viewpoint of a common man, always remains fixed, and likewise, a time interval of one hour also remains fixed. How the distances, measured on the surface of the earth, could contract? And, if at all, the distances do contract for light, then how could they retain their original shapes and sizes for the human-beings and other things? How any substance could have two different sizes at the same instant of time? Since the light always continues to pass-by the earth, why its size doesn't continue to shrink? Such questions appear to be beyond the wisdom of a common man. Such matters, being extremely complicated, the common man accepts this idea as it is, even without cudgeling his brain; he never tries to study this theory in detail. Unfortunately, I, myself, have never studied this theory, systematically.

The question that troubles me the most, is, how the light could pass-by a moving object with the same speed at that it moves past stationary objects, why doesn't it have any relative speed? Does the light not differentiate stationary objects from those which are moving with different speeds? Does the speed of light increases while passing-by a moving object, or such objects freeze at their places for a very short while? All of the possibilities questioned above are not feasible. Scientists all over the world, on the basis of the Michelson-Morley's experiment, believe that "the time dilates at the speed of light, and the distances do contract." I, somehow, feel that probably, misinterpretation of the aforesaid famous experiment has created some confusion, somewhere, at some level. This is perfectly correct that the light always moves with its own speed, but the contraction of the space or the objects, appears to be impossible and unbelievable. The light, because of its very high speed of about 300,000 kilometers/second, zooms past any object within a negligible fraction of the time which couldn't even be noticed, therefore, it appears to us that it has moved past the moving objects with the same relative speed, at which it normally moves. But in fact, these objects also keep moving simultaneously, without any change in their lengths, or speeds; they, therefore, also travel through extremely small distances, which are beyond measurements. We, therefore, feel that light always moves at a constant speed- *even in the reference frame of the moving objects, but this is not true.*

The Speed of Light and the Basic Mathematics

The speeds with which the known objects generally move around us, seem normal to us, but light moves almost infinite times faster than such objects. This could be understood by the following example. If we imagine that an observer is moving with the 99% speed of light, in this case the light rays would pass-by this observer with their normal speed, not with a relative speed of 300,000kilometers/second. This means that light would move ahead of this observer with a relative speed of 1% of its normal speed, which would be 3,000 kilometers/second, or 10,800,000 kilometers/hour. Normally, we, on the surface of the earth, can't see beyond 5 kilometers, therefore, this 1% speed of the light would be beyond the visibility limit of the observer. Other way round, light would take an extremely small time of 1.65 micro-seconds, to cover our visibility range of 5 kilometer, which is too small for human-beings to take any notice of. Therefore, the observer might feel that light has moved past him with an infinite speed. Now, if another observer moves with a speed of 99.999% speed of the light, then he will find that light is passing by him with a speed of 0.001% speed of light, that is, 3km/sec or 10,800 km/hour, which is 10 times slower than the earth's speed. Even this speed too, might seem infinite to him. However, if the observer moves with 99.9999999% speed of light, then he would find that light is moving with a speed of 3 meters/sec or 10.8 km/hr. The observer would now, easily identify this speed. All this is the *magic* of relative speeds.

It is envisaged in *relativity* that different observers, who are moving with different speeds while taking measurements of the distance traveled by a light-beam, might take different measurements, which might differ from the measurements taken by other observers. Similarly, the clocks carried by them might also show different readings. In spite of these differences, they would, still, find the same result. What I feel, that this is not at all weird or magical. Similar results could also be obtained by the most fundamental laws of the basic mathematics. *This is very simple, provided it may be kept in mind that both, the beam of light, and the observers, were moving independently with their respective speeds, that is, they were moving with definite relative speed with respect to each other.* No matter how slow the observer was moving, his speed can never be neglected, because he was also moving while taking the measurements. If, while computing the speed of light, this simple fact is kept in mind, then we would always find correct results. This is shown in the next section of this book.

Computation of the Speed of Light

If an observer, while at rest, observes that during a certain duration of time "t," a beam of light travels through a distance "d," then the speed of light "C," could be denoted by the expression C=d/t.

Now, if the observer is moving with a speed of 10% speed of light, then the speed of light, relative to him, would be 90% of its normal speed, that is, 0.9C. Therefore, he would determine 90% speed of light, instead of its 100% speed. In the said time period "t," the beam of light moving at this relative speed in the reference frame of the moving observer, would travel through a comparatively smaller distance. This might be considered to be a contraction of distance, but in fact, the said distance "d" would remain unaltered. The light beam, in reality, would still travel through the same distance "d," but the observer would also move through a distance of 0.1d. And accordingly, the observer would find that the beam has travelled through a distance of only 0.9d (d ⸻ 0.1d). He would thus find that 0.9d/ t = 0.9C, calculating back from this figure, he will find C=d/t, which is the normal speed of light.

In case the observer while moving with the above speed, allows the beam to travel through a distance "d," ahead of him, then that beam would take comparatively longer time to travel through a comparatively longer distance; this may be regarded as dilation of time, but in fact this longer time of t/0.9, was taken by the beam to travel through a longer distance. When the speed of light is computed, using this set of readings, he would get 0.9C=d/ (t÷0.9), or, C=d/t, as before. Calculating other way round, since the observer is moving at 10% speed of the light, he would also move through a distance of 0.1d, in the time period "t." And as such, in order to move through a distance "d" ahead of that observer, the beam will have to cover an actual distance of 1.1d. In order to move through this longer distance, the beam will also take a longer time of 1.1t. Thus, the observer, on computing the speed, will find C= (1.1d)/ (1.1t), or, C=d/t as before. The same would be true for all the speeds of any moving observer, moving with whatsoever speed.

Based on above example, it could be concluded that whatsoever might be the speed of any entity, its sped neither causes the time to dilate nor the distances to contract, both of them retain their normal values. Instead, the light, in the reference frame of different observers or object, apparently moves with different relative speeds. This relative speed of light is not real, it is only an illusion. Light, with reference to the space, or the point of its origin, always moves with its normal speed.

Interaction of the Speed of Light with that of the Other Moving Objects

It is absolutely correct that light, while surging ahead of other moving objects, moves with its own speed, however, other moving objects also keep moving with their respective speeds, which also remain unaffected by the speed of light. As a result, apparent changes, in the locations of some natural objects, are observed during some natural phenomenon. The results of such observations suggest that the light also does move with relative velocities in the reference frame of other moving objects. Outcome of certain experiments also indicates the same fact. A broad description of some of such observations is given below.

Aberration of Light

After Copernicus discovered that the earth orbits the sun, some of the scientists, during the period 1550-1600, suggested that in case the earth, really

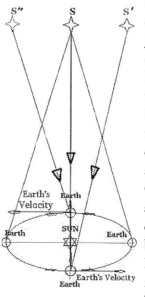

Fig - 4

moves around the sun, then the stars shall appear to deviate from their places. During the year 1725, James Bradley and Samuel Moleyneux, begin to observe movements of a star named Gamma (γ) Draconis. They observed that this star occupies its true or mid-position during the months of June and December, respectively. In the month of June it starts to shift toward the north, and touches the peak of its displacement in September. Thereafter, it turns back, and again passes its mid-position in December. Continuing its journey, it reaches the maximum southward displacement in March. These observations established that every 6 months, this star oscillates between its peak-to-peak displacements. In 1729, Bradley suggested that twice in a year, the earth while moving in its orbit, occupies the position of "Quadrature," that is, a position from where it casts an angle of 90° on the line joining this star to the sun.

The earth, from these points, starts to move either directly toward the star or in the direction opposite to it. This is depicted in Fig-4. The said star appears at its true position from both the positions of Quadrature. As the earth moves ahead on its curved path, a transverse component of speed is also generated in its speed, which acts in the direction perpendicular to the line joining the star to the Sun. This transverse speed gradually increases, till the earth doesn't reach the line joining the Sun to the star. Thereafter, this transverse speed starts decreasing and becomes zero at the second quadrature.

As shown in Fig-4, the star, from both the Quadrature, is seen at its true position denoted by S. As the earth moves past the left Quadrature, a component of speed, perpendicular to the incoming rays, is also produced in its speed. Light beam coming straight toward the observer would, therefore, not be able to reach him directly; instead, another beam would be seen by him, which was emitted previously, in the direction where the earth and the coming ray would reach together at a future point of time. The star would, therefore, appear to shift in the direction of the resultant speed of the earth's transverse speed and that of the light. When the earth would reach the line joining the star to the Sun, the star would appear displaced to its maximum position S'. Thereafter, this apparent displacement would gradually reduce and become zero at the second (right) Quadrature. As the earth moves ahead, the star would be seen to displace in the opposite direction, and at halfway to the left Quadrature, its apparent location would again shift to its maximum displacement S", but in the opposite direction.

Similar effect is produced when the raindrops are seen from a moving car. If no wind is blowing, then the raindrops shall fall in a perfectly vertical direction, but faster the car moves, more inclination is observed in their direction. Aberration is also similar phenomenon; the shower of photons comes directly toward us, but due to the earth's speed, these photons appear to come at the direction of the composite speed of the light and the transverse component of Earth's speed. *Apparent displacement of the star therefore, depends on the value of Earth's transverse speed. The light, therefore, appears to come from the direction of the resultant of Earth's speed and that of its own normal speed, which is merely an illusion.*

SAGNAC EFFECT

During the year 1913, French physicist Georges Sagnac, divided a beam of light, with the help of a half-polished mirror, into two separate beams. Next he, with the help of 3 or more mirrors, made both of these two beams, to propagate on two opposite branches of a closed path, such as a square or a circular loop. Both of these beams, after traveling through equal distances, were made to meet on a screen, at one point. This equipment was mounted on a platform, which could be rotated in the direction of propagation of any one of these two beams, or in the opposite direction. In the beginning of the experiment, while the equipment was at rest, no fringes were seen on the screen, which indicated that the light waves, in both of these beams, were in the same phase. As soon as the equipment was rotated in the direction of any one of these split-beams, characteristic interference fringes appeared on the screen. It is conspicuous from the above fact, that light waves in both the beams have now, shifted out of phase. This indicated that both these beams have now, to travel through different distances. In this experiment, the beams, traveling in the direction of rotation, had to cover a longer distance, because their path was also moving forward, whereas, the second beam had to travel through a shorter distance, because its path was moving in the direction opposite of the second beam.

It is explicit from this experiment that light doesn't move-past any moving object, with an unaffected speed of 3,000,000 kilometers/second. Had this belief been true, then irrespective of the fact that the equipment was stationary or rotating, the light should have taken equal time to travel through both of the paths, because both the paths were exactly equal in length. If, time dilates or the lengths contract, at the speed of light, then this should happen equally, in both the paths, even when the equipment was rotating. And accordingly, both the beams should have remained in the same phase. *The phase-shift noticed in this experiment, clearly shows that the speed of the path, in one of the directions, was added-up to the speed of light, whereas, in the second path its speed was subtracted from the speed of light.*

It is clear from both, "Aberration of light" and "Sagnac Effect," that the light, though, always travels with the constant speed of 300,000 kilometers/ second, it too, while travelling past moving objects, travels past them with an apparent relative speed. This relative speed can be calculated by adding or subtracting the speeds of such moving objects, to/from the normal speed of light, depending upon the directions of their relative motions.

ROSSI & HALL Experiment

Muons are very unstable elementary particles having unitary negative electric charge like electrons, but they are about 200 times as massive as compared to the electrons. Rossi and Hall, in the year 1941, proved that "Muons," live longer when moving at very high speeds, whereas, the Muons, when at rest, decay at higher rates. In other words, they proved that time ticks slowly at high speeds, or alternatively, the lifespan of the Muons extends at high speeds. This experiment is considered to be an irrefutable proof of relativity.

The muons are very unstable particles, which do not exist in normal conditions. They are generated at very high energies, for example, during experiments conducted in particle colliders; in the nature they are produced when cosmic rays interact with matter. Cosmic rays are shower of high energy subatomic particles, such as, protons and neutrons, which come from unidentified sources, which are located somewhere in the deep space. Muons are produced when cosmic rays impacts any atomic nuclei. The Muons, immediately after their births, start moving with almost the speed of light, in the same direction in which the cosmic rays were moving. The Muons are so energetic that they can penetrate through the rocks buried very deeply. They are found even at the depth of 700 meters below the earth's surface. The average lifespan of a Muon is 2.2 microseconds (microsecond means one millionth part of a second). On an average, Muons, during their entire life-period, travel through a distance of about 660 meters, or about 2,200 feet, thereafter they decay into one electron and a pair of neutrino-antineutrino.

Rossi and hall, based on the above properties of the Muons, compared the lifespan of the moving Muons, and that of the Muons at rest. They, for a time period of one hour, recorded the number of Muons, that is, their "flux," arriving at a detector placed on a mountain, at a height of 6,300 feet. A scintillator counter, comprising a thin plastic sheet that was cladded with a thick iron sheet, was used for this purpose. It was assumed that the muons, having lesser energy, wouldn't be able to penetrate through the cladding, therefore, they won't reach the counter. The Muons, having more energy, would pass through the scintillator, unrestricted. Only those Muons could be counted, which immediately after passing through the iron cladding, would lose all of their energy and come to rest; coming to rest would cause these Muons to decay. Such stationary Muons, while decaying, would produce a flash of light, which would be recorded in the scintillator counter. In this experiment they, at that height, counted 568 muons in an hour.

Rossi and Hall assumed that in case the "moving muons" and the "muons at rest" have the same lifespans, then only 27 Muons, having the same energy, should be able to reach the second counter that was kept at the sea level. Contrary to the above assumption, as many as 412 Muons were recorded at the sea level. On the basis of these results, it was concluded that the muons at rest decay much rapidly as compared to the muons moving with very high speeds. Or in other words, the lifespan of muons dilates at the near-light speeds. The speed of the muons was back-calculated, on the basis of the higher count of 412 found at the sea level, instead of the expected count of 27 numbers, which was found to be 99.5% of the speed of the light.

This experiment is considered to be a solid proof that the time dilates at near-light-speeds, or in other words, a proof of slowing down of the ticking rate of time, at the speed of light. However, I feel that the conclusion deduced from this experiment, depend on some assumptions, which do not have any solid ground. These assumptions are discussed below.

1) It was assumed that when the muons come to a rest, they decay instantaneously. Contrarily, the photons don't decay, even when they totally stop within the super-cooled sodium atoms, or within a magnetic field. Similarly, the photons, which, within the diamonds, move at almost 40% of their normal speed, have infinite life. Very long lives of photons at rest, or moving with a slower speed, indicate that the short lifespan of Muons shall not be linked to the speed; there must be some other reason for the same.

2) Lifespan of muons at rest was based on the assumption that whenever any muon would reach the plastic scintillator, the same would emit a flash of light, and the same will emit another flash of light while decaying. However, it was impossible to differentiate whether the second flash of light was emitted by the decaying muon or it was emitted by a new muon entering the counter. Therefore, the flux of muons recorded at the hilltop does not seem realistic.

3) The assumption that only 27 Muons will reach the sea-level was based on the count of the muons received at the height of 660 meters, whose lifespan exceeded 6.3 μ seconds; the number of muons that didn't stop in the counter after passing through the iron-cladding, was not considered. Therefore, the presumption of Rossi and Hall that only 27 muons would reach the second counter does not seem realistic.

4) Cosmic rays penetrate deep into the atmosphere, and on their way they persistently generate the muons at different altitudes. Whereas, the newly formed muons, after completing their lives, keep decaying regularly. If they decay immediately after penetrating the iron cladding, then this might be only a matter of chance that they might have decayed after completing their lives, not because they were forced to come to rest. This fact indicates that the count of decaying muons that was recorded at the hilltop, or at the sea level, shall not be totally attributed to their stopping at the scintillator recorder, because it

cannot be decided that which muon decayed because it was forced to come to rest, and which one of them decayed after completing its normal lifetime.

5) The cosmic rays during their journey toward the earth's surface continuously produce the muons at different altitudes. Accordingly, the new muons must have also been produced below the altitude of 6,300 feet (about 2000 meters) or even lower altitudes. The muons so produced might have different energies and life spans, therefore, they, during their life, can travel different distances. Therefore, this cannot be ascertained that at what time, or at what altitude, all the 412 muons, recorded at the sea-level, were produced? Probably, all of them might have produced at an altitude much below the altitude of 6,300 feet. In view of this possibility, it is not necessary that all the 412 muons that were recorded at the sea-level reached there after covering a distance of more than 6,300 feet, or they lived a longer life due to their near light speeds; instead, most of them were produced at a later point in time, at much lower altitudes. In view of this fact, it is not possible to confirm that the moving muons lived longer? In fact, it is not possible for any of the muons that were present at the altitude of 6,300 feet (or 2000 meters) to complete their journeys up to the sea-level. In view of the above possibilities, it doesn't look proper to link the lifespan of the muons with their speeds or dilation of time.

In view of the arguments given above, it appears that the data collected in the above experiment, don't truly represent the true lifespan of the muons while they are either in motion or at rest; the result obtained in this experiment, therefore, can't be considered to be realistic or reliable.

This phenomenon shall also be viewed from an alternate perspective. Since muons have high masses and speeds, they must possess extra energy as compared to the electrons, because the mass of a particle is considered to be the measure of its energy. As per the laws of "conservation of energy," any particle can neither be created, nor destroyed. This law attracts a question that is- "how and where from the muons were produced?" As per the "string theory" (please see chapter-9) any particle might be converted into another particle by changing its energy i.e. by altering the frequency of the vibrating strings constituting such particles. The energy of cosmic-protons, during the course of the collision of cosmic-protons and the atomic nuclei, is probably transferred to the electrons; thereby the electrons are converted into muons. The energy of impact probably causes these muons, after they are knocked-off from the parent atom, to move almost with the speed of light. Such conversion might be possible, because electrons and muons differ only in their masses. *This assumption of mine might explanation the Creation and Decay of Muons and a host of other unstable particles. This assumption of mine contradicts the belief that such unstable particles are elementary particles.*

Now, if the mass of the muons, that is, their extra energy, was resulted from the energy transfer caused by the collision, then this extra energy could be liberated at any moment. When the muons collide with other particles, then they may de-accelerate, change their direction of motion or might come to a total halt. This might result in the release of their energies in the form of a weak radiation. Moreover, the moving muons continuously ionize other particles, which come in their way; as a result, they gradually and regularly lose their energy. They may, therefore, liberate their extra energies after some time and convert back into electrons. Likewise, if their kinetic energy is lost due to resistance of the path or due to head-on collision with some other particle, they may lose their extra energy, and convert back into the electrons; their very existence depends on the extra energy.

In case above speculation of mine is correct, then, the decay of the Muons is resulted due to liberation of their extra energy. The Muons might lose their kinetic energy when they are stopped suddenly or gradually, which in turn might transform them back into the normal electrons. **In case this is possible, then the lifespan of muons shall not bear any relation, whatsoever, with either their speeds, or with the dilation of time, etc.**

Different Predictions of the relativity

(1) Gravitation and the Ticking Speed of Time

General Relativity predicts that near the massive bodies like stars and Earth, etc., the time ticks at a slower rate. This prediction is based on the belief that greater is the energy, higher will be the frequency of any wave. Accordingly, as any wave would move away from a region of higher gravity, it would lose some of its energy, and its frequency would also go on reducing. Reduction in the frequency would result in increased time-gap between two subsequent wavefronts. Any observer, stationed in the space, would feel that every event, down on the earth, is taking more time to happen. This assumption was, first, tested and proved in 1962, that is, after 47 years after this prediction was first made. In this experiment one clock was mounted at the top of a water-table and other at its bottom. When these clocks were viewed from a satellite, the clock, placed nearer to the earth, was found to run at comparatively slower rate. I believe that the clock placed on the earth's surface, would not have been seen through the water-table, otherwise the speed of the light rays, while moving through the water, was sure to have slowed down. *As a result, the conclusion deduced would surly go wrong.*

In case energy of the light-waves is really reduced while going away from the gravity field of a small planet like Earth, then *energy of the light-waves going away from millions times massive stars, must also reduce proportionately.* This effect is known as "gravitational redshift." The Black-holes are the best example of this idea, because they even capture the light-rays. If the gravitational redshift is a reality, then we might not be able to make an exact estimate of the energies of the different stars; their energies might be far-greater than what we observe from the earth. This in turn must affect the information collected through the light waves coming from the massive stars; their temperatures and masses, etc., estimated on the basis of the frequencies of the waves, received at the earth, might be far-below than their actual values. This possibility gives rise to a few questions, **"does the frequency of the light of distant stars, when observed directly from Earth's surface, is higher than the frequency of the same light when viewed through the "Hubble" or any other telescope installed in the earth's orbit?"** Do the properties of the photons differ at place-to-place, due to the change in the strength of the gravitational force that persists at different places?

(2) Relation between the Speed of Light and Time

Almost all the scientists, based on the discovery made by Michelson-Morley, believe that at the sufficiently higher speeds, the time dilates and distance contract. It is also believed that, as the speed of any moving thing increases, then the time starts to lapse at a slower rate, due to which, such objects probably move ahead in the future; at the speed of light the time comes to a total halt, that is, its ticking speed becomes zero.

In case above belief is true, then, time shall run with different speeds with respect to different moving things, which are moving with different speeds. Time of even slow-moving objects shall also be affected, but time-shift of such objects is said to be too small to notice. However, such a shift of time shall be cognizable, at least, in the case of those things which are moving with comparatively much higher speeds, and for considerably longer periods. This would mean that every moving thing shall reach to different points in the future. This means: *different things, moving with different speeds, should not be in the same instant of time; every moving object should be in a different point in time.* Depending upon the speeds of such objects, the time-gap between them would consistently increase. This might appear to be very thrilling, but if it could really happen, then the entire world would turn into a *"Time-Machine!"*

It is a well-known fact that we can see only the past of the stars; we can't see their present or the future. Obviously only past or present events can be seen, but it is not possible to see any happening beforehand, or any future object, no matter, how close in the future, it might exist; *how-come the rays, which have not yet emerged out of an object, can reach our eyes?* Moreover, we won't be able to touch that object - even if it lies at a fraction of one nanosecond ahead in the future; because it has no existence at that particular instant of time when anybody tries to touch it. Similarly, we can't touch the objects lying in the past too; we can see them when a light beam, emitted from them, reaches us at a later point in the time. This fact indicates that if we are able to touch any moving object, then such object should surely exist in that particular time-instant when it was touched; *objects, lying in a different time, can't be touched.*

If the fact that moving vehicles, moving with different speeds, sometimes do collide with stationary objects or with any other moving vehicle, is viewed in the above perspective, it would reveal that all such objects were precisely in the same point in the time; the time, for those moving vehicles, was not at all altered due to their speeds, not by even a smallest fraction of a nanosecond. *This should also be true for any object moving with any speed, not just for the objects moving at close to the light-speeds.*

Light is the fastest moving thing known to the mankind; probably this is the reason that time is considered to run with the speed of light. However, the speed of light doesn't remain constant in different mediums; within the water, it runs at 0.7 times of its normal speed. Likewise, it runs at ½ the speed within the glass, and at 0.4 of its normal speed within the diamonds. Time doesn't run with different speeds inside and outside of these mediums. Time is not a physical thing; it is merely a concept of the rate of happening of different events. No matter how fast different events are happening, the duration between such events could always be measured. Scientists believe that the universe, in the beginning, was expanding at a speed that was much faster than the speed of light. Since new events were continually taking place during that period, time was also running with the same speed, that is, faster than the light speed, instead of becoming standstill or even negative. In case the time slows down at the higher speeds, then any fast moving person would feel that everything behind him is taking longer to happen, but the events ahead of him, would appear to happen faster than normal. If he could move with the speed of light, then only one wave would always accompany him, therefore, he may feel that time has apparently stopped, but this would be, only, an illusion. Since, his movement through the space would be a series of new events; time would continue to run, even for him too.

Although, the light rays could be trapped* by super-coiling, or within a magnetic field, but the same is not possible with ticking of time. This proves that time moves independently with light. For an example, while observing light rays coming from distant stars, we see the glimpses of the time of the origin of those rays, but neither the time of origin of those rays could reach the earth, and nor the time of those stars would freeze; those stars would also move ahead in time. It is a fact that when any light ray moves with normal speed, or it is deflected, or totally stopped, even then the time continues to move on, obviously the time can't be stopped or diverted.

As brought out in chapter-4, under the section "Electron and its images," mankind has succeeded in making a camera that is capable to make video of the moving light-waves; naturally, this camera shoots at speeds higher-than-light speed, but not faster-than-time. **This fact proves that the postulate "nothing can move faster than light," doesn't apply to, at least, the aforementioned camera. When a man-made camera can take snapshots at the speed faster-than-light, then this may not be impossible for the Nature too. In other words "the speed of time is not limited to the speed of light; it may tick - even at faster rates."**

(3) The "Ticking Speed" of Time

Our concept of time is based on spinning of the earth, and its orbit around the Sun. When a spaceship, moving with the speed of light, moves past any planet, then neither the speed of spin of that planet changes, and nor the speeds of our Earth or Sun, etc., will be affected. This fact indicates that the speed of any moving spaceship can't change the time of the entire universe, everything would be at the unaffected time. If, the time freezes for any spaceship that moves at the speed of light, then by the point in time it would reach its destination, then, though the destined planet would be at its present time, the spaceship would reach there at a different point of time. In that case, the ship

---

*   See Chapter-4, "Some Least-known Properties of Light"

shouldn't be able to land on that planet, because of a long time gap between the times of the planet and that of the spaceship; instead it should disappear, or lost in the time. However, nothing like this can practically happen. This fact poses a question that is, "where the changes would occur."

In the example of GPS, it was seen that the ticking speed of the atomic clocks, carried by the satellites, really shifts by few nanoseconds. Their rate of ticking, therefore, needed to be adjusted in accordance with the formulae of Relativity. Ordinary clocks aren't capable to measure time, so accurately; therefore, CESIUM-133 clocks are used for this purpose. On the other hand, as elaborated in the previous paragraph, the speeds of the spaceships shouldn't affect the ticking speed of time, for at least, of other objects. This controversy raises a question that which of these two ideas are correct? And what is the mystery of the time-shift? In order to solve this mystery, and understand how and why the time measured by these clocks, is affected by the speed, and also by the depleted strength of gravitational force, it is necessary to first, understand the way of working of the atomic clocks. Only then it could be determined that what changes occur at higher speeds, where, and why?

Atomic clocks are based on a special property of the Cesium-133 atom, which is an isotope of the element "CESIUM." In these clocks "Hyperfine Transition" of Cesium-133 atom is counted very accurately. Please don't get panicky; a very simple overview of this scientific term is given here. We know that the electrons orbit the nuclei at different fixed energy levels known as orbitals. These energy levels, because of the interaction of the energies of the electron and the nucleus, may, sometimes, split into two or more energy levels, energies of these split energy levels differ from each other by very minute margins. Such split orbitals are called "Hyperfine Structures." Jumping of the electrons, from one hyperfine structure to the other, is called "Hyperfine Transition."

The Cesium-133 atoms comprise total 55 electrons, which orbit its nucleus at different energy levels; out of which, 54 electrons orbit in the 5 inner orbits, and a lone electron orbits in the outermost 6th orbital. The electrons, occupying the inner 5 orbitals, form stable pairs by aligning their magnetic poles in opposite directions of each other. The Hyperfine Structure is formed in the last, that is, the 6th orbit, where a single unpaired electron is left alone. Cesium-133 atoms are cooled in the atomic clocks to almost absolute zero degree, and then they are excited by the radiation of microwaves, having a frequency equal to the natural frequency of a Cesium-133 atom. As a result, the lone electron, orbiting in the last orbital, absorbs some energy from the microwave radiation, and jumps to a higher energy level of the hyperfine structure formed in that orbital. Thereafter, it liberates this extra energy and jumps back to the original energy level.

In Cesium clocks, transition of electron as described above, is repeated exactly 9,192,631,770 times or roughly 9.2 billion times in a second. Accordingly, the Cesium-133 atom absorbs or radiates microwaves of the above frequency. It is believed that this transition count of the Cesium-133 atoms always remains constant in the reference frame of the earth's speed and its gravity field. And therefore, ticking speed of time is determined by this count. Accordingly, duration of 1 second is decided by very precise counting of the frequency of this radiation. In order to adjust the time of these clocks, a signal of this radiation is sent to an oscillator, where the ticking speed of the clock, could be adjusted by adjusting this signal. In the above perspective, let us find out that how the ticking speeds of the clocks carried by the satellites, are affected.

As we know, atoms absorb energy from the higher energy fields, and similarly, they release energy into the lower energy surroundings. Accordingly, the electrons lose some energy in the weaker gravitational field prevailing in the space, and as a result, they jump from a higher energy level to a lower energy level, that is, a little closer to the nucleus. On the other hand, because of very high speed of the satellite, they gain some energy, and are pushed away, to the corresponding higher energy levels. A combination of both of above effects might compel the electrons to occupy slightly higher energy-level than what they occupy at the earth's surface. The electrons therefore, might take slightly longer time to complete their orbits, which in turn, might reduce the transition count of the electrons. Therefore, counting of the fixed number of say 9.2 billion transitions, might take slightly longer time period as compared to one second. This might be the cause of apparent slowing down of the rate of ticking of the time, whereas, the time might continue to tick at a constant, unchanged rate. Similarly, if the lone electron, orbiting in the last orbital, loses some energy, then it would go a little closer to the nucleus. As a result, the number of transitions per second might increase. The time would, therefore, appear to run faster, because the counting of the fixed number of 9.2 billion Transitions will be completed in less than 1 second. *This means that the very scale of the atomic clocks, for measuring time, would change, instead of any change in the ticking speed of the time. These clocks would, therefore, measure the same time-period differently, under different conditions. This is analogous to the old fashioned wall-clocks, in which the scale for measuring the ticking rate of time was affected due to variations in the temperature,*

rather by the variation in the length of the pendulum. Correctness of this speculation can be verified by the following example.

For the last 14 billion years, that is, since the inception of the universe, various stars located in the central part of our galaxy, are orbiting the galactic center with an average speed of about 250 km/Sec, or more. If time really slows-down at higher speeds, then during the said time period of 14 billion years, all these stars, in comparison to the Galactic Centre, should have moved ahead in time, by about 500 years or more. Similarly, electrons, in the Hydrogen atoms, orbit the nucleus at a speed of about 2300 km/Sec, that is, at about 0.07% speed of the light. Moving with this speed they, as compared to the atomic nuclei, should have moved ahead in time by about four-hundred-thousand years. If the speed of expansion of the universe is also considered then the time-gap between the stars and the galactic centre or between the electrons and the atomic nuclei, would increase manifold. ***This means that, electrons, within any atom, are orbiting a nucleus that exists at a far remote point in time, not in the same time. A question arises in this scenario that "what will cause the electron to move in the orbit, and around what object?"*** Similar would be the case with the Galactic Centre and the stars orbiting it. ***Had the time shift been possible, then the structure of the entire universe and that of the matter as well, would have shattered long back.*** Contrary to above, matter and the universe, both have maintained their existence since the inception of the universe. ***This fact indicates that the ticking speed of the time is not at all affected by the speeds of the electrons, or the stars.***

It seems from the foregoing discussions that ***"time" doesn't shift due to the speeds of the moving objects or due to any variation in the intensity of the gravity field. Instead, it is the scale of the atomic clocks for measuring time, which might get altered. In case, this speculation, of mine, is correct, even then the importance and utility of the relativity or atomic clocks would not, at all, be diluted.*** Very precise calculation of time is required to dock any spaceship with a space-station, or landing a probe on any planet. Such calculations could, only, be done by the formulae of relativity, and such a precise measurement of time is possible by atomic clocks only. However, we might have to modify our existing concept of the "time," and its capacity to tick at the variable speeds.

(4) Slowing-down of the Process of Aging

The concept of aging, in relativity, is linked with the belief that the rate of ticking of the time changes due to the variations in the speeds and also in the strengths of the gravitational fields. However, as discussed hereinbefore, any change in the ticking speed of time doesn't seem feasible. It is also believed that the process of aging of the living beings would, at the speed of light, come to a total halt; they won't age, at all, if they travel at this speed for infinitely longer time periods. I feel that since the aging-process of the living beings depends on biological processes, the same could only be slowed-down, if this process could also be slowed-down.

Whenever we, the ordinary people, talk of speeds, we believe that we are at rest. We judge the speed of any moving thing in the reference frame of the earth's surface, believing that the earth is at absolute rest. But, the earth, the Sun, the Milky Way or any other galaxy, or any of the celestial bodies in the universe, are not stationary, all of them are moving with considerably high speeds. The entire universe is expanding with the near-light-speed, and thus we are also moving with the same speed; this speed can't be considered to be negligible as compared to that of the light. *However, our aging process does not seem to be affected, in any way, by these different speeds.* This fact gives rise to a question "does the speed really affect the process of aging?"

We have, since very long time-period, conceived a preconception, rather a misconception, that light and time travel with the same speeds. This is the reason, why it is believed that time totally stops at the speed of light. Or the other way round, time has zero relative speed in the reference frame of the speed of light. However, if a light beam is deflected, or its direction is reversed by a mirror, then the time prevailing at the source of that beam or at the earth, couldn't be changed or reserved. *This fact signifies that only the glimpses of time, not the time itself, travels with the light.*

The effect of speed, on the process of aging, could be understood by an example of a manned spaceship which is sent with the speed of light, to an exoplanet located about 10 light-years away from the earth. During the entire journey, any of the passengers of the said ship, would see only one wave of light coming from behind, and therefore, he may feel that the time has totally stopped. Now, in case that ship, after a period of 10 years, reaches the destined planet, then it would mean that during the entire duration of last 10 years, the ship had been moving ahead by 300,000 kilometers, every second. Accordingly, new events would have continuously kept happening all the way. Since the time is simply a concept of duration between two or more events, or more accurately, the rate of their occurrence, it would mean that time also kept running all the way. Had the time halted, then the ship couldn't have moved from its place, because no event could happen in the frozen time. If time didn't stop for the ship then how it could stop for the astronauts sitting inside? How could the time, keep ticking outside of the ship, if it had stopped for the astronauts sitting within? Different times can't exist outside and inside of the ship. It could, of course, happen that the astronauts might be crushed to death, due to the extreme pressure produced due to the very high rate of acceleration. In that case, time will surely stop forever, for such passengers, *however, if they reach their destination, live or dead, then it couldn't be said that the time had stopped ticking during the said journey.*

The spaceship probably, on attaining the speed of light, might disappear from the sight of the earthly people, and the radio contact might also be totally snapped. Under these circumstances, the fact that what would happen to the passengers of the said spaceship could only be explored after that ship returns from its journey. In case the time really stopped during the journey period, then though20 years would have elapsed for the people who stayed back on the earth, whereas the astronauts would still be in the same time when they started their journey. In other words, the astronauts after returning to the earth would find themselves 20 years behind the current time. When it is not possible to see the objects located in different points in time, then how the astronauts would be able to see the earth or land on it? If, at all, they succeed to land on the earth, then could the people living at two different points in time, could see, talk or meet with each other? Could two different times prevail on the earth, at the same instant? During this interval, the earth would have gone 20 times around the sun, and 7300 times on its own axis; how this time gap could be bridged? No clarification on these points could be given at this moment, because such journeys have not yet been performed. Nobody, therefore, knows the truth. But if such journeys are performed in the future, then the only possibility that I can visualize that all the astronauts, in that case, would grow older by 20 years. *No real effect of speed, on the aging process of the living beings seems to be feasible.*

(5) Relation between the Mass and Speed

The mass of any particle is believed to be a measure of its energy. The *Relativity Theory* further envisages that the matter and energy are interchangeable. Accordingly, it is also believed that the mass of any moving object should increase due to the extra energy of its motion, and therefore, more energy would be required to increase its speed further. As a result, requirement of energy, to increase the speed, would increase exponentially. As the speed of any object, approach the limit of speed-of-light, the requirement of energy would increase infinite times, and so would be the mass of that object.

Scientists also believe that the energy of any object, i.e., the mass of any object, could be increased by adding external energies like kinetic energy, etc., to it. *Since, the laws of science shall always remain same, it shall also be possible to increase the mass of a piece of matter, by adding extra energy to it in any other form too, that is, by heating or exposing it to a strong radiation, etc.; energy of an object is thought to represent its mass,* isn't this is true? Probably, this aspect has never been verified by anyone or reported by any of the sources.

If the mass of an object really increases by increasing its speed, then reverse of this shall also be true; mass of any object shall decrease by decreasing its speed; if this presumption is correct, then mass of an object, at the absolute zero speed, might become zero. This possibility indicates that matter might decay at the position of absolute rest or at the zero intrinsic energy. Since, position of absolute rest doesn't exist anywhere in the entire universe, this possibility couldn't be verified. However, if the particles don't decay at the position of the absolute-rest, then their intrinsic energies, that is, their masses too, might remain intact.

We all know that the objects, which appear to be stationary, are actually moving with the earth. Scientists believe that the universe is expanding with almost the speed of light. Therefore, the stationary looking objects are also moving with the universe, with very high speed. In spite of this high speed, no effect of speed could be seen on the masses of different objects. *This fact indicates that either the universe is not expanding at the near-light-speed, or its speed has no effect on the mass of any object. The latter possibility puts a question mark on this concept of Relativity.*

(6) THE FABRIC OF THE SPACE-TIME

This is a common belief that the interstellar space is totally empty, contrarily the same isn't an ordinary empty place; it is supposed to be filled with infinite amounts of energy and matter, both of which are distributed throughout the interstellar space in a random manner. In fact, the universe is a manifold or a combination of three entities, which are energy, matter and space (distances). Einstein, in his theory of relativity, suggested that time is not separate or independent of the space; it combines with the same to form the interwoven continuum of space-time, which, like other physical things, could be stretched, folded, contracted or twisted like a fabric. Ripples or waves of light and other kind of radiations, like those formed on the surface of water, are also supposed to form in this fabric. Rotating masses are supposed to drag-along the space-time around them. Einstein also envisaged that the fabric of space-time has an inherent property to expand, and accordingly, the far-parts of the space-time are moving away from us, at higher-than-light speed. It is believed that space-time is spread in two dimensions only. *If it is so, then all the galaxies shall lie in the same plane in which the Milky Way is located. If any of the galaxies is seen in any other plane, then it could be inferred that the aforesaid notion might be wrong; space-time is not spread in a two-dimensional plane; instead, it is spread in a three-dimensional space.*

The distances between various stars are so vast that they need to be measured in light-years. The time, due to these vast distances and relative motions of different celestial bodies, is supposed to differ from place to place. That is the reason that the fourth dimension of time, has come into being. *However, the stars that were born at the same point in time would have aged through the same time-period, no matter how far-off they are located from each other. But due to very large distances in between, such stars appear to exist at different points in time, which is only an illusion. In fact, they don't exist at the locations where they appear to be, instead, they exist somewhere else, in their respective present times.*

This fabric is thought to be so strong that it holds the entire universe; all the stars are spread over it like the pieces of straw floating on the water-surface. This fabric is thought to be so stiff that trillions of stars are spread on it in one plane. On the other hand, various small objects, like meteors and asteroids, etc., pierce through it, and keep falling on the earth and other planets. *The fact that this fabric can't even bear the mass of small objects like meteors, poses a question mark on the strength of this fabric, and also on the very existence of the fabric of the space-time, which has never been proved.*

(7) SPACE-TIME and the GRAVITATIONAL FORCE

Relativity envisages that gravitation is not a force like other forces; it is merely a consequence of warping of the fabric of space-time. It is also believed that planets move in a straight line, toward their nearest massive body, but due to the curvature of space-time formed around different massive bodies, they appear to move in orbits.

This concept of gravity has been, from time to time, explained on different television channels, by the help of a simple equipment, which looks like "Trampoline," which is a device used by kids to jump. In this equipment a flexible sheet is mounted on a strong frame, and if any heavy object is placed at the center of this sheet, then this sheet sags-down, or warps below that object, in the manner as shown in fig-4A. Another equipment, made of plastic or metal sheet, is also exhibited in most of the Science-Museums, in which a whorl shaped conical slope is created in the central part of this equipment, like the one as shown in Fig 4-B. The gradient of its curved slope increases gradually toward its central opening. When a coin is rolled down the slope of any of the said equipment in the direction transverse to the radius of the said curved slope, then the coin instead of moving in a straight line moves around the central opening in a circular path. It is believed that the planets also move on their orbits, in a similar way.

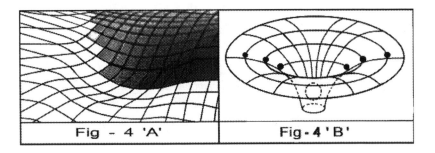

In both of the said equipment, objects moving in circular paths can, at a glance, convince anybody that planets do orbit their stars due to warping of the fabric of the space-time. However, on contemplating a little, a host of doubts comes up. Some of these doubts are discussed below.

a)   The flexible sheet, mounted on the equipment shown in Fig-4A, sags-down due to the gravitational pull of the earth. On the other hand, no force pulls the fabric of space-time, from the below. The same, therefore, shall not sag-down beneath the celestial bodies.

b)   Both, space and time, permeate in all the three dimensions, therefore, massive bodies shall displace the continuum of space-time all around evenly, in accordance with their shapes, as is done by any object, which is submerged in water; sagging-down of this continuum, like a two dimensional sheet, neither seem to be logical nor feasible.

c)   The coins, because of their initial velocity and the pull of the gravity, move in circular paths in both of the equipment. In case the same experiment is carried out on-board a spaceship, in micro-gravity environment, then the coin won't go round the curved surface of any of the aforesaid equipment. Instead, they would move in straight lines.

d) The prediction of Relativity that "the celestial bodies follow the nearest thing in straight line," attracts a question that what force causes the planets to move in a particular direction, or where from they get the energy to move continuously, and in a definite direction. This is against the laws of science.

e) ***Relativity*** predicts that the curvature of the Space-Time compels different planets to follow its curvature. If this prediction is correct then the same Space-Time, while expanding at near-light-speed, does not pushes different planets of the solar system and different stars of the Milky-Way, in the direction of its expansion? In other words, why the sizes of the solar-system and the Milky-Way are not expanding along with the expanding universe, with the speed of light

f) Since the gravitational force is a consequence of warping of space-time, massive bodies shall not attract any object toward their centers of gravity. Instead, the gravitational force shall appear to act along the varying inclinations of the curved space. Accordingly, no effect of gravitation shall be felt in the flat portions of the said fabric, at the flat portions of the space-time that extends beyond the outer edges of the indentations made by different massive objects. If the above prediction is correct, then different galaxies located far-away from each other, on the flat portions of space-time, shall not attract each other. Contrarily, galaxies attract each other from the far-off distances.

g) Since the celestial bodies orbit massive bodies, due to warping of the space-time, they should appear to orbit at different altitudes of the curved surface of the space-time, in the manner as shown in Fig 4B. Accordingly, the shapes and sizes of different indentations made in the fabric of space-time shall be visible very clearly. Contrarily, different planets of the Solar System, and various stars of different spiral galaxies, are spread over almost flat surfaces, not along any curved surface.

In case stars and planets are not moving directly on the curved surface of the space-time, then neither they would push the space-time nor shall the curved space be able to compel them to move in the orbits. Therefore, the flat distribution of stars, within the Milky Way, suggests that the space-time isn't warped, at least not in the shape as depicted in Fig-4B. The aforesaid fact raises a question that do the massive bodies really warp the fabric of space-time, and does the gravitational force is really a consequence of the warping of the fabric of space-time? The fact that nothing could move without any force, again gives rise to the same question that what force causes the celestial bodies to move in definite orbits, and in an orderly manner?

Probably, Einstein assumed that the curved paths* made in the space-time, are like closed rings. According to this concept, the celestial bodies, which are trapped in these curved paths, follow the nearest thing in a straight line, but the curvature of these paths, persistently pushes these celestial bodies and compels them to follow these closed ring-shaped paths. As a result, such celestial bodies, though moving ahead in a straight line, appear to move in circular orbits. This is analogous to the toy trains moving on fixed circular tracks. Though the train moves in a straight line, but due to the curvature of the track, it appears to move in a circular path.

If the above idea is correct, then these curved paths should necessarily be very stiff and strong so that they may exert adequate pressure on the celestial bodies moving through their respective curved paths, and thereby compel them to follow the curvature of these paths. How strong should be these paths, made in the curved space-time, can be understood by yet another example; if an ordinary ball is rolled-down the kid's slide, then it will easily roll-down along the curvature of the slide. But what would happen if that ball is replaced by a steel ball weighing 5-10 tons or by a very heavy ball fired by any cannon? The slide would, probably, be totally destroyed. The masses of the bodies, moving through the space, are millions of trillions times greater and heavier in comparison to any cannonball, moreover, they move with much higher speeds. This implies that the paths, made in the space-time, should be extremely strong. Now the question arises that could two nonphysical things like an empty place or merely a distance (space) and the time interval between two or more events, when combine together, become so strong and stiff that it may withstand the pressure of massive celestial bodies? This is clear from the fact that in reality, the trains, moving on the steel tracks, could easily follow the curvature of the track, but the same train can't run on the paths made on the surface of water. Similarly, direction of a moving ship can't be changed, simply by any path made on the surface of water.

If the curvature of the space-time compels celestial bodies to change the direction of their motions persistently, then this would result in continuous loss of their energies; more massive is the celestial body, proportionately, more energy it will lose. Relativity envisages that heavier objects, while in motion,

---

* These paths are known as "Geodesics," which is shortest distance between two points on a curved surface like that of the earth.

emanate gravity waves that ripple through space-time, at the speed of light. These ripples, like other waves, carry away energy from the objects, which emit these waves. The said energy-loss shall result in gradual shortening of the orbits of all the celestial bodies. Therefore, they, after some time, must gradually spiral toward the stars, which they are orbiting respectively. In case celestial bodies are really losing energies, then the said loss of energy should result in gradual and continuous contraction of the orbits of all the planets, and also the sizes of all the galaxies and their clusters. Contrary to the above possibility, the entire universe is continuously expanding instead of contracting. It can be inferred from above fact that the celestial bodies either do not produce gravity waves while moving through the space-time, or alternatively, no such fabric of space-time does exist.

In the absence of any proof that the fabric of space-time does really exist, it is hard to believe that gravitation is not an independent force. If gravity is not an independent force, then what is the explanation to each of the following questions?

1. While the earth moves in its orbit, why the atmospheric air, due to its inertia, is not left behind? With what force it is bound to the earth? Why it is not blown away by the Solar Wind?

2. Why the surfaces of the liquid substances always maintain even levels? And why do pressure is generated due to the head of water columns or atmospheric air? What force produces weight in different objects or bodies?

3. What force restricts us to lift heavy loads?

4. Why all the massive celestial bodies are spherical in shapes?

5. *Relativity* envisages that the planets, in the absence of any force, move like freely falling objects. If it is so, then why they don't directly and radially fall into the nearest star, or why the objects, which float freely within any spaceship, in zero-gravity condition, don't continuously accelerate forever? Nothing can roll down a slope in the zero-gravity condition, or move all by itself; a force is essentially required for this purpose.

6. Nebulae (gas clouds) are normally several hundred thousand times more massive than the stars. Such a huge mass must make a huge indentation in the space-time. When planets don't need any force to follow the nearest star, then the same shall also be possible for other objects too. Accordingly, any nebula shall rotate, as a single body, about its axis, which never happens. This fact implies that planets also need a force to move in their respective orbits.

7. If gravitation is not a force, then how the high-tides occur in the sea? How tidal effect occurs on the solid surfaces of the moons of the planet Jupiter, namely "Io" and "Europa."

8. Trivial bodies like the meteor and asteroid, etc., fall regularly on the earth from time to time. This fact puts the strength of the fabric of space-time under question mark. If this fabric is not strong enough to bear the loads of even small bodies, then how it bears the mass of massive stars and their planets?

9. Whether the man-made satellites are established in the pre-existing geodesics around the earth or their paths are calculated on the basis of the gravitational force of the earth?

10. *Relativity* predicts that celestial bodies, while moving on their orbits, push the fabric of space-time, and the space-time also pushes back these bodies with an equal force. This concept gives rise to a question- "why the air blanket of the earth, or the creatures living on its surface, are not crushed by the immense pressure created between these two?"

11. *Relativity* predicts that the celestial bodies having lesser masses fallow much massive bodies due to curved space. However, different planets in the solar system and different stars in the Milky Way are seen to spread over almost flat planes, not on any curved surface. This fact indicates that different stars and planets etc. do not move along the curved space. This means that the curved space does not compel the celestial objects to go round any massive body, there must be another reason for the same.

12. In case the earth orbits the sun because it follows the curvature of the space-time (as shown in Fig- 4A/4B), then the strength of Sun's gravitational field should have almost equal strength all along the earth's orbital path. Defying this possibility, strength of the gravitational field at any space station, located a few hundred Km away from the earth, is almost zero. This means that curvature of space-time is almost zero at this place, which cannot compel the earth to orbit the sun. On the other hand, the moon orbits the earth from a distance of 380,000 km. This means that curvature of space-time, at almost equal distance from the sun, is not uniform. This fact clearly indicates that Earth do not orbit the sun due to curved space, there must be another reason for the same.

13. If gravity is not a force, then how the planet Neptune causes irregularities in the path of the planet Uranus? Astronomers have observed that massive planets, orbiting any star, cause the stars to wobble. This

fact raises a question, "what force compels the stars to wobble? This phenomenon, in the absence of independent force, seems impossible.

14. Relativity predicts that all the things, which move through the curved space, shall follow its curvature. If above belief is correct then, whenever the moons of different planets happen to cross the paths of their planets, they shall be distracted by the bigger indentation that compels the planets to orbit their own star. Furthermore, since the curved paths, on which any moon orbits its planet, is made in the inclination of a bigger indentation, therefore, the moons of different planets shall orbit their respective planets in different inclined planes. In that case no eclipse of the sun or the moon would have been possible. This fact indicates that celestial objects do not move along the curvature of space-time.

15. The far-parts, of the space-time, are thought to expand with very high speeds; further is the part, the higher is the speed of its expansion. However, this uneven speed of expansion doesn't distort or elongate galaxies or planetary systems. This fact indicates that space-time, while expanding, doesn't push celestial bodies. This inference further suggests that celestial bodies are, probably, not moving in their orbits due to the indentations made in the space-time.

16. Since the celestial bodies are supposed to lose their energies very slowly by emission of the gravity waves while they move through the space, their orbits are supposed to contract gradually. On the other hand, release of very huge amounts of energies by the quasars, magnetar-flares, gamma-ray bursts and supernovae, etc. have no effect on the size of their orbits. This anomaly indicates that the energy distribution or any variation therein, have probably no effect on the sizes of the orbits of the celestial bodies.

17. **How the gas clouds collapsed without any force like gravitation? How the universe, or the galaxies, was formed? How the stars are created in the absence of gravitation, or they end up in supernovae or even in the black holes? (See Chapter-11 "Life Cycle of the Stars" for the details)**

At least first 10 to 13 questions must have been considered, at the time of formation of relativity theory. Whereas, on the basis of the new discoveries, the remaining 4 to 5 questions might have come up during the next 10 to 50 years. Clarifications to such questions are given, from time to time, on the basis of relativity. However, the existence of independent gravitational force is probably not totally negated in the current era. It is believed that gravitational force acts through its carrier particles called "Gravitons," however, gravitons could not yet be detected. The scientists should now make it clear "whether gravity is a force or it is a consequence of warping of the fabric of the space-time;" only one of these two concepts can be correct, not both.

Anyhow, based on the questions raised above, it does not appear logical, at least to me, that gravity is merely a consequence of warping of the space-time; instead, the existence of the fabric of space-time doesn't appear to be logical. Had gravity been not a force, then meteor, etc., instead of falling on the earth, should have kept floating in the space. Similarly, the speeds, of the falling objects, can never go on increasing until any force doesn't act on them persistently; *this indicates that gravitation is a force, independent of the fabric of space-time.*

(8) Deflection of Light near the Massive Bodies

General Relativity predicted that the light rays too, shall follow the curvature of the space-time, and accordingly, the light rays while passing-by any massive body from a close distance, shall deviate from their straight paths. This prediction was, after about 50 years, found correct, when the light was found to deflect while passing at a very close distance from the Sun. This was considered as a proof that space-time really warps near the massive bodies. But the Sun is not alone; the fabric of space-time shall also warp near numerous other bodies as well, whether massive or small. These bodies move along the curved surface of a huge, bowl shaped, indentation made in the space-time. Now, if the light rays really deflect due to curvature of space-time, then they shall follow this rule everywhere: rays shall invariably be deflected by curved space, near each and every celestial body whether big or small. However, light doesn't bend near small bodies or by their curved paths. This fact indicates that either light is not affected by each and every curvature of the space, or the space-time doesn't warp near smaller bodies. Since, the light deviates near very massive bodies only, not everywhere, bending of light doesn't appear to be a universal rule.

The phenomenon of bending of light-waves toward the gravity centers of the massive bodies is known as "Gravity Lensing." *The fact that light bends only at very close distances around very big bodies like the sun, etc., indicates that only very powerful gravity fields are capable to bend light, not the weaker ones. The aforesaid fact also implies that even very massive bodies can warp very small portions of the fabric of space-time, that too in their very close vicinities only, not at the far-off distances i.e. near the planets etc. If this inference is correct, then the planets, orbiting the massive bodies from far-off distances, must orbit them due to some other reason, not due to the warping of space-time.*

The wave nature of the light was established by James Clerk Maxwell in 1860-65. Since then, it is believed that waves can't be affected, by any force such as gravitation. Scientists still have faith in the aforesaid belief. Contrary to this belief some Indian scientists have succeeded in trapping photons in the magnetic field. (Please see chapter-4, "Some Least-known Properties of Light") If, magnetic force is capable to affect light waves, that is, a shower of photons, then why any other force can't do the same? *This fact suggests that gravitation, in the capacity of independent force, might also affect light waves or the photons, though from very close distances only; this force loses strength very sharply with even very slight increase in the distance.*

(9) The Limit of Speed

The Theory of Relativity is based on the postulate that "Nothing can move faster than Light," and also that "only the waves without any intrinsic mass can move with this speed." Contrary to this belief, cosmic rays, which are, in fact, shower of sub-atomic particles such as protons, neutrons and nuclei of Hydrogen and helium, etc., are found to travel with the speeds which are very close to that of the light. Likewise, Muons, which are 200 times heavier than the electrons, also move at speeds very close to the speed of light. The jets emitted from the quasars, also travel with the speed of light. These jets have a composition which is very similar to that of the cosmic rays. Even the entire universe, with all the galaxies, stars and planets, etc., are also believed to be expanding at the near-light-speed. *This fact indicates that massive particle and even massive bodies can also move at the speed of light.*

We all know that even the light, whose speed is highest among all the known moving things, can't escape the black-holes, whereas, the effects of its gravitational force, and also that of the magnetic force, are surely felt from very large distances. This fact puts up a question, *how the magnetic force escapes the black-hole? Does the black hole exert its magnetic force at faster-than-light speed?*

Pulsars are very compact stars, which are many times heavier than the Sun, and which rotate on their axes at very high speeds. Very powerful pulses of radio-waves are emitted after regular intervals, from the poles of the pulsars. Scientists believe that spinning magnetic poles of these stars, produce rotating polarized currents, which in turn, produce the said radio pulses. Some of the scientists believe that though these pulses travel at the speed of the light, but the source, from which these pulses are emitted, moves at a speed 6 times faster than the speed of the light. ***This belief indicates that faster-than-light speeds may be possible in the Nature.***

As per the information available on the Internet, some scientists have developed equipment, which are capable of transmitting radio-signals at faster-than-light speeds. During November, 2011, neutrinos were also found to travel at speeds faster-than-light. During the same time-period, that is, December, 2011, MIT, USA, exhibited a camera (**Chapter-4, "Electron and its images"**) which can take photographs at the speed faster than light. *When a camera, developed by the mankind, can work at the speeds faster-than-light, then the Nature may also be able to do so.* ***In case, the aforementioned speculation is correct, then the speed of light is not the limit; speeds faster than that shall also be possible, at least under certain conditions.***

(10) Relativity and Propagation of the Waves

General Relativity suggested that all types of the energy waves ripple through the fabric of space-time which is analogous to the two-dimensional water-ripples. This idea is very widely accepted worldwide, because it successfully explains how waves travel through the space and how they bend near massive bodies. In spite of the worldwide acceptability, this concept doesn't give a clear picture that how the spherical waves undulate while propagating in three dimensions. A two dimensional fabric can't spread in all the three dimensions, or if the energy waves propagate in all the three dimensions, then the space-time should also spread in all the three dimensions, not like a fabric. This possibility suggests very clearly that space-time, if it exists at all, is not like a two-dimensional fabric, it should also spread in all the three dimensions. But in that case the space-time would neither warp beneath the stars and planets, like a two dimensional fabric, and nor its warping may result in the gravitational force. Besides the explanations given earlier, in the Chapter-5, on propagation of light waves, few more possible anomalies that support this idea are discussed below. These anomalies put up question on the very existence of the fabric of the space-time.

It is believed that when any massive star, on the way to become a black-hole, collapses due to its own gravity, the curvature of the space-time in the immediate surroundings of such a body, increases gradually. Finally, curvature of the space-time becomes infinite. Gravitational force, of such a collapsing star, increases to such an extent that the fabric of space-time immediately surrounding the black-hole, is drawn within such a star, and, as a result, a hole having infinite curvature is ripped apart in this fabric all around the newly created black-hole. The light rays, which happen to pass through this hole, are trapped in its infinite curvature, where they keep moving in a closed loop or keep hovering there forever. The outer edges of this hole, made in the space-time, are known as the "event horizon."

Surprisingly, in spite of the fact that though, the medium of space-time doesn't exist around the black-hole, even then its magnetic force finds the way out, to spread beyond the event horizon. This fact suggests that the medium of space-time is not necessary for the propagation of the virtual photons of the magnetism. In case virtual photons of the magnetic field, emanating from the black hole, don't need the medium of space-time to spread all around, then this should be possible for the light-carrier photons too. And if this is possible for the light, then any other kind of the energy waves shall also not require the medium of the space-time, for their propagation. As brought out earlier, in the chapter-5, I personally feel that the possibility of propagation of energy without any medium shall be thoroughly examined. Secret of the duality of particle and the wave nature of energy radiation shall also be explored.

The concept of rippling of the waves through the fabric of space-time, as proposed in the Theory of Relativity, points toward numerous other anomalies in the proposed mode of propagation of the waves, it also puts up question on the very existence of the fabric of the space-time. Such anomalies are discussed below.

Relativity envisages that the light waves ripple through the fabric of the space-time, whereas, the space-time itself, is expanding with about the speed of light. If both of the above assumptions are correct, then the light should become almost stagnant or still relative to the expanding fabric of the space-time, because whatever distance light will travel in the direction of expansion, space-time will also expand by the same amount. On the other hand, whatever distance light would travel in the opposite direction, the expanding space-time would drag it back to the starting point. *This means that the light, in the direction of the expansion of the Universe, will move with the expanding space-time, whereas, it should not be able to propagate in the opposite direction. However, the fact that light moves spherically, in all the directions with equal ease, indicates that either the light-waves do not ripple through the space-time, or else the space-time is not expanding, at least, not with the speed of light.* Both of these assumptions of the Relativity cannot be correct simultaneously, and therefore, this point needs thorough scrutiny.

Space-time is supposed to adopt the curvature of the earth, at least, in its near vicinity. In case, the light-waves really ripple through the space-time, then light traveling closer to the earth's surface, should travel parallel to the earth's surface, along the curvature of the space-time. **However,** the straight line of vision of the living beings is a proof that light **does not** travel on any curved path; we, because of the earth's curvature, are unable to see the far-off objects located on the earth's surface. Contradicting relativity, the aforementioned fact tells very clearly that light, i.e., the shower of real photons propagates in a straight line; it **does not** follow the curvature of the space-time. *All the arguments* made *to prove Earth's shape, that is, its spherical shape, prove that light travel in a straight line. Moreover, this fact raises a question that does light really need the medium of space-time to travel, or does any such medium at all exists in the* reality.

The way all the galaxies and other celestial bodies are floating on the fabric of the space-time, requires that it should have very high tension, which should be the same or fixed all over this fabric. A question arises in this context, "if the tension of the sheet of space-time always remains fixed allover, then how different energy waves, having different frequencies, travel through this sheet simultaneously and in the same time instant." To me it seems impossible, because on the one hand different sorts of energy-waves, which have different frequencies, would probably need different tensions, of the space-time, to propagate, and on the other hand, any occasional variations in its tension would cause all the celestial bodies to rock at their respective places, or at least, their Gravitational Fields should vary. I personally, feel that this might not be possible. In this perspective, I feel that this fact needs very thorough verification.

It is also believed that all the celestial bodies are resting on the fabric of the space-time, which holds them at their respective locations by pushing them from the beneath. However, if black-holes really rip open holes in this fabric, then nothing would be left beneath them. This possibility raises a question that how the black-holes keep hanging in their respective locations? Why don't they fall down? These questions point toward yet another possibility that if black-holes, which are million times heavier than any stars, can remain floating without the support of the space-time from the beneath, then this should be possible for all the other celestial bodies too. In that case, the existence of the space-time would become unnecessary. The celestial bodies would, still, be able to remain in their respective orbits by the gravitational force; this possibility is discussed hereinafter, in the next chapter "The puzzle of Gravitation." This possibility suggests that the existence of the fabric of space-time shall also be thoroughly examined.

Had gravitation not been a force, independent from the curvature of space-time, then gas-clouds could not have collapsed to create different stars, and nor the stars would ever end up in supernova type explosions; black holes could never be formed. The existence of gravitational force seems to be a must, for the creation of the universe and its proper functioning (please see forthcoming chapters 10 to 12). The whole universe, in the absence of any binding force, would have scattered, thinned-out and disappeared in a vast emptiness. Moreover, persistently increasing accelerations of the free falling objects, suggests that a force, that is, the force of gravitation, is necessarily acting upon them.

8: THE PUZZLE OF GRAVITATION

Although Relativity doesn't cognize gravity as an independent force even then the scientists, of the later generations, have perhaps different ideas; the Standard Model of Particle Physics envisages that only a single "super-force" existed before the big bang, which later on split to create the *Gravitational force* along with *three other fundamental forces,* which are *The Strong Nuclear force, The Weak Nuclear force* and *The Electromagnetic force.* All the four fundamental forces are supposed to work in a similar way, that is, by emitting and absorbing their force carrier particles. With a little contemplation, it can be seen that gravitational force is much different from the rest of the three forces. Properties and strengths of the remaining three forces undergo changes at high temperatures, but the strength of the gravitational force remains unaffected, which works with the same vigor at temperatures ranging from absolute zero to hundreds of billions of °C. All the other forces repel like forces, but gravitation always attracts, it never repels. Normally, all the other forms of energy always flow from the points of their higher densities to the lower densities, so that the density of the energy at such points reduces gradually. Contrary to this, the gravitational force always attracts everything toward the point of its highest density, that is, the center of gravity. This property of the gravitational force causes the massive bodies to collapse and shrink in size. Gravitational force can crush the matter and compact them into a point of almost zero size, where this force becomes strongest amongst all the other forces. The discussions made under the chapter-7, *"Analysis of Relativity,"* suggest that gravitational force is not a mere consequence of the curvature of the space-time, it is an independent force. If gravity has not been a force, it wouldn't have the capacity to squeeze massive bodies within themselves. It is evident from this fact that gravitation is an independent force with a separate identity. Probably, Gravitation is not a property of any particular kind of particle; it is the common property of all sorts of matter-particles. The strength of the gravitational force of any object, because of the virtue of this fact, always bears a definite ratio to the combined mass of the total number of all the matter-particles contained within that object.

While contemplating over the birth of the universe, the problem that worries the scientists most is the strength, rather the lack of strength of the gravitational force. They expect that "since all the four fundamental forces were created by splitting of a single super-force, all of them should have equal strengths." However, gravitation is much weaker among the remaining three forces, almost billions times weaker. Probably, everyone has seen that even a small magnet can lift a small pin against the gravitational force of the earth. This fact might appear most ordinary to the commoners, but the same is a matter of great concern to the scientists. At a glance it might seem that even a small magnet can overpower the gravitational force of the entire earth. However, a series of questions arise at this conclusion, which are, 1) whether the entire gravitational force of the earth was centered only on that pin? 2) Whether the same magnet could lift comparatively heavier objects? 3) Would it lift the same pin from a much longer distance? 4) If a small magnet is stronger than the earth's gravitational force, then can it also affect the orbits of the moon or any other celestial body made of iron?

The answer to all the above questions would certainly be in negative. In case the distance between the pin and the magnet is increased a little, then it would certainly fail to lift the same pin. On the other hand, if the whole mass of the earth could be compressed to a small point, then its gravitational force would become so powerful that not just a small magnet, even the most powerful crane would not be able to lift the same pin.

It is clear from the above discussion that before jumping to the conclusion that even a small magnet is stronger than the Earth's gravitational force, an important fact has been probably ignored persistently, till now, that is **"the longest range-of-effectiveness of the gravitational force."** The strong and weak interactions respectively, remain effective within the range of the atomic diameters only. Although the magnetic fields of the celestial bodies, permeates through very long distances, but the electromagnetic force acting between the nucleus and the electrons, remains active within a very limited region only. On the other hand, gravitation is capable to attract the celestial bodies spread over distances of several thousand light-years, or even further. However, similar to the rays of light, the intensity of the gravitational force also goes on decreasing with increasing distances.

In the above scenario, it could be seen that the earth is exerting the gravitational force on the said pin, from its center of gravity, that is, from a distance of almost 6,550 kilometers. Whereas, the magnet can lift the said pin from a distance of a few millimeters only, that is, from a distance that is about one billion times shorter as compared to the distance from which the earth exerts the gravitational force on the same pin. Therefore, it wouldn't be proper, to say that even a small magnet is one billion times stronger than the earth's gravitational force.

Gravitational force acts over very long distances - even at such far-off distances where all the other forces become ineffective. However, its effectiveness depends on the masses of different objects and distances among them. This could be very well understood by the following example: Our Moon is located at about 380,000 kilometers away from us. From such a long distance we may not feel the force of gravitational attraction exerted by the moon - even then it produces tidal waves in the huge masses of the seawater. Similarly, the sun also, from a distance of about 150 million kilometers, produces tidal waves in the seawater. *The fact that the tidal effect is produced in the sea on its surface that faces massive bodies like the Sun and the Moon, not on the opposite surface, indicates that the gravitational force exerted by these bodies produces such an effect.* This fact also indicate that **the tidal effect is not produced by the curvature of the space-time, which shall be the same for both, seawater and the sand particles, whether they are lying on the surface facing the sun/moon or opposite to it.** Further, anyone can observe that *the sun and the moon respectively, exert attractive force on the seawater and the sand particles lying at the same distance from these bodies, in a similar manner, but tidal effect is produced in the seawater only.* The fact that both, Sun and Moon, are not capable to produce a similar effect on the sand particles lying on the sea beach**, *indicates that* more massive is the object greater is the gravitational force acting on it.**

Although the earth and the moon are located at about equal distance from the sun – even then the moon has been captured by the earth's gravity. This has become possible because of the smaller mass of the moon as compared to that of the earth, and due to its shorter distance from the earth. The Sun because, of this reason, is unable to exert as much force on the moon as the earth does. This further means that besides the distance, mass of various objects also has an important role; the combination of both, that is, the mass and distance, decides the strength of the force acting between any two objects. The structure of the entire universe depends on this property of gravitational force. Although the gravitational force is considered billions times weaker than the other natural forces, it carries out its role properly. Had the nature of gravitational force been a little different, from what it actually is, then either the universe would have collapsed to a single point immediately after the big bang, or it would have expanded at an infinite rate, and therefore, it would have defused in the endless space. Whatever duties the nature has assigned to the individual forces, it also has bestowed matching properties upon them, so that they may perform the assigned work efficiently. Or the other way round, it may also be said that the creation of the universe was done according to the properties of these forces.

And therefore, there is no point in comparing their strengths; the nature has bestowed all the four forces, with different properties and different strengths, so that they may discharge their duties properly.

Sir Isaac Newton proposed that the gravitational force, acting between two objects, could be calculated by the formula $(m_1.m_2)/d^2$, where "m_1" and "m_2," represent their respective masses, whereas, "d" is the distance between them, measured from their respective centers of gravity. The distance between the center of gravity of two or, more objects is, therefore, extremely important. The denser object, out of two objects of the same mass, would be smaller in size, therefore, the distance between its surface and the center, would be shorter, due to which its gravitational force would become more intense at the surface of the denser one. When any star collapses due to its own gravity, and becomes a black hole, then the intensity of its gravitational force increases a lot. As a result, any black hole, in comparison to the original star, exerts much stronger force on the objects located at equal distances from their outer surfaces. This can be understood by the example of an optical lens, which can focus light rays on a very small area, and make a piece of paper to catch fire. In the same way, when entire gravitational force, of any massive object, is concentrated at one point, then its intensity increases to such an extent that even the atoms of that object are crushed and compressed into a zero-sized point.

As per the prevailing concept, the strength of gravitational force, acting between two objects, decreases in the inverse proportion of the square of the distance between these objects. However, gravitational force doesn't act in two dimensions only, instead, the same permeates spherically in all the three dimensions. And as such, its strength should decrease in the inverse proportion of the volume, instead of the area, that is, in the inverse proportion, of the third power of the distance (d^3) from its center. According to Newton's Formula, the value of force, acting between two objects, is taken as $(m_1.m_2)/d^2$. Now, the question arises that, how a smaller object can exert force of the same magnitude on the much massive object, as the bigger object exerts on the smaller one? In fact, the value of the total force, acting between two objects, should be the sum of the attractive forces that the individual objects exert on each other. However, smaller objects are, normally, not able to exert any appreciable attractive force from the larger distances, because their gravity fields fail to reach out to much longer distances; only bigger objects attract the smaller ones. In case both of the objects have considerable masses, and the distance between them is comparatively shorter, then the total force, acting between the two, shall be the sum of the forces exerted by each one of them individually on the other one. This idea needs thorough verification.

The way, the gravitational force performs its function, could be understood by the example of light. Any distant star could be seen from a very long distance of billions of light-years, whereas, it is not possible to see the candlelight from the same distance. This doesn't mean that the rays emitted by a candle, won't reach us from far-off distances. Different light sources, depending on their energies or the intensity of light emitted by them, could be seen from different distances; this has no relation to the speed of light. The candlelight could not be seen from far-off distances, because its intensity, after traveling through even a small distance, defuses to a great extent due to continuous expansion in all the three dimensions. In other words, the number of photons per unit area, that is, the flux of light, diminishes to such an extent that it becomes difficult to see their source, the candle; it is the intensity of the light-source, which matters. Any source of light, normally, emits a flood of successive light-waves, which propagate one after another. Therefore, the intensity of light, that is, the flux of photons per unit area, at any particular distance from the source, normally remains almost the same. As a result, when any object comes out of the shadow of any other object, then the same would be instantaneously flooded with light; it doesn't matter, how far-away that object is located from the source. ***Such objects do not have to wait for the fresh light waves, to come from the source, to illuminate them***.

Gravitational force might also work in a similar fashion. Everybody might be conversant that the telescopes, having bigger lenses, instead of smaller ones, can see a faint light in a much better way. Similarly, a battery of photocells can produce more power than a single cell. Analogous to this fact, any massive star would exert more force on a massive object than what it would exert on a smaller object located at the same distance, or even closer. The gravity field of any celestial body, unlike the deep gravity wells as envisaged by Einstein, probably permeates spherically, all around its source, like an invisible halo. The ambit or the reach of the gravitational field of any object might extend to infinite distances, but as the distances go on increasing, its intensity becomes so weak that it might not exert any appreciable force on other objects from a large distance. A small object, situated within the gravitational field of any massive body, may or may not exert any appreciable force on the said massive body, or on any other small object situated in that field, but the massive body, depending upon the distances, and masses of different bodies, would exert much stronger force than that any smaller objects would exert on the same object. Wherever any small object would move within the limit of effectiveness of any pre-existing gravitational field of the said massive body, the strength of gravitational force, acting on that object, would be adjusted immediately and automatically, according to the varying distances between both of them. *Analogous to the light waves, gravitational force would not be required to travel repeatedly between these two bodies.* This would mean that **within the ambit of any gravitational field, the gravitational force, acting among two or more bodies, would immediately be adjusted according to their varying distances, without depending on the speed of the gravity.** However, any celestial object would not exert any appreciable force on any star or any known celestial body beyond the limit of effectiveness of its gravity field.

Earlier, before the formation of the *general relativity theory,* it was believed that if any celestial body moves from its place, then the force acting amongst all other bodies, located at infinite distances, would change instantaneously. This concept is only partially correct that too within comparatively shorter distances. As explained in the previous paragraph, the strength of the gravity field of any object can neither remain constant nor be effective at infinite distances. In fact, the distances between the stars located within any galaxy, are far too long in proportion to their masses; as a result, the stars, because of inadequate field strengths at larger distances, are unable to affect the movements of the planets of the nearby stars, or snatch away their moons. Similarly, no star is capable to affect the speeds of other stars or shift them or their planets from their respective orbits. All the stars, within any galaxy, remain attached to its central black hole only, without disturbing other stars. **It is a matter to ponder that if the gravitational force of any star, depending upon its mass and also the distance from other stars, fails to reach out to even the nearest stars, then how the same can affect all the stars of the entire universe?**

Although the Gravity field, of any supermassive black hole, permeates beyond the outer edges of the host galaxy, it becomes so feeble that it may not be able to exert any appreciable force on the normal sized stars, beyond that limit. In spite of this limitation, the same black hole, of course, attracts extremely massive bodies like supermassive black holes located in the centers of other nearby galaxies. However, at such a long distance the black hole of any galaxy is not able to exert any appreciable force on the stars of other nearby galaxies, orbiting their respective black holes. Because of this reason, other galaxies will not at all affect the rotational movements, of any star, or its planet, or any other celestial body, orbiting their respective stars or planets, etc.; they would continue to orbit their respective gravity centers, without any disturbance, whatsoever.

Galaxies, of different sizes, are spread all over in the universe, and are located at different distances from each other. The gravity fields of their central black holes, depending upon their masses, permeate up to different distances.

The gravity fields of all such black holes, because of very large distances among other galaxies, become so weak that the gravity field of only the most massive black hole, among other black holes of other nearby galaxies, is able to attract smaller black holes of the galaxies located within the ambit of its gravitational field. Therefore, analogous to the whirlpool formed within the washbasin, smaller black holes, with their respective disks of stars; orbit the nearby galaxy that has the most massive black hole in its center. Such whirling structures of galaxies are known as Local clusters of galaxies or local groups of galaxies. In such constellations of galaxies, all the stars of the galaxies, orbiting the most massive black hole, continue to move on their respective paths, without being affected, in any way, by the gravitational force of the black holes or stars of the other galaxies.

Different local-clusters of galaxies are located at even much greater distances than the distance that exists among the black holes of different local-clusters of galaxies. So that only the biggest black hole situated in the centre of a particular local cluster, is able to exert force of attraction on only the biggest supermassive black holes of the nearby local clusters of galaxies. As a result, strong gravitational bonds are developed among the biggest supermassive black holes of different local clusters of galaxies. Gravitational force causes all the nearby smaller clusters of galaxies, having black holes of comparatively lesser masses, to orbit that local cluster of galaxies, which have the most massive supermassive black hole in its center. In this way still bigger clusters of galaxies are formed which are known as "Super-Clusters of galaxies."

The distances, between different super-clusters of galaxies, are so vast that even the most massive black holes fail to exert any appreciable force on the other supermassive black holes that are located in the centers of the other super-clusters. Due to this reason, the super-clusters are floating almost freely in the space. Formation of still bigger whirling configurations of super-clusters of galaxies becomes impossible in the absence of any strong attractive force acting between these freely floating super-clusters of galaxies. Such super-clusters are not connected directly with each other; instead, they are connected to each other, one by one, like the links of a chain, by very weak gravitational force that acts between the central black holes of each super cluster. Because of this type of bondage, the super clusters are joined together like spider's webs. Such structures are known as "Filaments". These Filaments can form very long chains measuring to billions of light-years. Webs of such chains are spread in the entire universe, all around. However, in the absence of any strong bondage between them, even a feeble force can cause these super-clusters to move away from each other. In this expanding universe, only these super clusters are perhaps drifting apart, not the other whirling structures that are held together by strong bondages of gravity. Such rotating structures are probably stable in shapes, because of strong gravitational bondages.

Whenever galaxies happen to come very close to each other, the attractive force, acting between their respective black holes, might increase exponentially. Accordingly, they might start to come still closer gradually, spiraling toward each other, and finally they may collide. After such collisions, they totally merge into each other within a few million years, and form a much bigger single galaxy. After such collisions, the black holes, of both the galaxies, start orbiting each other to form a pair of binary black holes. Eventually, the smaller black hole might fall into its bigger companion. Likewise, if a much smaller galaxy comes very close to a massive galaxy, then the bigger one may stretch the smaller one, like spaghetti, which after some time, may add up to the bigger galaxy like an extra arm. In this case, the smaller black hole would start orbiting the massive one from quite a distance. The smaller black hole would gradually approach the bigger one, through a spiral path. In the due course of time, either the same, after reaching too close to the bigger one, would finally, merge with it or it would be thrown out of such merging galaxies, to the far-off distances. Such supermassive black holes, which have been thrown out, would gradually accrete stars from their surroundings, and thereby they would build new galaxies in the due course of time. All the previously mentioned activities depend only on the distances and masses of different galaxies, and their respective black holes.

9: THE STRING THEORY

According to this theory, the whole universe, that is, all the known and unknown things, all particles whether real or virtual, space-time and all types of energy, etc., are thought to have been made of oscillating string-like objects, which do not have any dimensions other than the lengths. The universe is supposedly comprised of a web formed by these strings. Particles are now supposed to be **waves** travelling on these strings. Different types of particles are thought to be collection of nodes (points of zero amplitude) on these vibrating strings. These nodes are formed at such places where two threads of the said web meet each other.

String theory envisages that instead of having different types of elementary particles, we have a single type of one dimensional object known as fundamental or elementary string, which is the basic constituent of the matter and all other entities. The same string when oscillates in a different manner appears as a different particle. In other words, different vibrational states of the same string appear to us as different elementary particles. This is similar to a musical instrument in which a single string, when vibrates in a different manner, produces different musical notes. Any change in the frequency of these strings, results in change of places of the nodes and their count per unit length; as a result the same string is converted into another kind of particle. One of the vibration states of the said string has properties similar to the hypothetical *"Graviton."* This theory also envisages that two pieces of strings, by virtue of their inherent properties, can join together to form a single string or a single string can divide or split into two different strings. This theory is though, very hard and complicated for the common man, scientists believe that anything can possibly happen in the world of particle science.

These theories now have 5 different versions in which strings can perform different types of vibrations. It is envisaged that the total numbers of dimensions are not limited to only 3 or 4; instead, there may be as many as 9, 10, or many more dimensions, even as many as 25 to 26 dimensions are possible. Scientists believe that possibly the gravitational force, while traveling through all these 26 dimensions, dilates to such an extent that it loses most of its strength, and thereby it becomes so weak.

In the big bang theory, it is not clear that how the universe begun from nothing, or zero. String theory has tried to remove this anomaly also. Before formulation of this theory, the universe was thought to be only one and single, but the string theory envisages multiple universes having multiple dimensions. Such a constellation of different universes is called "multiverse". These multiple universes may be like different slices of bread, which are known as "membranes" or simply "branes." It is believed that collisions of two or more "branes" result in explosions similar to the big bang. Such explosion did not happen only once in the history, such collisions might be repeated several times, after regular intervals; explosions similar to big bang are among regular activities of the multiverse.

It is very hard to understand that what these extra dimensions are. All the distances, in all the directions, can be measured in the known three dimensions. Every country on this globe has different cities; every city has different buildings, and every building has its own set of measurements of length, breadth and height. However, all these measurements taken at different places, come within the known three dimensions; it is very hard to imagine any other dimension. On the other hand, scientists believe that any single line can be considered as a separate dimension. Scientists believe that perhaps the "Large Hadron Collider can discover these extra dimensions," but this could not be done so far.

×   ×   ×

Scientists have observed that when subatomic particles are made to collide at high energies, then different kinds of new particles are produced. The particles so produced include some known elementary particles and some rare particles like the muons, mesons and positrons, etc.; thereafter these newly created particles decay almost instantaneously. The law that "particles can neither be created and nor destroyed" poses a question that is, "where do such new particles come from, and how do they destroy?" On the other hand, the string theory envisages that if a state of vibration of a string is altered, then such particle is converted into a new particle. I feel that if this is possible, then the energy of collisions might be momentarily absorbed by the colliding particles, due to which the natural order of fluctuations, that is, frequencies and the amplitudes of the strings comprising these particles might be altered. This change of frequency might, in turn, convert the colliding particle momentarily, into an entirely different particle. A short while afterwards, when the energy of collision departs, in the form of a photon or any other particle like photons, or neutrinos, etc., then these particles might be converted back into the original particles. Similarly, the energy of collision possibly, might also split the composite particles into their constituent sub particles.

CLARIFICATIONS NEEDED ON THE STRING THEORY

String Theory has been formulated with the hypothetical 9, or even more dimensions, to maintain conformity with *The Theory of Relativity, Quantum Mechanics and the Standard Model of particle physics, etc.* Scientists believe that multiple dimensions might really exist, but because of their compact near-zero sizes, we fail to cognize or take notice of them. Scientists have many expectations from this theory because it can provide solutions to many problems remaining unresolved up till now. However, in order that the common man may also understand this theory, the following points need further clarifications:

1. What are these extra dimensions? And why do they affect the gravitational force alone; why not the electromagnetic force, or any other force as well?

2. With what stuff these strings are made of? And where from these strings get energy to keep vibrating continuously? If they are made of energy, then how energy could be confined in any particular place; why it doesn't dilate or flow to some other place of lower intensity?

3. Since, all types of the energy waves vibrate at very high frequencies, therefore, these strings should have very high tensions. These strings might possibly be of two types; the first type may have open ends and second types of strings may be of closed ended type. Now, the question arises that "where the ends of these strings are tied to, and how such a high tension is produced in both the types of these strings?"

4. In case a particle, due to change in its frequency, may really be transformed into another particle, then how the tensions of these strings are adjusted or varied to match the new frequency?

5. If the same string could be transformed into different particles, then how it is possible to transform their masses and different charges, etc., such as electrical charge and the color charges, etc., into another kind of charge? For example, electrons and protons differ very widely, not only in their masses, but in their electrical charges also. How is it possible to transform an electron into different particles, that is, sometime in quark, sometimes in a proton and sometimes in an antielectron, by merely altering its frequency?

6. Different particles, depending on their energies, are supposed to have different masses. If the same particle is transformed into another particle of higher or lower mass, then its energy should also increase, or decrease. This means that such particles would either gain energy, or

lose it. The law that "energy could neither be created nor be destroyed," puts a question on this concept "where from such particles gain extra mass, or what happens to the mass they lose?" This is contrary to the laws of Science.

7. When two particle beams are made to collide, then, at times, different types of new particles are produced. Some of such new particles immediately decay and produce some other elementary particles. The fact, that new particles are produced only after collision, not at the time when their energy was increased, indicates that *"it is the energy of collision that produces new particles, not the higher energy imparted to such particles."* This point needs clarification.

8. From the above probability, it appears that some of the energy of the collision is momentarily transferred to the colliding particles. Due to this reason, the same string might start to vibrate in a different manner instead of vibrating at its natural frequency. As a result the same string might behave like a new kind of particle, and after the extra energy absorbed by it, is released, the same string might transform back into the same or any other elementary particle. This idea needs thorough verification.

9. In case different particles of more than one kind are produced after such collisions, then new strings should also, compulsorily, be produced. This possibility raises a question that "where from these new strings are produced?" This contradicts the law that "nothing could produce from zero, or nothing." A similar question also arises that is, "where the strings, of the decayed particles, disappear after the decay of any such particle?"

Scientists might have the answers to all of the above questions, but in order that common man too, may understand this theory, answers to above questions shall also be included in this theory.

PART- 3

THE
UNIVERSE
&
ITS
FUNCTIONING

10: THE UNIVERSE AT WORK

The meaning of the word "Universe" is probably known to everybody, but perhaps, some of them don't know that how big it is. The entire ambit of the universe, or its total span, could, probably, not yet be seen. We have, by very powerful telescopes, seen stars spread over the distances ranging from 13 to 14 billion light-years. Up till now, about 200 to 400 billion galaxies have been seen in the known universe. Out of which, every galaxy contains several hundred billions of stars. The mankind, in spite of such a vast expansion of the universe, didn't know till 1924, that stars also exist beyond the Milky Way. Before that period the Milky Way was, naturally, assumed to be the entire universe.

In the ancient times all the stars, except for the planets, were thought to be stationary. Afterward, people realized that as the earth moves ahead on its path, some of the stars, which are located comparatively nearer to us, appear to slightly change their positions relative to the distant ones. This is similar to the phenomenon of looking out of a moving train; when we peep out of the window of a running train, then the nearby things, such as the ground down below and the trees, appear as if they are moving with very high speed in the opposite direction, whereas the distant things appear to be almost stationary. The aforesaid apparent displacements of these stars enable the scientists to measure their distances relative to us.

Our Milky Way is, in fact, a medium-sized galaxy in which about 200 billion stars are distributed in the shape of a disk. This disk measures about 100 to 125 thousand light-years diameter-wise. On the other hand, the thickness of this disk is only one thousand light-years, that is, about $1/100^{th}$ of its diameter, or even less. In the beginning, probably, based on this fact, the universe was believed to be two-dimensional in shape; contrarily, the universe, in fact, should spread in all the three dimensions. The universe comprises approximately 400 billion galaxies, many out of them, are much bigger in comparison to the Milky Way. The biggest galaxy, seen up till now, is about 60,000 times bigger than our Milky Way. All the stars, contained in the Milky Way, are not distributed evenly in a totally flat disk; this disk bulges-out, like a ball, in its center. All the stars, of the Milky Way, are not equal in their sizes; some of them are bigger than our Sun, and some are smaller than it. The biggest known star is almost 2-3 thousand times bigger than the sun. Even much bigger stars may exist in such a vast universe, in one or the other galaxy. As against the vastness of the universe, we, with the naked eyes, cannot see beyond a few hundred light-years. It may be inferred from this fact that when we can't even see the entire Milky Way, then how is it possible to see the entire universe.

Earlier, we have seen that none of the stars, or the galaxies, is stationary in the whole of the universe. Accordingly, the Milky Way, containing several hundred billion stars, is rotating very slowly around its center known as the galactic-center. The stars, located in the middle part of our galaxy, including our Sun, orbit the galactic center at an amazing speed of almost 250 kilometers/second. Our galaxy is so big that in spite of such a high speed, it takes a very long time period of about 250 million years to go round once about its axis. Besides the rotational speeds of different galaxies, the entire universe, comprising all the galaxies, is thought to be expanding with the near-light speed. We are also moving with the same speed, but we are unable to feel it, that's why we think we are stationary.

The stars, located very close to the galactic center, might appear to have much higher linear speeds, and on the other hand, the stars located near the outer edges of any spiral galaxy, appear to trail behind other stars. Probably this is the reason that ***Relativity*** has predicted that as the distances of the stars increase from the center, their rotational speeds should dropout gradually. Contrary to above prediction, scientists, on actual measurements, have found that in fact, the rotational speeds of the stars follow almost a flat pattern; stars at increasing distances maintain almost same speeds, or they move with slightly increasing speeds. Probably this is the reason that stars appear to maintain almost the same ***relative locations*** with respect to each other.

If our Milky Way is seen from the above, from a distant point, then it would look like a spiral of stars, as shown in the Fig-5 "A." An imaginary cross-section of a spiral galaxy is shown in the Fig-5 "B," which shows that the stars, located very close to the galactic center, might orbit with all possible angles. A realistic side-elevation, of a spiral galaxy, is also depicted in the Fig-5 "C."

Fig- 5A

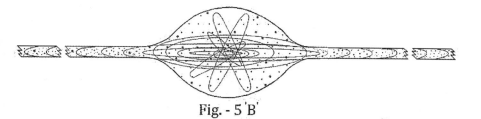

Fig. - 5 'B'

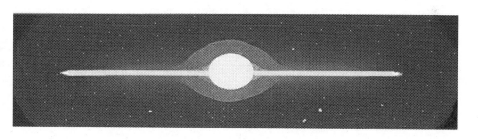

Fig – 5 'C'

All the stars are so far-away from us that they look like point-sized shining objects. Wherever we look at the night sky it appears all the same, in all the directions; small bright spots are seen spread all over the sky. The galaxies are located at such far-off distances that it is not possible to even see them with the naked eyes. Despite this limitation some astronomers, during the middle of the 18th century (around 1750), who used to observe the sky with only most primitive telescopes, predicted that all the visible stars might lie in a single band, which is now known as the "Milky Way." They also predicted that this band should appear like a flat disk. However, it took almost 150 years before this idea could be fully accepted. Since different stars, located at equal distances from the center of this disk, rotate with almost equal speeds, it is difficult to make out the difference between their speeds; they appear to be stationary with reference to each other, however, after long and patient observations, the stars located nearer to us may be seen to move in the background of the distant stars. The amount of the said displacement of the nearby stars, gives the idea of the distances of the furthest stars.

The ancient philosophers believed that the universe always remains in the steady-state; nothing ever changes in any corner of the universe. But contrary to this belief, the universe is a very active place; on the one hand, numerous stars regularly take birth at different places, and on the other hand, different stars at different places end up their lives with violent explosions. Sometimes a massive star or a black hole swallows another star, and at another place, a star, after running out of its fuel, collapses into a small but much denser body. At yet another place, two galaxies may merge into each other as a regular feature of the universe. In fact, the entire universe is the workplace of the nature, where numerous events happen continuously, but at different places, which are located at far-off distances from each other. Enormous changes take place everywhere in the universe at the different places; the phenomena of creation and destruction go on side by side. However, every new event takes place in such far-off places that we can't see or even imagine what is going on all around. Since we can't see or notice any change going on at different places, the universe falsely appears to us to be identical in all the directions. In fact, the universe is neither eternal nor immortal. Scientists, these days, believe that long back in the past, the universe started with a very powerful explosion known as "big-bang," and since then, it is expanding at a very high speed. It is also believed that one day, the whole structure of the universe will shatter. Different scientists during different times have devised different theories to describe the functioning of the universe. A broad outline of some of such theories is given below.

BACKGROUND OF THE "BIG BANG" THEORY

Probably, based on the fact that the universe appears to be identical from all the directions, the Russian scientist, Friedmann, in the year 1922, made two very simple assumptions: (1) the universe appear identical in whichever direction we look at & (2) this will also be true if we were observing the universe from anywhere else. Both of these assumptions in general, may appear to apply to the whole of the universe, but in fact they don't apply to any particular portion of the universe. Neither all the galaxies nor all the stars are identical; the distances between them are also not identical. Based on the fact that the universe appears to be identical from every direction, it should not be assumed that the earth is at the center of the universe. Scientists believe that since the universe is apparently identical from everywhere, it appears the same from the earth also. *I, however, feel that there may be another reason as well; since we, in all the directions, can see only up to a limited distance, we always remain in the center of the limit of our visibility*. Anyhow, it is not possible for us to see that how the universe looks beyond this limit or how far it has actually expanded in all the directions. In spite of this limitation, all the theories, about the beginning and end of the universe, are based on the aforesaid predictions made by Friedmann.

Our true understanding of the universe began in 1924, when Edwin Hubble focused a powerful telescope on an apparently empty tract of the space. To his astonishment, he found that the portion of space, which was thought to be empty, is actually full of a host of other galaxies. In 1929, Hubble made yet another discovery that almost all the galaxies are moving away from each other with very high speeds. This discovery brought a revolution that divided the world of science into two separate camps. One of the groups of the scientist interpreted that the universe could not be static, and also that it must have had a beginning sometime in the past. The other group, including even Einstein, firmly believed in the steady-state. This controversy continued almost for the next 40 years. Finally, in 1970, Roger Penrose and Stephen Hawking proved that in the remote past the universe begun with a powerful bang that is the reason that it is expanding continuously. This theory, eventually, brought the *end* to the concept of the "Steady-State."

×   ×   ×

George Gamow, the American Physicist of Ukrainian origin, in 1948, suggested that early universe must have been very hot, dense and would have been glowing with white-hot light (having a white-hot color temperature). Afterward, Robert H. (Bob) Dicke and Jim Peebles, based on above speculation, suggested that apart from scattering the matter-particles (that later on condensed into galaxies) a tremendous blast of radiation also must have been released by the "big bang." They also argued that light from very distant parts of the universe, would just be reaching us now in the present era. Therefore, we may still be able to see this radiation as microwave radiation, because of cooling down and very great redshift caused by the expansion of the universe. Accordingly, they started preparations to find out any such residual or relic radiation.

After some time, that is, during 1964-65, Arno Penzias and Robert Woodrow Wilson, who were unaware of the aforesaid prediction of Dicke and Peebles, accidentally discovered a microwave radiation, which appeared to be coming from all the directions. This radiation remained almost unchanged day and night and even throughout the year; it didn't vary even as the earth was spinning on its axis and orbiting the sun. If a very powerful telescope is focused beyond the visible stars, then a very faint glow could be seen. Scientists believe that this glow is coming from the surface of the last scattering of the big-bang. The "Background Microwave Radiation," discovered by Penzias and Wilson, was unanimously accepted as the proof of the "Big-Bang," and as well as that of the predictions made by Friedmann that "universe is identical in all the directions." As predicted, by George Gamow, Dicke and Peebles, this microwave radiation was believed to be the residual radiation of the big-bang.

From the inception of the civilization, the religious people and the philosophers have conceived various concepts about the beginning of the universe, but none of them had any proof to support his idea. And therefore, it was logically not possible to know that how the universe was born. In the present era scientists have two clues that are: (1) all the galaxies are running away from each other & (2) the residual background microwave radiation (discovered by Penzias and Woodrow Wilson) that always remains unchanged. The present hypotheses of the big-bang and expanding universe is therefore, based on at least a few grounds.

Almost at the same period, that is, in the year 1965, Rogar Penrose, on the basis of *The Theory of Relativity,* proved that a massive star while collapsing under its own gravity might get trapped into a region of the zero surface-area, i.e., it may shrink to zero volume, and become a "Black Hole." Stephen Hawking and Penrose, by reversing the direction of time in the above theorem, proved in 1970, that *if the theory of relativity is correct,* then the universe would have begun with a big-bang. This simply means that the *correctness* of the concept of the "big-bang," totally depends on the *correctness* of the *unproved postulates of Relativity.*

I personally feel that whenever any process is reversed, then we should know that up to what limit it could be reversed. If this limit is not known, then we would never know that at what stage this process of reversing should be stopped. This may be understood by the example of the relation between the volume of the gases and their temperatures. When the temperature of a gas is increased or decreased by 1°c, its volume also increases or decreases in a ratio of 1/273 of its original volume. If a graph is plotted, showing the above relation between the volume and temperature of the gases, then it would show zero volume at -273.15°C, that is, 0°K; below this temperature the graph would even show negative values of the volume. Since gases liquefy on cooling below a certain temperature, the volume of any gas can neither become zero, and nor negative. This fact clarifies that in the practice we shall not reverse a process beyond a certain limit. If we go beyond this limit, then the results, so obtained, would not be true or realistic.

On the basis of this fact, it may be said that if we don't know that when and at what stage did the universe start to expand, then how it would be decided that how much back in the time, we can go? Therefore, it cannot be imagined that what exactly had happened in the beginning? Whether the universe at its birth was only point-sized, or bigger? This means that the said theory of the birth of the universe is based only on assumptions. Since the scientists didn't have any clue other than the expanding universe and the background microwave radiation, no better theory of its beginning could have been formulated perhaps. Anyhow, I have come to understand that somewhat similar description of creation of the universe is given in the "Rig Veda" also; though I am not very sure about this fact.

A brief overview, of the "Big Bang" theory, is given herein below:

THE "BIG BANG" THEORY

In this theory, it is envisaged that before the beginning of the universe, infinite energy was concentrated in a very small point, which was even smaller than the size of an atom. This point was infinitely hot and dense, millions of billion times hotter than the cores of supergiant stars. Space and time were also believed to be encapsulated in the said point, where they had infinite curvature. Scientists believe that space and time also began with that Bang. Since all the laws of the science and mathematics break down at infinity, it is not possible to find out that what existed before that point, or what was the reason of starting of the universe with a bang?

Nobody knows that when and where the "big bang" occurred or what was the cause of this explosion. It is estimated that the said explosion occurred approximately 13.79 billion years back in the past. Some people say that the explosion, in that point, was stronger and louder than the blast of billions of hydrogen bombs exploding together, and on the other hand, it is also said that it was much milder and quieter. Whatsoever it might have been, the energy, so released, started to expand at higher than the light speed. It is envisioned that this energy would have spread all over in all the three dimensions, like an expanding sphere. All the matter particles, and subsequently the universe, were created within this expanding energy.

I envisage that the energy so liberated, could have expanded in any one of the following ways.

1) *Had all the energy been released in one sudden spurt, then all of it would have expanded like the surface of a bubble, or a thin walled hollow ball. In that case it should enclose a vast empty space measuring billions of light-years. Two opposite portions of its surface would move away from each other with a speed more than the speed of light. Therefore, it would not be possible to see or receive any radiation from the opposite surfaces of this expanding bubble. We would probably see only a small portion of the inner and outer surfaces of the said thin-walled bubble.*

2) *Alternatively, that point might have emitted energy for a few billions of years and thereafter it gradually ceased to emit energy. In that case the universe would have formed like a hollow sphere having a thick wall and two distinct surfaces, that is, outer and inner surfaces. By now these surfaces might have become faint due to continuous expansion.*

3) *As a next possibility, energy might have continued to ooze out of that point. Newer waves of energy, would have kept following the earlier ones, due to that the universe might appear similar in every direction, like the interior of a solid sphere. In case energy is still oozing out of that point, then we shall probably be able to see its source, but to best of my knowledge, no such source of energy has ever been seen.*

It is not possible to find out that in what manner the universe did exactly expand. However, scientists have predicted that in the initial phase, the universe and the space-time, both expanded together, at a speed much faster-than that of the light. Expansion of energy at such a high speed might have cooled it down very rapidly, accordingly, it cooled down in about trillionth of a trillionth second, to such an extent that energy started to convert into matter particles. At that time, it was still so hot that the particles formed at that point in time, consisted of quark-gluon plasma. The particles, so formed, had such high energies that they were still moving randomly in the form of countless eddies that were whirling and swirling in all the possible directions. The particles, due to their random speeds, must be colliding with each other. It is believed that in the beginning, there was only one single force known as "Super-Force," but within one billionth second after the big bang, this super-force divided into the four fundamental forces, that is, the "strong nuclear force," "weak nuclear force," "electromagnetic force" and the "gravitational force." Even at that moment, the newly created particles possessed such high energies, and they were moving with such a high speed that none of these fundamental forces were able to have any effect on them. Therefore, these particles, created within the expanding universe, continued their uncontrolled and random motions; unrestricted expansion of the energy resulted in the continual reduction of its temperature.

Almost after one second of the big bang, the temperature of the expanding universe fell-down to about ten-billion degrees centigrade, which was still about hundred-thousand times hotter than that exists in the core of the sun. At this temperature, some of the energy would have converted into very light particles like neutrinos, photons, electrons, etc. and their antiparticles. The types of particles that were produced at that time would have depended on the rate of fall of the temperature. These particles, because of their random motions, must also be repeatedly colliding with each other. Collisions of particles with antiparticles would have resulted in the annihilation of both of them. This would have resulted in production of more photons. Scientists believe that, due to some unknown reason, production of normal particles would have marginally outnumbered antiparticles; otherwise, the universe would not have survived. ***Contrary to the above belief, I feel that the nature probably knows* that what exactly it should do under any particular condition. The difference between the numbers of particles and antiparticles produced at that time was probably not merely a coincidence; probably, following the laws of nature, they were destined to be produced in that manner only.***

After about 100 second of the big-bang, the temperature would have fallen to one billion degree centigrade that persists in the cores of the hottest stars. At this temperature, some particles, like quarks, would not be left with sufficient energy to escape the attraction of the strong nuclear force. As a result, they would have started to clump together to create protons and neutrons, which,

---

*   See chapter-4, "Particles and Antiparticles".

in turn, again combined with each other to create nuclei of lighter elements, like Hydrogen and Helium. Nuclei of some other light elements, like Lithium and Beryllium, etc., also would have produced at that time in small amounts, but it was not possible to produce much heavier elements. Production of such nuclei of different matters would have stopped within 3-4 minutes of the "big bang," but the electrons, because of their very high energies, and very high temperature would have been moving with such high speeds that the electromagnetic attraction of the newly born nuclei was unable to capture them to form atoms. Therefore, while the universe continued to expand, the electrons continued to move freely, eluding the attraction of the newly created bare nuclei of different elements.

The universe, for several hundred-thousand years thereafter, continued to expand without any further activity. At that time, photons contained within the expanding energy, might have been interacting with the electrons and nuclei. It is believed that photons, at that time, were coupled with the bare-nuclei, and thereby a white-hot opaque fog of hydrogen plasma was formed. At that point in time the universe was not emitting any light, because the photons were not free; they were coupled with atomic nuclei. This period is known as the "Dark Age of the Universe". After about 379,000 years of continued expansion, the temperature dropped-down to a critical limit of, say, 3000°C. At this temperature the electrons and nuclei didn't possess enough energy to overcome the electromagnetic attraction among the two. Therefore, nuclei captured the electrons almost instantaneously, and formed the atoms of very simple elements, mostly Hydrogen and Helium. It is believed that at this temperature the photons would have decoupled from the nuclei and spread out in all the directions. As a result a sudden flash of bright light would have emitted from the infant universe. Scientists also believe that, this radiation, from the very hot early universe, might still be around today in the form of the photons, which would have cooled down to only a few degrees above absolute zero. Accordingly, these photons would now, be reaching us as microwave radiation. The "cosmic background microwave radiation" reaching us from all the directions, is thought to be the signature of the leftover or relic radiation, which was emitted for the first time from that white-hot fog. This radiation is also considered to be the indisputable proof of the big-bang. Presently, the color temperature of this microwave radiation has dropped down to almost 2.7°K.

Scientists believe that this microwave radiation was emitted from a set of points in the space, which were located at such a vast distance that these photons, emitted at the time of photon-decoupling, are being received now. These sets of points are known as the ***"Surface of last Scattering."*** In other words, this radiation which is supposed to have been emitted from the said "white-hot fog," about 13.7 billion years ago in the past, is being received now after covering the vast distance between the said sets of points of its origin and the existing location of our Earth.

At that point in time, the particles, because of their random speeds, might have collided with other particles, and as a result these particles might have coalesced together. Soon more particles would have started to accumulate in different places, due to which localized denser accumulations of matter-particles, in countless numbers, were formed in different places. Probably, for the same reason, numerous clouds of gas and dust were gradually produced all around. In the due course of time, these clouds might have grown bigger. The clouds located closer to each other would have developed gravitational bonds due to which bigger clusters of clouds would have formed in different places. However, those clusters of clouds, which were separated by very larger distances, might have continued to expand with faster-than-light speeds. The larger clouds, due to the random motion of the particles within, might have fragmented in yet smaller and denser areas. Gradually, in the next few million years, the localized denser regions of these clouds would have continued to collapse under their own gravity and would have become stars. The universe is supposed to have been created in the aforementioned way.

×   ×   ×

MY TAKE ON THE BIG-BANG THEORY

In case the universe was expanding at faster-than-light speed, then it would not have been possible for the gravitational force, which is supposed to move with the speed of light, to reach out to the particles moving ahead with the higher speeds. However, gravitational force of the particles moving in the front lines must have reached out to the particles following them from behind, because both, the gravitation force and the particle coming from behind, were moving toward each other. Due to this reason the speed of expansion of the matter particles, would have slowed-down gradually, which after de-coupling probably enabled the photons to move ahead of them. *Even in that case, photons couldn't move ahead of the fabric of the "space-time," which was moving with a faster-than-light speed, otherwise their speed would have become more than twice the speed of light.*

When the matter-particles were first produced, it is not known at what exact speed the universe was expanding? Since the entire matter was produced in the first 3-4 minutes, that is, within a very small region, the gravitational force should have immediately pulled-back all these matter particles, and squeezed them into a zero sized point. But contrary to this possibility, the universe persisted to expand; *apparently the matter particles, because of their very high energies and speeds, couldn't be affected by the force of gravity.* It is also not know that at the time of decoupling of photons what was the exact speed at which the universe was expanding? *However, since space-time was also expanding along with the universe, at a faster-than-light speed, it doesn't seem possible for the photons, to move ahead of either the fabric of the space-time, or the expanding universe.* **In that case the flash of light could have travelled along the expanding space-time, with the same speed, but in that case it might not be able to propagate in the direction opposite of it.**

The fact that "photons always appear to come from the place of their origin", puts the concept of "relic radiation" under the question **"if this radiation was originated at the time of decoupling of the photons, then why it doesn't appear to come from the point of its origin, that is, from a very small region, instead of appearing to come from all the directions?" This fact suggests that this radiation is not coming from the point of the Big-Bang; it is not the relic of the "Big-Bang."**

PROBABLE LOOSE-ENDS OF THE BIG-BANG THEORY

1) In case the speed of expansion of the universe, at the time of emission of the said first glow, was lesser than the speed of light, then that glow might have moved ahead, leaving behind the slow-moving universe. Since the photons always move ahead, in straight lines, it shouldn't be possible for them to come back; therefore, we shall not, at all, be able to see that first glow. On the other hand, if at that moment, the infant universe were moving at a faster-than-light speed, then that glow would have been left behind the expanding universe. Afterward, when the universe would have slowed-down, then after sometime, that glow would have overtaken the speeding Earth. Only at that moment, the said first glow could be seen that too, for a very short moment only. ***However, in that case it should appear to come from the point of its origin, not from all around.*** After that moment, the glow would have moved ahead, therefore, we should not be able to see that glow again; it just could not keep hovering on the earth forever. ***In this scenario,***

*the microwave radiation, of identical properties, coming from all
the directions, shall not be considered as the "relics of the first glow."*

2) The probable way in which Universe might have expand, is depicted
    in the Fig- 5D, Given below-

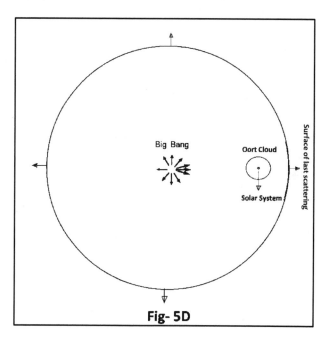

Fig- 5D

After Big Bang, the Universe did spread out spherically from the point
of big-bang, in all the directions. Thereafter the Earth was created in
the expanding universe after about 9 billion years. It is clear from Fig-
5D that *we are not at the center of the surfaces of last scattering,
therefore, different parts of this surface must be moving away
from the earth with different speeds.* As a result, the said microwave
radiation, reaching us from the different directions, should come with
different amounts of the redshifts; *it shouldn't appear to be identical
in all the directions.* Moreover, since the portion of the said surface,
lying at the other side of the point of the "big bang," is moving in the
direction opposite of that of the earth's direction, the same shall move
away with more than the speed of light. Therefore, no radiation shall
come from this side of the said surface. *This fact suggests that the
said microwave radiation might be coming from a surface, which
is surrounding the solar system from all around spherically so that
its size always remain stable with reference to the solar system, and*

whose temperature is about 2.7°K. I feel that the Oort cloud (Opik-Oort cloud), which is a surface of very cold, icy gases, ice lumps and the leftover planetesimals, and which surrounds our solar system spherically, from a distance of about 1½ light years, might fulfill all of the above requirements.

3) Light emitted from the oldest galaxies, located about 13.2 billion light-years away from us, could still be seen as light waves. Therefore, the glow emitted almost about 0.5 billion years earlier, shall also reach us as light waves, not as microwaves.

4) At the time when the first glow was flashed due to photon-decoupling, that is, 13.8 billion years in the past, the earth was not born; the same was created almost 9 billion years after the said emission of the first glow. During this period of 9 billion years, the first radiation emitted from the surface of the expanding matter, would have diffused in the space. However, the radiation emitted from the said surface at a right point in time, much before the birth of the earth, would have reached the early Earth after its birth; thereafter, subsequent radiations would have persisted to reach the earth regularly. Therefore, the radiation received now, shall not be considered to be the "leftover radiation of the first glow; the same was actually emitted much later."

5) Since the first glow was emitted when temperature of the expanding matter had dropped down to around 3000°C; the *first glow,* couldn't have been *"white-hot,"* as believed, *instead it should have been orange or dull red.* Thereafter, the temperature, of the surface of the last scattering, would have continued to drop-down. As a result, the frequencies of the waves, emitted from this surface, at different points in time, and their respective color temperatures, would have persisted to reduce gradually.

6) The early universe would have been very small. Therefore, the fact that the first glow should appear to come from the point of its origin, contradicts the belief that the microwave radiation seen today is the relics of the said first glow. The said glow emitted 13.8 billion years in the past, cannot come from the future location of its source, i.e., "the present location of the surface of the last scattering." Of course, the matter scattered by the big bang, must also have spread along with the expanding universe to far-off distances, *that expanding matter can't emit the said first glow forever.* Moreover, since the fabric of the space-time is not stationary, it is also expanding with almost the speed of light; it should not be possible for the light waves to travel

in the direction opposite of the direction of that of the expansion of the universe. *The only condition that light may propagate in any direction, with its normal speed, is that light shall be able to propagate without the medium of the space-time.*

7) Space-time is believed to have born with a "big bang." Expansion of the universe - even at the speed of light would, therefore, certainly result in thinning of the density and distribution of the continuum of space-time. Accordingly, its strength should also go on diminishing. In due course of time the space-time should defuse infinitely, thereby it might lose all of its strength. Moreover, since the area or volume of the space-time at its far-parts, is increasing at an exponential rate, it must expand at different rates, at different places. Since the universe, immediately after the "big-bang," was expanding at faster-than-light speed, it, at its outer edges, should expand at a rate hundreds of trillion times higher than that of the light, which is impossible.

8) The formula $E = mc^2$, suggests that energy amounting to at least 90 billion times greater than the entire mass of the universe, would have released from the big-bang. Energy always flows out from its higher density to the lower density. This fact attracts a question that is, "how such a huge amount of energy could accumulate in an atom sized point that too against its nature to flow outwards," and also that "where did such an enormous amount of energy come from?" Such questions are not unnecessary, they indicate the possibility that something must have happened before the "big bang." How the entire universe could be created out of nothing? What was special about that point that energy, violating its nature, accumulated in that very point only, not anywhere else? What was going on within that point, which resulted in the explosion of energy? And what was the reason that the said point exploded exactly at that particular point in time? All these questions clearly indicate that something must have happened before the "big bang," such as the creation or accumulation of energy in that particular point. This accumulation of energy finally resulted in the said Explosion. Since *"time"* is the concept of the duration between two, or more events, therefore, *if some events did really happen before the "big bang," then the "time" surely did exist beforehand; it was not created by the "big bang."*

9) It is believed that nothing existed before "big bang," except that point that contained space-time and the entire energy; curvature of space-time before the "bang," was said to be infinite. Now, the question arises

that if nothing existed, then in what place the universe was expanding? In case the aforesaid notion that nothing existed before the big-bang, is correct, then a vast void and limitless-emptiness would have been permeating all around. After "big bang," the universe and space-time would have expanded within that very emptiness or the void. The term "Space," merely defines the distance between two or more objects; it is nothing except the concept of distances. In what manner, the distances measured, within that "primitive void," differ from those, measured in the present day interstellar space? The universe is presently expanding within that primitive-void, and day by day, it is growing bigger and thinner. After a few billion years in the future, the universe would gradually dwindle-away and become so sparse that finally it would defuse completely. *However, the death of the universe would not be the death of this void; it would continue to exist. Neither this void was born, nor would it die with the universe. That primitive, empty place is, in fact, the "space;" it surely did exist before the birth of the universe. Both, space and time are not physical things; none of them was born with the "big bang," both surely did exist before the "big-bang."*

×   ×   ×

At this juncture, I am unable to withhold myself, from raising an irrelevant issue which is not, at all, concerned with the subject-matter in any way.

Above questions raised on big-bang are neither against any religion, or community, and nor do they, in any way, intervene or question the moment of creation. The God has bestowed the mankind with a bigger brain and an unquenchable curiosity, so that he may not just try to understand the unknown things, he may also succeed to understand them. It is rightly believed that nothing could happen against God's wishes. If he hasn't granted permission, then such thoughts would not have come-up in anybody's mind. This effort of the mankind is in accordance with the God's wishes. God has definitely blessed the mankind with the extra curiosity and bigger brain, with a special purpose; we shall not negate his wishes.

In case anyone has felt offended by above thoughts, then I tender my apology for the same; I have no intention to offend anyone or any religion in the world, I respect them all equally.

SIZE, SHAPE AND AGE OF THE UNIVERSE

It is believed that our universe was born about 13.8 billion years ago, and since then the stars, moving with very high speed, have spread in all the directions over a distance of nearly about 13.79 light-years. On the basis of this fact, it seems that the universe is expanding with an average speed of equal to the speed of light almost. In the year 1929, Hubble observed that almost all the galaxies are running away from each other; further away the galaxies are located, faster are they moving away. Based on this fact, it was implied that the speed of expansion of the universe is increasing continuously. Later, in 1970, it was envisaged in the "big bang" theory that the universe, in the beginning, started to expand with greater than light speed. *It could be deduced from the above fact that in the beginning the speed of expansion would have first slowed down, and after some time, it started to increase. This fact was, later on, confirmed, when in the decade of 90's, some scientists, while observing an exploding star (supernova), found that billions of years earlier in the past, stars were moving at comparatively much lower speed. Now, since the present speed of expansion is marginally below or equal to the speed of light, the average speed of the expansion of the universe, should be much below the speed of light. Based on this fact it could be deduced that the universe might have taken much longer than 13.7 billion years to spread through the distance of 13.7 light-years. Since this conclusion differs from the prevailing belief, it could not exactly be said that what is the actual age of the universe or what is its actual size?*

There is no single opinion on the shape of the universe. Some people think that it has spread over a two-dimensional sheet and some people think it looks like a three-dimensional sphere. Yet another group thinks that its shape might be like a doughnut, toroid, or an "O" ring.

Scientists believe that the universe is almost 13.7 billion years old, whereas, the estimated age of our own galaxy, the Milky Way, is around 13.2 billion years. On the other hand, furthest galaxies are also located at the distances of around 13.2 billion light years. This means that our galaxy and the aforesaid furthest galaxies would have born at almost the same time, at close proximities to each other, that is, about ½ a billion (500 million) years after the "big bang." It may also be predicted that these galaxies, at the time of their births, would have located very close to the place of the big-bang. As the universe expanded, all of these galaxies would have moved in different directions, but with almost identical speeds. Our Earth was born billions of years thereafter. Then how is it possible that the light rays, emitted from those so-called furthest galaxies, much before the birth of the earth, are reaching us now? This is explained by the help of Fig–6 "A," given below.

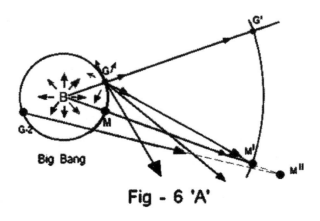

Fig - 6 'A'

The place of "big bang" is denoted in Fig–6A, by the letter "B." The locations of the Milky Way and one other galaxy born at the same time are respectively shown by the letters M and G. The present locations, of these two galaxies, are respectively shown by M' and G'. These two galaxies, immediately after their births, would have started to travel in different directions, that is, toward their present locations, and at the same time, they would have emitted light rays continuously, in all the directions. Both these galaxies were moving, with the expanding universe with almost the same speeds, therefore, by the time the Milky Way would arrive at its present location M', the said galaxy "G", after traveling by almost equal distance, would also have moved from its original location to its present location at G'. As shown in figure "6A," the galaxy G at the time of its birth would have emitted light rays in the direction of the future location of the Milky Way, that is, toward M'. These rays, after covering a distance of several billion light-years, would reach us now. During this journey of the aforesaid rays, and that of the Milky Way, the Earth would have born about 5 billion years in the past, within the solar system. When these rays would reach the earth at M', the said galaxy, instead of its present location G', would appear at its original location G, from where the incoming rays were first emitted.

Likewise, the rays emitted from yet another galaxy G-2, which was born at the same time, but on the other side of the point of the "big bang," would not yet have reached the earth. The rays emitted by the said galaxy G-2, in the direction of the future location of the Milky Way, shown by M", would probably reach the earth in the next few billion years. This means that we, at present, cannot see all the existing galaxies or the entire universe.

×   ×   ×

The galaxies, which born at the same time-period after the "big bang," would have immediately started to move in all the directions with equal speeds. Therefore, since then they should have traveled through equal distances, and by now, they would be located at equal distances from the point of the "big bang." The shape and size of the universe would depend on the fact that whether the space-time did spread on a flat, two-dimensional sheet of the space-time, or spherically in all the three dimensions. If all the galaxies are located on the surface of a hollow sphere, then due to limitation of our vision, they may appear to lie on a two-dimensional sheet. In that case we may be able to see either a very small flat portion of the total surface of such a sphere, or alternatively, the galaxies located within the range of our sight, may appear to have spread on a spherical cap. But probably we won't be able to see the entire surface of such a sphere.

Irrespective of above fact, whether the galaxies are spread in two-dimensions or they are spread in three dimensions, within a spherical ball (not on its outer surface alone), the surface of the last scattering, which was created in the first instant, would be moving in the front, ahead of all other surfaces of galaxies, and the same would be followed by different surfaces of galaxies, which would lag behind one after another, in the order of their creation. In that case, some galaxies would be moving ahead of the Milky Way and some galaxies might be following it. A schematic diagram of the universe expanding in this manner is depicted in the Fig–"6 B."

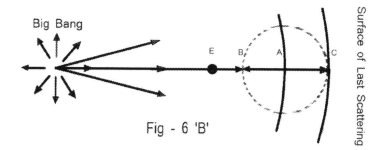

Fig - 6 'B'

A surface of galaxies, which is moving ahead of the Milky Way, but behind the surface of last scattering, is shown in this figure as "A." Since its inception i.e. even before the birth of our Earth (E), the said surface of galaxies "A," would emit light rays, in all the directions. Now, consider that a ray of light was emitted, at a right point in time, toward the future location of the earth, which is shown by the letter "B." The earth, immediately after its birth, would also have started moving in the direction of the expansion of the universe. By the time the earth would reach the point "B," the rays emitted from the surface "A," would also reach the same point "B," which is the present location of the earth. As a result, the surface "A" would appear to be located still at "A," from where the incoming rays were originally emitted. However, by this span of time, the said surface "A" would also have moved from "A" to its present location "C." Likewise, all other galaxies and stars must have moved to comparatively greater distances as compared to the distances at which they appear us to exist.

On the basis of the above example, it may be envisaged that the universe might have expanded even beyond its estimated ambit of 13.7 billion light years. If in the present era, we can see the oldest galaxies located at a distance of 13.2 billion light-years, then subject to the condition that such galaxies do still exist, they would have moved further away from the locations where they presently appear to exist, by a considerably longer distances. Therefore, we probably cannot find out the exact speed of the expansion of the galaxies; their apparent speeds relative to the earth could only be calculated. If this presumption is correct, then the actual expansion of the universe and its age, both, might be much more than what we have estimated.

NEBULAR THEORY OF STAR FORMATION

Apart from the visible stars, massive clouds of gas and dust, known as "Nebulae," also exist within all the galaxies and in the interstellar space. Such clouds might spread over very large areas, measuring up to hundreds to thousands of light-years. These clouds, depending upon their size, may contain several hundreds of thousands time more mass than that of our Sun. These clouds mostly consist of molecules of different gases like Hydrogen, Carbon-mono oxide and Helium, etc., and therefore, they are also known as "Molecular Clouds." These clouds also contain small grains and dust-particles, solid objects like pieces of ice lumps, small quantity of heavy elements and various other compounds. So far, total 118 types of molecules, of carbonic and inorganic substances, have been seen in such clouds. Since the stars are continuously formed within these clouds, they are also known as the "stellar nursery."

Large quantities of gas and dust molecules are spread all over very thinly within the different nebulae. The gas molecules and dust, etc., due to their mutual attraction, start to accumulate in different places. As a result, several dense gas clumps are formed within any nebula. Larger clouds gradually shrink or collapse within themselves, first, due to accretion, and then due to gravitational force, to form numerous dense cores. Accumulation of the gas, around different such cores, causes these clouds to fragment into yet smaller dense regions. Masses, of these dense pockets, may range to several times the mass of our Sun; their sizes may vary from 1 to 5 light-years or even more. Scientists believe that due to some *unknown reason*, the gas surrounding these cores, start to rotate slowly; **the reason of generation of this rotating motion could not yet be established.** Anyhow, the gas and dust, from these rotating clouds (known as "protoplanetary disks"), gradually start to accrete onto their central regions. As a result, gravitational force of these central regions increases gradually, which causes them to gradually squeeze within themselves. In the next few million years these cores, because of increasing pressure within their cores, grow immensely hot and start to oppose further compression; finally, balance is created between the gravitational crunch and outward pressure. Several hundreds of such hot cores may be created within a large cloud simultaneously, at different places. With time, these hot cores become seeds of different stars; masses and sizes of these seeds depend on the respective sizes and masses of their parent gas clumps.

Scientists believe that the gas clouds flattened out due to the centrifugal force generated because of their rotating motion. This is analogous to making the raw pizza bases, or "the Rumali Roties (a sort of very thin Asian bread)." Pizza bases are made by rotating and tossing the flat dough cakes in the air, on the similar lines it is believed that gas clouds also expand and flattened-out because of their rotatory motion. The sizes of these planetary-disks may range from ½ to 100 light-years in diameter, or even bigger that depends on the mass and amounts of gas contained in their mother clouds. When any such rotating gas disk that envelops the dense core, collapses inward, its rotational speed, gradually increases due to the conservation of its angular momentum. As a result their rotational speed increases, which further results in slowing down the process of direct accretion of gas onto the central core; it is also believed that the gas and dust contained in the central part of this envelope is instead forced to spread outward. In spite of this, the core gradually grows bigger in mass, and in due course it becomes a young hot star known as "Protostar". Persistent compression of the gas causes the temperature of the core to increase gradually; when its temperature reaches up to about 3000°C and above, the core, from time to time, emanates bipolar jets along its rotational axis, this is illustrated in Fig-7. Magnetic activities are also associated with these jets. It is also believed that these core shed off, theirs excessive angular momentum, through these jets.

Fig - 7

The said rotating gas envelopes, or the Protoplanetary Disks, gradually become thin and less opaque, and eventually they disappear, due to continual accretion of large amounts of the gas and dust onto their cores. As a result the Protostar continues to become more massive; it also continues to grow hotter due to continual compacting. As a result, the young star, after about 1 million years, becomes visible. This stage of star formation is known as "T. Tauri Star." During about next 10 million years, the young star continues to accumulate mass, and it also continues to emanate bipolar jets. Gradually, its core is heated up to a temperature of about 8 to 10 million degrees. Nuclear-fusion of the hydrogen atoms is triggered at a right temperature; as a result the young star becomes a fully functional star. In due course of time, when the amount of gas falling onto the cores reduces, the bipolar jets gradually disappear.

FORMATION OF THE PLANETS

Scientists believe that rotation of the gas in the protoplanetary disks, produces friction between gas and dust particles, this friction heats them up. These particles, on heating up, tend to stick to each other. Radiation of heat from the hot core helps to accelerate this process of sticking of dust particles together. By the time the star reaches the T. Tauri stage, the gas enveloping the disk, becomes thin, and because of the reduced friction, it starts to cools down. This results in condensation of the less-volatile materials, which in turn results in formation of small grains near the central part of the disk. Within next few hundred-thousand years, the dust particles coagulate to form about 1 kilometer-sized objects, called "planetesimals." Gas and dust start to accumulate on these planetesimals at a much faster rate. As a result the planetesimals, within next 2-3 hundred-thousand years, grow up as big as the Moon to Mars sized objects. These bigger bodies act as the seeds or embryos of the future planets. Thereafter, these seeds start to suck large quantities of gas and dust from their near surroundings, and start to grow at runaway speeds. Generally, rocky and metallic planets are formed in the regions lying in the near vicinity to the central core, because large portions of the available gas and volatile matter are sucked-away by the star itself. Normally gas-giants, like Jupiter and Saturn are formed at larger distances from the star, from where the star doesn't suck much gas and where temperature remains low. It is estimated that it might have taken a time period of few hundred-million years in the formation of our Sun-like stars and their complete planetary systems.

PROBABLE LOOPHOLES IN THE NEBULAR THEORY

Though this theory enjoys very wide acceptance world-wide, but it doesn't clarify the following points, at least, to my satisfaction:

1) There is no explanation of the points that (a) "why and how the clouds start to rotate, even before the formation of the stars?" And (b) "from where they get the energy to rotate, and how is it decided that in which direction will they rotate?"

2) There is very vast difference between flattening of the pizza base, and the protoplanetary disks. *No force attracts the dough cake towards its center; on the other hand the gravitational force of the dense cores, always attracts the protoplanetary clouds toward their centers.* Thus, the conventional explanation, of flattening of protoplanetary clouds, doesn't seem satisfactory, at least to me.

3) Since all the molecules of the gas and dust, rotate with almost same speeds, the possibility of any friction between them, seems to be very remote.

4) The stars spin at a much slower speeds as compared to the speeds of the protoplanetary disks. The earth orbits the sun once in a year, whereas, the sun completes one spin around its axis in 11 years. The explanation that "the excessive angular moment of the rotating stars, is released or vented through the bipolar jets", is unable to fully satisfy, at least, me. No proof is available to support this prediction.

5) If planets are formed due to coagulation of dust particles, then the internal structure of the comets and asteroids, etc., should be granular in structure. But direct proof of this is not available. If samples are collected from the asteroids/comets then this fact could be verified.

6) No proper justification of formation of bipolar jets is available.

7) It is not clear that at which particular place the planets would form and why, that is, how and why dust particles would start to coagulate at any particular place only?

It is believed that supernova type explosions, by compressing the molecules of the gaseous clouds, trigger-off the process of star-formation. But the primitive stars were born millions of years before any such explosion could take place. This signifies that star formation was not triggered by supernovae; of course, *such explosions must have provided raw materials and the solid cores to facilitate formation of the next generation of stars; planets might have formed due to accretion of gas and dust on smaller fragments, of different sizes, those were scattered here and there by the explosions of the dying stars.*

ALTERNATIVE SPECULATION ON STAR FORMATION

An alternative speculation, on formation of the stars, is given below; *effort has been made to clarify the doubts raised above.* However, this speculation needs thorough examination.

The earliest stars were born about tens of millions of years after the "big bang." By that time the expanding gas, which possessed diamagnetic properties, would have cooled down nearly to absolute zero degree. Probably the interstellar gas would have become superconductive at such a low temperature. After the "big-bang" this gas and dust would have expanded in very uneven and inhomogeneous manner, due to which dense gas clumps would have produced at numerous places. These dense clumps might have been surrounded by thin and sparsely distributed gases. Gravitational collapse would have further fragmented these bigger clumps into different smaller and more compacted cores, which might have contained different quantities of gas. All these compacted gas pockets would have spread all over, at different distances from each other. These dense cores, due to continued accretion of gas/dust from their surroundings, would have persisted to gain mass; such accumulation of mass would have caused their gravitational force to gradually grow stronger. In the beginning, these cores simply persisted to accrete mass at an exponential rate, and so did their gravitational force.

Initially the gravitational force of these compact gas pockets would have been very weak; therefore, the centers of these gas pockets would have sucked gas, only from very close distances. As a result, the cores of these gas pockets, as a first step of star formation, would gradually collapse inward. Analogous to the formation of the water-whirl in the washbasin (Chapter-3, "Puzzle of the Whirl"), gas from all the directions would have, first, flown towards the centers of these pockets radially in different straight lines; this would cause congestion around the core. As a result these gas-currents, in due course of time, would have adopted different curved paths as shown in fig-7A and fig-7B. Thus, it could be seen that whirling motion in the gas was caused by the gravitational force; it didn't start due to warped space or any other reason. Cores of these gas-pockets too, because of the formation of the gas-whirl, would have started to rotate. Their rotational speeds would have depended on the distances from where the gas was being sucked. Every current of superconductive gas flowing in a spiral path, would produce a magnetic field along its rotational axis (Chapter-2, "London Moment"). When, the gravitational force of such rotating cores, gained more strength, they, as the next step, would have sucked thinly distributed super-cooled gas from larger distances too. In accordance with the polarity of the magnetic fields of the cores, different gas currents coming from outside, would also have adopted spiral paths, swirling in a particular direction.

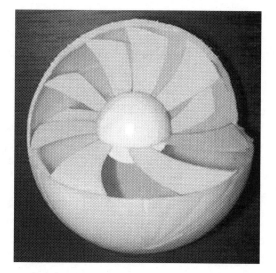

Fig- 7A

Fig- 7B

In the beginning, the gas clouds have neither regular shapes, and nor homogeneous gas distributions. Therefore, different gas-currents, flowing towards the rotating core, would have been drawn from different distances and directions; each of such currents would carry different amounts of gas. The gas-current, coming from the furthest corners of the cloud, would have the highest speed due to the acceleration produced by the gravitational force. The gas-current that would be flowing with greater speed and carrying greater amount of gas, would generate the strongest magnetic field amongst all others. This strongest magnetic field would create its mirror image (See chapter-2, "superconductivity") in all the molecules of the superconductive gas-currents, which are rushing toward the central core. As shown in Fig-7B, this strongest magnetic field would gradually push different gas currents toward its magnetic-equator, and finally establish all of them in the plane of its magnetic-equator; this would, as a next step, create a rotating disk of gas around the core, in the plane of its magnetic equator. The spiral motion of all these gas currents would produce a centrifugal force in the molecules of the swirling gas currents, and thereby give these currents a stable shape and path.

In due course of time the surrounding disk would grow bigger and rotate faster. This in turn would also enhance the strength of the magnetic field of the core rotating in the center of the gas envelope. More massive the core becomes its gravitational and magnetic fields, respectively, would also grow stronger. Similarly, as more quantity of the gas would rush towards the core more opaque its surroundings would become. Gradual compaction of the core would have heated it up; the same would therefore start to radiate heat. In due course of time, gravitational crunch would turn these rotating cores into red-hot spherical balls or embryos of the future stars. However, due to the opacity of the gas envelope surrounding these cores, it would not be possible for anybody to see the early stages of the star formation, that is, the process of compaction of these cores, till they don't become adequately hot and start to emit strong-infrared radiations. By this time, a zone of hot gases, having no superconductivity, would have created around the core; this hot region would be surrounded by a very cold region of super-conductive gases. As the magnetic field of the core would assume adequate strength and reach out to this cold zone, its mirror image would be gradually created in every molecule of the superconductive gas lying within the said magnetic field. At the same time, both the poles of this magnetic field would repel these mirror images, from both the sides, and gradually compel them to occupy the plane of the magnetic equator of the core. Thus the in-falling matter, right from the initial stage of star formation, would be organized in a two-dimensional rotating disk. The speed of rotation of this disk, or gas envelop, would depend on the distance from where the gas is drawn and the gravitational force exerted by the core, that is, on the acceleration that would be generated in these gas-currents coming spiraling toward the central core.

As was seen in Chapter-3 (Puzzle of the Whirlpool), the maximum rotational speed, in any whirlpool, is generated at its outer edges; this speed gradually drops marginally as any spiral current approaches the central drain. Galaxies also exhibit a similar pattern of the rotational speeds. Probably, the rotational speeds of the gas-disk, rotating around any collapsing core, might also follow a similar pattern. In spite of the fact that their rotational speeds keep reducing persistently by a very slight margin, curvatures of their spiral paths would go on increasing rapidly, and accordingly the value of the centrifugal force generated in the gas molecules, also increases gradually. As a result, such disks finally, separate-out, from the respective cores, and from the parent cloud also. Thus, such gas-envelops would, as a second phase of the star formation, become independent units.

It could thus be seen that the rotating core and its rotating gas-envelop, both were though created by the gravitational force of the core, but both of them were created by the gas coming from different distances and also at different points in time. Therefore, depending upon different speeds of gas rushing from the outer edges of both the both of these units, that is, the core and the rotating gas envelope, both of them would have different rotational speeds and different angular momentums as well.

Since similar process within any nebula might start simultaneously, at numerous other places. And, as a result, several hundred to millions of such cores, of varying sizes and masses, might have formed within a big nebula. Since a similar process created all such cores and their rotating gas envelopes, their magnetic polarities and directions of rotations, etc., would also have been the same. These cores, because of similar magnetic polarities, would repel each other. Initially, such cores, at the time of their creations, would have simply continued to accrete mass from their respective envelopes, no other activity, because of their inadequate gravitational strengths, might have been possible.

In the due course of time, different cores, due to continuously increasing temperature, would have been converted into numerous whirls of red-hot gases of different sizes and masses, and the gas envelops would have become protoplanetary disks. Gravitational force would have further compacted them and turn them into swirling spherical fireballs or the embryos of future stars. Bigger cores would continue to collapse until nuclear fusion did start within them, thereafter they would become complete stars; smaller cores would have become either failed stars or planets.

In a few million years after the "big bang," different fireballs, or the protostars, would have become so massive that their gravitational force would have reached-out to much longer distances. As a result, they would have started to draw gases - even from the surroundings of the smaller fireballs that would have been located in their near vicinities. Amongst a local group of such neighboring embryos of different masses and sizes, gravitational force of the biggest amongst all the other fireballs, would have become so strong that it would have started to attract even the smaller fireballs one after another, which would have located within its gravity field. As these smaller fireballs along with the loose gases, move toward the bigger ones, on different curved paths, speeds of these smaller fireballs, would have kept increasing gradually, and the curvature of their paths would also increase. As a result, the centrifugal force produced in these smaller fireballs would finally, establish them in different stable orbits around the biggest one. In this manner a supergiant whirlpool of gas, would have formed around the most massive fireball. Smaller fireballs, orbiting the biggest one, would have become integrated parts of the said giant gas-whirl. The smaller fireballs, while orbiting the main one, would also continue to suck gas and dust from the regions lying in their near vicinity. Since the gravitational force of the biggest core would have been much stronger than that of the smaller fireballs, it would suck more gas from larger distances including the areas lying around the smaller fireballs too. This would probably, starve the smaller cores, which would be able to suck only limited quantities of gas, from a much shorter distance. As a result, either the rate of growth of the smaller fireballs would have been slowed-down, or it might have totally stopped at some stage of their growths. In the absence of a fresh supply of the gas, the much smaller fireballs would cool-down and, depending on their masses, might turn into either smaller stars or planets of different sizes. All of the newly created stars/planets would have been surrounded by few planets and their moons too. All such smaller objects would respectively orbit their nearest massive objects.

Such process, of star-formation, if spread over a very large area, might result in the formation of a whirling configuration of the stars, in which several stars along with their families of different planets etc., orbit a massive star, like the one shown in Fig- 7C. Such a configuration of the stars could be said to be primitive, mini or dwarf galaxy. Such mini galaxies containing first generation stars, might have formed in the early universe, which kept growing by accreting more mass. In due course of time, bigger galaxies would have captured smaller ones, and grew still bigger. The giant sized central stars of such mini galaxies would have, in due course of time, become black-holes. Explosions of the stars like hypernovae and supernovae might have scattered star-dust and debris in the form of numerous solid cores of different sizes. In the due course of time the gas ejected by such explosions, would have accreted on such solid cores, and as a result the second generation of stars and their planet would have been created.

Fig- 7C

The bipolar jets emanated by the young stars under the process of making, are very much similar to the jets emanated by the "Quasars," and also those jets that are produced just before the death of the super-massive stars due to Hypernovae explosions. No clear explanation of the formation of such jets is available even as of today. At the present, it is believed that stars and black holes shed off the excess material swallowed by them through these jets. *However, an entirely different idea of the formation of these jets, though speculative, is given in this book at the chapter–13, "Quasars."*

×   ×   ×

DEATH OF THE STARS

The law of the nature that "anyone or anything that was born, is sure to die, one day or the other," is irrevocable. Even the stars and universe are not exempted from this law.

Immense energy is produced, deep within the cores of the stars, by fusion of the Hydrogen atoms to form the Helium atoms. In this process a very small amount of matter is destroyed and converted into energy. The stars, in order to shine continuously, must, necessarily, accumulate a very large quantity of gas that would last for their entire lifetime. Any star, of the size of our Sun, need to burn hundreds of million tons of hydrogen within a small period of one second. The stars, during their average lifetime of 10 to 14 billion years, continuously burn Hydrogen at the above rate. Massive stars, in order to maintain their temperatures and shapes against gravitational collapse, need to burn fuel at much higher rates. Due to this reason the massive stars run out of fuel in comparatively much shorter periods. The life span of a star depends on the total stock of the fuel it has accumulated, and the rate at which they consume their Hydrogen stock. This is an irony that bigger the star shorter is its lifespan. The bigger stars complete their lives within a very short period of even ½ billion years to 1 billion years as against the life span of 10 billion years of averages sized stars of the size of our Sun. The stars smaller than the sun, may have much longer life.

It is the huge stock of the fuel, which provides life to the stars, but the stars, whether bigger or smaller, one-day run out of their fuel. Thereafter, the gravitational force, which gives birth to all the stars, also becomes the cause of their deaths. However, stars of different sizes and masses end up their lives in different ways. Although the stars are said to have died, but some activities still continue within their remaining cores - even after their so-called deaths. Life never accepts defeat so easily; the gas envelope separated-out from the star-core, provides raw material for the formation of the second generation of stars, and the ***seeds of life were*** also ***produced*** from the chemicals produced by the explosion of the different dying stars.

A Brief description, of the different stages from which the stars of different masses pass through before their deaths, is given below:

Brown Dwarfs

Non-shining celestial bodies, which are marginally smaller than the stars, are called "Brown Dwarfs." Such bodies are, in fact, *"failed stars,"* which fail to trigger nuclear fusion. Star must possess at least 80 times as much mass as that of the planet "Jupiter," so that they may support Hydrogen-fusion. Celestial bodies, which are 3 to 70-80 times as massive as the Jupiter is, develop as failed stars. Such failed stars, while in the process of their formations would have become very hot due to the heat generated in this process; they, therefore, glow like stars or at least with red light. Nuclear fusion would also have started, to some extent, in the cores of some of the bigger bodies, but this process could not sustain any longer in the absence of the required temperature and pressure. Whatever amount of energy is produced within these stars, they radiate-out almost the same amount of energy. As a result, these stars gradually cool-down with the passing time. They retain their shapes due to natural repulsion between atoms. It would be wrong to say that they die immaturely; in fact, they couldn't grow fully for lack of adequate quantities of gas.

The surface temperature of such stars normally ranges within 5-6 hundred degrees to 1000 degrees. At this temperature some radiation, in the form of infrared waves and dull-red light, is radiated from these failed stars. Charged particles and X-rays also emanate from such bodies from time to time. Such radiations indicate that they are not completely dead; instead, some nuclear activity is going on in their cores. These dwarfs also have magnetic fields of their own and may have a family of some planets and moons orbiting these planets. Such a system of failed stars and its planets could be said to be the "Mini Solar System." Since heat in adequate quantity is not generated within these dwarfs, they, in the next few billion years, may become very cold and the activities within their cores may stop totally. Even after this fate their gravitational force would continue to exist. In case they assume some extra mass from any collision with other celestial bodies, or in some other manner, then they may also turn into small stars. But if this doesn't happen, then they would remain as dwarfs forever.

Red Dwarfs

Smaller stars having mass of up to half the mass of the sun or even lesser, are also capable of supporting nuclear fusion, but at a much slower rate. Lesser is the heat generated, duller and redder is the light emitted from these stars. And therefore, they are known as "Red Dwarfs." These stars can also have families of planets and their moons. In case these stars don't get any further mass, then they would continue to burn their fuel for very long periods of time, but at very slow rates. The surface temperatures of these stars remain around 3 to 4 thousand degrees, due to which they shine with luminosities of around $1/10^{th}$ of our Sun, or even 1/10000 times lesser. Such stars might be far-more in number as compared to the visible stars, however, because of their faint light, it would be very difficult to observe or find them out. The luminosities of such stars would go on diminishing with depleting fuel, and because of that it would become still harder to see them. Since such stars burn their fuel at a very slow rate, they have much longer life as compared to the sun sized stars. These stars, because of their much longer life, might be capable to live - even after the end of the universe. However, even such stars are also not eternal, some day or other, they also would run out of the fuel. Thereafter, they would cool-down very slowly.

<u>Red Giants</u>

When the bigger stars, having mass ranging from ½ solar mass up to 10 solar masses, consumes about ⅔rd of their total fuel, then nuclear fusion within their cores, gets slowed-down. This, in turn, reduces the heat produced. As the outward pressure, created by the heat of their cores, gradually diminishes, gravity becomes dominant. This causes the gas envelopes of their cores, which mostly comprises Helium and Hydrogen, to suddenly contract and collapse. This sudden collapse has two consequences which are, 1) more hydrogen enters into this hot zone, & 2) Temperature of the core raises again that reignites nuclear fusion in the Hydrogen layer that immediately surrounds the Helium layer formed deep within their cores. Heat, generated by the nuclear fusion, again causes the star to expand. And as a result the process of nuclear-fusion spreads in a bigger region. This causes any such star to expand more rapidly, up to even 10 to 1000 times of its original size; its luminosity may also increase by 1000 to 10,000 times. Any Sun-sized star may swell up to 100 to 200 times, of its original size. At present the diameter of our sun is about 15 hundred-thousand kilometers, however, in the next 4 to 5 billions of years, when it would consume most of its fuel, and would be inflated by about 100 times of its present size, it may reach up to the earth's orbit, or perhaps it may swell further, to an even greater extent and may reach up to the orbit of the Mars. Expansion of these stars, to such a great extent, causes their heat energy to spread-over a much bigger volume. This results in dropping of their surface temperatures to about 3 to 5 thousand degrees. Such stars, at this temperature, appear to be red or orange-red, and as such they are known as "Red Giants."

When the process of nuclear fusion reaches the outer layers of the stars, then their gas-shells swell to such a great extent that the grip of gravity, on their outer gas layers, becomes very weak. As a result the outer gas layers of the red giants are blown or thrown away by the radiation pressure and the shock-waves produced by the nuclear activities going-on in their cores. In about next 1 million years or so, the entire gas shell of such a star is disposed of, leaving behind the bare core which is very dense and hot. The gas so liberated accumulates around the star like a hollow shell or ring, which is known as "Planetary Nebula." Such rings are short-lived, and therefore, in about next 10 to 50 thousand years, they gradually expand and thinned out to such a great extent that they become completely invisible.

When any massive star, much more massive than the sun, uses up its fuel completely, then its core is squeezed to such a great extent that the temperature of its core shoots up to several hundred million degrees. Such a high temperature facilitates the nucleosynthesis of much heavier elements. Such stars, after running out of their fuel, swell to many times bigger than the red-giants. Such massive stars, depending on their sizes, are called "Super-Giants" or "Hyper-Giants." Being much massive and heavier than the red-giants, they end their lives in different fashions, which are briefed hereinafter.

White Dwarf

What could happen to a star, when it runs out of fuel, and how its cores could support themselves against gravity, was first proposed in 1928, by an Indian student **Subramanian Chandrasekhar.** According to his calculations, any dying star having about 1.4* times the mass of the sun, or lesser, would, after using-up all of its fuel, and disposing off its gas envelope, eventually stop contracting and settle down as a white dwarf; this would become possible because the repulsion between the electrons would finally counter-balance the force of gravity. The compact material formed due to contraction of the cores of such stars, is called "Electron Degenerate Matter." And the small, but very dense cores left over after the end of the Red-Giants, are known as "White Dwarfs."

In the beginning the dense core left behind after the death of a Red-Giant, glows with very bright white light, due to its residual heat energy. It may glow with luminosity 250 times greater than that of the sun. But in the absence of any nuclear activity, it gradually cools-down, and due to that its glow gradually goes on diminishing. The white dwarfs formed after the deaths of stars of different masses, differ in their sizes. The white dwarf left over after the death of a star as massive as our Sun, would be almost equal to the earth in size, that is, about 13,000 kilometers in diameter. White dwarfs, after a few billion years of their formations, would cool-down to such an extent that they would not emit any light. Such cores are known as "Black Dwarf." A black dwarf is, probably,

---

*   This limit of mass is known as *"Chandrasekhar Limit"*

made of pure diamond that measures several thousand kilometers in size, but because of its mass and gravitational force, we neither bring it to our earth nor start mining of diamonds on its surface.

The leftover core of a so-called dead star, in fact, isn't a dead celestial-body, that is, a totally inactive body. In case any other star or big planet collides with it or it sucks sufficient matter from any other nearby source, then the process of nuclear fusion may restart within its core. If its mass persists to grow, then after a certain critical limit of mass, it would shrink further and convert into a "Neutron Star," with a powerful explosion.

Supernovae and the Neutron Stars

The most intense and luminous interstellar glow is known as "Super Nova." The word, "nova" means a new star, that is, supernova means a very bright new star. In fact, the glow of a supernova is produced by the explosion of a dying star, which emits very energetic and extremely luminous glow, for a very short period of time. However, its remnant core, and the gas envelope, may continue to shine for a few weeks to a few months. Such explosions may emit as much energy in their brief life period as the sun could do in its entire life span of about 10 billion years.

The process of nucleosynthesis in the bigger stars is carried out at much rapid rates, therefore, the cores of the bigger stars, having about 3 to 10 solar masses, generate temperatures of hundreds of million degrees. Such a high temperature enables these stars to start fusing the Helium atoms too. The process of fusion of Helium atoms produces some heavier elements such as Selenium, Carbon, Nitrogen and Oxygen, etc. However, nucleosynthesis of Helium atoms does not produce much heat; therefore, the star begins to contract under its own gravity. Therefore, for a smaller period of time, nuclear fusion spreads in the inner layers of its gas shell. This process being short lived it causes repetitive swelling and contraction of the core. The star eventually inflates very rapidly and grows much bigger – even much bigger than the red-giants.

The process of nucleosynthesis generates temperatures as high as 8 billion degrees within the cores of still bigger stars, which is about 60 times higher than the temperature of the core of our Sun. At this temperature the atoms of the element "Iron" are also produced. The gravitational force tries to fuse the iron atoms too, but it fails to do so; much higher temperature is required for this purpose. The element Iron is said to be the enemy of the stars, because it absorbs almost their entire energy (heat). As a result, the process of atomic fusion comes to a total halt. In the absence of any resistance in the form of outward pressure, the entire matter contained in the cores of such stars, is suddenly squeezed into a very small point. The crushing force, in such big stars, is so strong that even the mutual repulsion between the electrons fails to counter it; as a result, all the electrons enter into the nucleus and convert all the protons into neutrons. Finally, the inward rush of the matter is halted by the mutual repulsion among the neutrons. This sudden halt of the in-rushing matter creates a powerful shock wave. The matter rushing inward is not just halted; it is rebounded back. Consequently the in-rushing matter bounces back with very high speed. The shock wave, so produced, shatters the gas shell of the dying star, and sweeps the gas-shell off, up to very large distances. Some very heavy elements are also produced during such explosions in very small quantities, because of very high temperature generated in this process. What is left behind after the total destruction of such a massive star is only a very small and dense core having a radius of about 20 to 30 kilometers. Almost all the mass of such a big star squeezes into this dense core. This compact matter is known as "Neutron Degenerate Matter," whereas the remnant core is called "Neutron Star."

Binary Stars and their Deaths

Some stars, during the process of their formation, are born alone, such as our sun, and some of them might have taken birth in pairs of two or even in a group of more than two stars. At the beginning, the seeds of these stars, because of their low masses, would not be able to exert any appreciable force on each other. But as they grow bigger, their mutual attraction would also grow stronger. Ultimately, because of almost equal masses they would start orbiting each other, more precisely the point of their common mass. In such pairs, the star having more mass is known as "Primary Star," and the other one as "Secondary Star." The heavier one of these two stars, runs out of fuel comparatively much earlier and becomes a white dwarf, due to that it becomes almost invisible. The secondary star, which is a little lighter in mass, becomes a red giant. This red giant, therefore, appears to orbit an invisible object. Sometimes, another star, having a family of several planets, might also orbit a binary pair of stars. Such a congregation of stars is known as a "Triplet of stars."

During the year 1963-64, scientists were greatly surprised to see that a giant star was not just orbiting an invisible point, but the gas from its gas-envelop was gradually spiraling toward that invisible point, where it just continually disappeared. Astronomers first thought that the primary star, in a binary pair of stars, must have collapsed and transformed into a white dwarf, whereas, the other one, orbiting it, would be a red-giant. And as such, because of very small distance between the two, the white dwarf is gradually snatching away gas from the gas envelope of its companion. This invisible point was given the name of "CygunusX-1," which was later on accepted to be a black hole.

In such a pair of stars, when the invisible white dwarfs accumulate adequate mass, then nuclear action might once again start in its core. Such a dwarf, after assuming adequate mass, might end up in a supernova and become a neutron star. Such explosion may throw away the gas-cover of its companion or even its remnant core too.

Hyper-nova

Massive explosions causing deaths of extremely massive stars say 10 to 30 solar masses or even bigger, are known as "Hyper-novae". These stars use up their fuel within half a billion to 2-3 billion years. Thereafter, they end their lives with explosions like a supernova, but hundreds of times energetic and vigorous than that. Very powerful bipolar jets of charged particles and gamma ray radiation, etc., are also emitted just before such explosions, from the poles of such dying stars.

Extremely high temperature, matching with the energy of the hyper-nova explosion, is generated at the time of such explosions. During that extremely small fraction of time, when this extreme temperature is produced, very heavy elements like Silver, Gold, Platinum and Uranium etc. are also produced. Since these elements, are created within a very limited time-periods, they are so rare in the nature.

Fig- 8

An imaginary picture of "hyper-nova," is depicted in Fig-8, above. Probably, the gas shell and debris of the dying star are thrown mainly in two directions, 1) charged particles and energy radiation is mostly swept away in the directions of both of its poles, and 2) The gas shell and debris are thrown away in the direction of its magnetic-equator, this debris might spread like a doughnut. This might be related to the strength and direction of the magnetic field of the star. What actually happens could only be established by the astronomers and the scientists.

Quark Novae

A very powerful explosion, much bigger than the hyper-nova, was observed about 9 to 8 years earlier from now, i.e. sometime in 2006-07. The energy of this explosion suggested that probably still bigger star had exploded. The gravitational force of such a massive star would be so strong that even the mutual repulsion between neutrons would fail to stop gravitational collapse, which would be finally halted by mutual repulsion of the quarks. Such an explosion is known as "Quark Nova," which is much more energetic and stronger than the hyper-nova. The dense core, left behind such explosions, is known as "Quark Star," which is made of "Quark Degenerate Matter." Such stars, on the name of the strange quark, are also known as "Strange Stars."

Electroweak Stars

It is speculated that if still bigger star explodes, then even the quark degenerate pressure would fail to support their cores. It is believed that gravity would squeeze the quarks completely, and would burn them down, and thereby convert them into Leptons. Such a great temperature is generated in this process that the electromagnetic force and the weak nuclear force merge into each other to become one single force. Such stars support themselves by mutual repulsion between leptons. Such dense cores are called "Electroweak Stars."

Black-Holes

The next stage of star-collapse is the *"Black Hole,"* which is discussed separately in the next chapter (chapter-12) of this book.

×   ×   ×

The Spark of Life

In the beginning only very light elements such as Hydrogen and Helium, were created after the "big bang;" no heavy element could be created at that time. However, some heavy elements have also been seen in the oldest galaxies. This means that extremely massive stars were formed in the infant universe, which might have very short lives of, say, about ½ billion years. Heavy elements and their different compounds would have been created within the cores of the first-generation stars and also during their explosions. Subsequently, these chemicals would have spread all over the universe due to explosions similar to hyper-novae and supernovae. The second and third-generation stars and their planets would have formed from star-dust and debris of these first-generation stars. The chemicals like Nitrogen, Oxygen, Silicon, Calcium, Carbon, Phosphorous and their compounds like water vapor, Carbon-di-oxide, Methane, Ammonia and oxides of different elements, etc., were also formed by these explosions. All these compounds are the raw materials, from which the life did evolve* afterward. In brief, the life was created by the death of stars. Death of the stars also resulted in the creation of the next generation of stars and their planets, which provided places like different planets, where various life-forms originated in due course of time. Deaths of stars have provided us home such as Earth like planets, to live and flourish. It is a cruel reality of the nature that "the death of one is the life for other."

We knew, beforehand, that the entire universe and all the living beings are made of different matter particles. It could now be seen from the 'life cycle of stars' that the force of "Gravitation" is nature's main tool of creation of the stars and planets, and the same force causes their destruction too. The raw materials, for evolution of life, were also created indirectly by the same tool that spread them all over in the universe. In fact, gravitation is merely a property of matter, which was created by the "Big-Bang." Thus, matter and all of its intrinsic forces are responsible for the creation of the universe and eventually the origin and evolution of life.

Up till now we have found-out the answers to some of the eternal questions except for the question that wherefrom the energy was created that resulted in the "Big-Bang." Answer to this question is still eluding the mankind.

---

*   Please see Chapter-17.

PART – 4

FEW
UNRESOLVED
MYSTERIES
Of the
Universe

12: THE BLACK HOLES

Black holes are point sized celestial objects having immense masses; they are the most compact objects, and are totally invisible. Black holes, because of their infinite gravitational force, can swallow anything from their vicinity; even light rays cannot escape them. The existence of black holes was envisaged as early as 1783, but this idea was not accepted until 1965, when based on *Relativity*, Roger Penrose proved their existence. It is not at all possible to see the black holes, but the effect of theirs gravitational force could be felt at far-off distances. The stars, located very close to the galactic center of our milky way, are orbiting some invisible object, at very high speeds. This fact indicates the presence of a very strong gravitational field at the galactic center. Moreover, gases from the gas-shells of several stars, which are located within our milky way, have been observed to spiral into some invisible point, where such gas disappears forever. Sometimes a dark, and point sized small object could be seen in the background of bright light or behind the gas falling into these objects. Such invisible bodies are possibly the black holes. The gas spiraling toward any massive black hole becomes so hot that it periodically emits X-rays, radio rays and infrared rays, etc. Possible location of the black holes can also be predicted by locating the sources of such radiations.

When the fuel of a massive star is exhausted, then the entire matter existing in its core collapses into a small point. And as a result, that star becomes a black hole. Scientists believe that the process of gravitational collapse is so rapid that the star would start to spin on its axis at a very high speed. Therefore, on the basis of *Relativity,* it is believed that the entire energy of such a star would be instantaneously carried away by the gravitational waves. As a result the star would shed-off all of its energy within that very instant, and would settle down in a stationary state, and as a result it would also cool-down to 0°K. Thus, the star would turn into a black hole, that is, an extremely small object of zero activity and zero energy. Such a black hole, because of its immense gravitational force, would continue to suck gas and nearby objects. The core, due to the velocity of the infalling gases, would start to rotate - even then, it would be impossible to see it, because it would not emit any sort of radiation.

THE GRAVITY WAVES

Before we discuss anything about **Black holes,** let's find out what *"gravity waves"* are and how a moving object could dissipate its energy by these so-called gravity waves?

Waves are normally produced by the periodic vibration of particles of any medium or a piece of matter about an average position. Einstein predicted that the massive objects while moving through the space, produces gravity waves, which ripple through the fabric of space-time with the speed of light. It was predicted that similar to any other wave, gravity waves also carry away energy from the fast moving objects producing these waves. Sophisticated equipment of the modern era has found that the earth is very gradually moving closer to the sun, and accordingly the earth, within the next 4 to 5 billion years, might fall into the sun. But one example goes against this prediction, the moon is gradually moving away from the earth, instead of coming closer to it. Both, the earth and the moon, shall follow the same rule, but in reality they do not follow the same rule. Therefore, it is very difficult to establish the fact that whether both, the earth and the moon, are really losing their energies by way of emission of gravity waves?

If gravitational waves are produced by the movements of celestial bodies, then such waves would complete their one frequency after any of such body producing the gravity waves, completes its one orbit. Celestial bodies take very long time periods to go round their centers once. The earth completes its one orbit in one year, the sun takes around 250 million years to go-around the galactic center once, whereas, any galaxy may take many times more time to orbit a bigger galaxy. If gravitational waves are produced by the movement of these bodies, or collections of celestial bodies, then their frequency periods would be so large that it might not be possible for the mankind, or his equipment, to even take notice of such waves.

The intensity of the gravitational force of any celestial body depends upon the mass and compactness of such bodies, if any one of the two quantities varies or fluctuates, then the intensity of gravitational force, at its surface, would also vary. Sudden periodic changes in any of these two entities may also produce gravitational waves. This means that sudden change in the size or mass of a massive body would momentarily create powerful gravitational waves that might be detected. Such waves would possibly be produced by explosions like supernovae/hyper novae, or by collision between two massive stars, etc.

Scientists, since the time long past, are very minutely observing several pairs of binary stars/black holes, to detect gravity waves. In 2010, scientists said to have succeeded in detecting gravitational waves coming from a far-off pulsar, which is spinning at a very high speed. But the question is, "why not all other pulsars emanate gravity waves?" Since the properties of the gravitational waves are still unknown, the aforesaid lone evidence doesn't appear to be adequate to establish this idea. Rotating magnetic field of the aforesaid pulsar might also produce some other kinds of waves, which might have been mistaken as gravity waves. Supermassive black holes, billion times heavier than the Pulsars, spinning at very high speeds, are located at the centers of each galaxy. *Such supermassive black holes might be much better candidates for this purpose; the galactic center of our own galaxy is the nearest one of them. However, no gravity waves coming from these objects could be detected so far.*

The energy of any object is normally carried away by similar types of waves. For example, sound waves or light waves can not carry away heat energy of an object; this could be done by the infrared waves only. Analogous to this fact, only gravitational energy should be carried away by the gravity waves, thereby *it should become a body without any gravity field*. In other words, the loss of heat and kinetic energies, by the gravity waves, does not appear to be logical. *In case the energy of the moving objects is carried away by gravity waves, then the black holes must shed-off their entire masses too, because mass is considered to be the measure of the energy.*

The energy, possessed by any object, is of two types 1) intrinsic energy due to its own mass, and 2) the heat and kinetic energy, etc., which it might acquire from some other source or from the high energy surroundings, therefore, these kinds of energies are not intrinsic to any object. Heat energy, of any hot object, is continuously dissipated by radiation, due to that its temperature persists to fall gradually; however, its kinetic energy would reduce, only by friction, not by radiation of heat energy. The fastest rotating pulsar (a kind of neutron stars) rotates on its axes, at the speed of around 800 revolutions per second. At this spin speed, a pulsar, of about 20 miles (32.28 km) in diameter, would have a linear surface speed of about 80,000 kilometers per second, that is, almost $\frac{1}{4}^{th}$ of the speed of the light. Since no energy loss due to friction is possible in interstellar space the kinetic energy of any object, as per the law of conservation of energy, remains intact; it is not carried away by its speed or the gravitational collapse. Gravitational force causes any object to just contract in size; heat and kinetic energies of that object as well as the quantity of matter contained within it, i.e., its mass, would remain unaltered – even at such a high rotational speed. Since the entire energy of a black-hole, would concentrate in a zero sized volume, value of its rotational speed and temperature, both should increase to infinity. In fact, the kinetic energy of any compacted body would be stored within it in the form of its momentum, i.e., in the proportion to the product of its mass and the rotational speed.

In case the aforesaid pulsar assumes some extra mass from somewhere else, and contracts further to become just ½ of its size diameter wise, then its volume would reduce by 8 times. As a result its rotational speed shall increase by 8 times, that is, double of the speed of light or at least equal to it, if not greater than that. A very large inertia would be generated in such a massive body which would depend on the product of its mass & speed. *The mass of any object could not be simply carried away by increasing its rotational speed, and therefore, it shall retain its angular momentum.* In order to stop the speed of rotation of such a massive body, and bring it to a total halt, a very strong force would be required to break its inertia; *it cannot come to rest all by itself.*

The Black holes are formed by the collapse of extremely massive stars, which are comparatively much more massive than the pulsars. They would naturally possess comparatively greater mass and inertia. *Any star after becoming a black-hole retains is mass, which is evident from its gravitational force; neither any object can exist without mass nor it can exert the force of gravitation. This simply means that the entire energy of a collapsing star is not carried away by the gravity-waves, as is envisaged in Relativity. Therefore, the inertia of any black hole should also remain intact.* Such a massive body cannot be brought to rest instantaneously, without applying a very strong brake. It is not clear that *wherefrom this force is produced to bring the spin of such a big mass to an instantaneous halt?* Such a big force cannot be produced all by itself, and therefore, its speed should not come to a halt automatically; instead, according to the law of conservation of energy, its speed should increase in the inverse proportion to its volume. Had it been possible to shed off the energy by means of gravity waves, then the spinning black-hole should also shed off its entire energy, i.e., its entire mass too. *In view of this anomaly, this idea appears to be merely a speculation without any proof, especially when the very existence of the space-time couldn't yet be proved. Moreover, how the gravity waves could be selective, that is, how can they take away only one kind of energy, that too instantaneously, not gradually?* Contrarily, it appears to me that intensities of its heat and kinetic energies too, might become *infinite* due to the concentration of the entire energy of the core into a very small place, instead of becoming zero. *Since gravitational force of a black hole doesn't allow any energy wave to escape, its entire energy shall also remain confined within its core.*

All the natural forces, that is, the "Strong Nuclear Force," "Weak Nuclear Force," "Electromagnetic Force" and the "Gravitational Force" are intrinsic properties of different matter particles. Therefore, energy, that is, the capacity to do work, could be derived from any of the above forces. This means that

"Energy," in the form of these natural forces, is confined within the matter itself. According to the famous formula $E = mc^2$, the energy of any piece of matter, could never drop down to zero value until its mass, that is, the value, of "m," doesn't become zero. *If the above formula and the belief that "mass is the measure of energy," are both correct, then the energy of any celestial body, because of its mass, could never depart from it.* This means that till such time the matter-particles are intact, their intrinsic energy would also remain intact. For example, the black hole, located in the centers of our galaxy, has been exerting gravitational force since last 13.2 billion years, on each and every star of this galaxy, but its strength has not at all attenuated. This fact is evident from the truth that our galaxy is gradually growing in size, by continual accretion of mass by swallowing matter from outside. *In case the gravitational force of any massive body causes any smaller body to move,* **then none of these two bodies would lose any mass, or their intrinsic energy; simply some of the potential energy of the smaller object, would be converted into kinetic energy.**

Above idea could be understood by the example of permanent magnets. Permanent magnets are, these days, made of various types of alloys and mixtures, such as Neodymium-Iron-Boron ($Nd_2Fe_{14}B$), Yttrium-Cobalt (YCo_5), Samarium-Cobalt ($SmCo_5$ & Sm_2Co_{17}), Alnico, Ceramic and Ferrite magnets, etc. Such magnets have very long lives. Pole strengths of such magnets don't diminish even by a bit, by repelling or attracting other magnets or objects for even millions of times. This becomes possible because of the special structure of their molecules; more particularly, because of the manner in which electrons are arranged within their molecules, or atoms. The electrons within their molecules are arranged in such a way that their magnetic fields always remain aligned. The molecular structure of these magnets, rather the manner in which their electrons are arranged, doesn't change by performing any amount of work. And, therefore, the strength of their poles doesn't weaken by a bit; magnetic force is an inseparable property of the matter-particles. Electrons, since last 13.7 billions of years, have been orbiting the atomic nucleus, due to their mutual attraction; their energies have not depleted even by a bit – even after exerting force on each other for such a long time. This is possible because the force-carrying particles could be exchanged in any number. *Thus, it could be concluded that energy could not be separated from the particles; it is intrinsic to them.* The energy of the universe would always remain proportional to the total mass of the matter existing within it; not a bit more or less. *Therefore, it should not be possible to carry away the intrinsic energy of any object, regardless of the fact that how fast it is spinning or how much force it is exerting on the other objects.*

FORMATION OF THE BLACK HOLES

The modern theory envisages that when a massive star collapses under its own gravitational force, then the curvature of space-time, around such stars, increases due to the concentration of its mass in a smaller area. To me this appears to contradict the idea that gravitation is not a force; how an object could collapse in the absence of any force? Anyhow, it is believed that the light rays, passing at close vicinity to such a collapsing body, would follow the increasing curvature of the space-time, and go on bending toward the center of that star. Thus the angle of deflection of those light rays would go on increasing, and in turn, make it difficult for them to escape. Increasing redshift would cause the light-source to apparently grow redder and dimmer. Soon the entire matter of the star would be squeezed into an atom sized point that would cause the curvature of the space-time around that point, to become infinite, the star would be surrounded by space-time of zero surface area. Probably, this is known as *"singularity."* Gravitational force, of the collapsing body, becomes so intense that it rips open a hole of infinite curvature, in the two-dimensional fabric of the space-time that immediately surrounds that collapsing body. Persistent deflection of the light rays in the same direction along this hole would compel them to move along the edges of this infinite curvature, that is, in a closed circular path; they would fail to escape from this curvature. According to the theory of relativity, nothing can travel faster than light; if light can't escape, neither can anything else. The black hole, therefore, couldn't be seen; only its gravitational force could be felt from the outside. The gravitational force of a black hole becomes so intense that it drags every nearby thing, into its point sized core, and merges the same with itself. One can see only what happens outside of the edges of the infinite curvature; not from within this limit. Since no radiation could come out from inside of this infinite curvature, any information of the events happening inside couldn't be obtained. The region of infinite curvature, from where the light rays can't escape, is called "Event Horizon." This event horizon acts as a one-sided door, or a nonreturn valve that allows everything only to enter this horizon; it doesn't allow anything to come out.

As the black hole grows bigger, it catches different objects and light rays, from far-off distances, and therefore, the region of infinite curvature would also go on increasing. Scientists believe that no two rays would run on the same path; since the size of the event horizon persists to increase, the light rays, trapped within this region, should move on parallel paths, that is, away from each other. ***This belief has given rise to a problem; since the size of the event*** *horizon, that is, the hole created in the fabric of the space-time, continues to increase in size, no medium of space-time would be left for the earlier rays to move on their circular paths. The problem thus arises that "where or in what medium do the rays that were moving along the smaller circles, would move?" When no medium would be left for such rays to run, where would they undulate and how?* This in turn poses a still bigger problem that *"do the light rays actually ripple through the fabric of space-time and do they need a medium to propagate; do they really undulate while propagating?"* A possible mode of propagation of the light waves has been discussed earlier in the Chapters 5 and 7 of this book, which may also be referred to.

ALTERNATIVE ANGLE ON FORMATION OF THE BLACK HOLES

The theories prevailing in the present era, envisage that *"Relativity"* alone can give a proper explanation of the formation of the "black holes," that is, they are formed due to the formation of the infinite curvature in the space-time. Similarly bending of the light waves, near the "black holes," could only be explained by the curvature of space-time. *It is, therefore, a matter of contemplation that in case the existence of the fabric of the space-time, or correctness of the relativity theory, couldn't be proved, then how the formation, of "black holes," could be explained?*

In view of above problem, an alternative angle, as envisaged by me, on formation of the black holes, is discussed below in brief. This angle is independent of the Relativity Theory.

The roots of the belief that the force of gravitation couldn't affect light waves in any way, goes back to about 150 years in the past, when James Clerk Maxwell established that light is a member of the electromagnetic wave family. It was thought that if light could be affected by gravity, then after some time light-waves should also come back to the earth, like the cannonballs. Speed of light was probably not considered while conceiving above belief. Contrary to the aforesaid belief, the spaceships, only because of their very high speeds, are able to escape the earth's gravitation. Anyhow, as per the prevailing theory, the black-holes are formed because the light waves are trapped in the infinite curvature of the space-time; this means that the gravitational force accomplishes this work indirectly, not directly.

According to the modern concept, photons, because of their momentum, propagate through infinite distances. In order that any particle could have momentum, it is necessary that it should have at least some mass, may it be negligible. We have earlier seen that photons could be trapped in the solution of nano-sized magnetic particles (Chapter-4, Some Least-known Properties of light). The above fact suggests that analogous to the magnetic trapping, the gravitational force, in the capacity of a real and independent force, might also affect, or even capture, photons, provided they have, at least, a little mass. The value of the gravitational force, acting between two objects, depends on their respective masses and the distances between their centers of gravity as well. The photons emitted by distant sources, while coming towards the earth, normally move at a considerable distance from the massive celestial bodies, therefore, such photons persist to move unaffectedly. However, when photons pass-by the surface of any star, from a very close distance, where the gravitational force is very intense, then in spite of their negligible masses and high velocities, gravitational force diverts the photons toward the star's center of gravity. Gravitational force of any black hole is million times more intense than that of the stars, therefore, when any photon happens to pass by a black hole, from very close distance, its gravitational force might attract such photons, with very powerful force. Consequently, photons might bend toward the black holes, or even fall abruptly into their cores, through a spiral path. If this is possible, then the belief that "the Event Horizon is created due to infinite curvature of the space-time" would be wrong.

In case the fabric of space-time doesn't exist, even then as speculated above, the "black holes" could still be formed directly by the gravitational force. *In that case formation of the wormholes would not at all be possible.* The existence of the wormhole totally depends on the existence of the fabric of the space-time, whereas no direct proof of the same is available. On the other hand, it is logically pointed out at several places in this book that force of gravitation can't be resulted by the curved space, and also that medium of space-time is unnecessary for propagation of the light. In view of the aforesaid possibilities, the existence of the wormhole doesn't seem feasible.

In the above perspective it is clear that no photon from the near vicinity of a black hole can come back to our eyes, this is the reason why we cannot see anything beyond the event horizon. Yet another possibility might also exist, though the same is very remote. When the matter falling into the black hole reaches the event horizon, its speed might reach the limit of the speed of light, and thereafter, it may surpass even this limit also; this might also be a reason that nothing could be seen beyond this limit.

SIZE OF THE BLACK HOLES

German scientist Schwarzschild, in 1915, proposed that stars having 3 solar masses or even more, could become black holes, but even some of the neutron stars might be more massive than this limit. Quark-stars/strange stars and electroweak stars, etc., might be many times more massive than the aforesaid limit. Therefore, any black hole must be much more massive than this limit.

Scientists have predicted that all the matter contained in any black hole, is squeezed into an atom-sized point. In the absence of any information coming from within the black holes, it is not possible to find out that in what form or state, do the matter exist in this point, or how big in size its core could be. It is also believed that magnetic force is created due to the circular motion of the electrons, but this concept doesn't seem to be correct in the case of the neutron stars. It is believed that the electrons, in such stars, enter into the nucleus and convert all the protons into neutrons. If this concept is correct, then no magnetic field could be generated in the absence of any electrons moving in a circular path. Contrary to this concept, neutron stars have very strong magnetic fields. Likewise, the most compact stars, that is, the black holes, besides the gravitational force, have very strong magnetic force too. This fact indicates that the matter particles, even after having been squeezed and crushed to the last limit within the cores of the black-holes, retain at least these two properties (Gravitation and Magnetism) of the matter. In other words, matter might exist within their cores in some compact form or in any other state in which matter particles don't lose the properties of matter. As we know, even a small quantity of matter contains trillions of atoms, whereas a supermassive black hole might contain several million times the mass of the sun. It could thus be imagined that the atoms in infinite numbers might exist in the point sized cores of the black-holes. Scientists believe that all of these atoms might occupy the same place measuring even lesser than the size of an atom. However, it seems to me that matter, ***in the form of particles***, might not be able to do so.

The size of the core, of a black hole, would depend on the fact that to what extent the matter could be compacted. A bigger black hole, formed by the merger of two identical black holes, would contain twice as much matter as compared to the original ones; its gravitational force would also be doubled. It would then squeeze the total matter with twice the force. In this scenario there could be three possibilities: 1) In case it would be possible to squeeze the matter further, without any limit, then as believed, the core of such a black-hole would again be compressed to zero size, 2) in case it would be possible to compress the matter only to some extent, then although the final size of the new black-hole would be reduced in size, but couldn't be compressed back to the zero size, and 3) if the matter was already compressed to the full extent, then it would not, at all, be possible to reduce its size any further; it too, would become double in size (volume wise).

Above discussion suggests that there is, at least, a slight possibility that the core of any black hole might also have some size; at least the core of the supermassive black holes might have some size, *because the infinite heat energy trapped within the black-holes would resist the compression of the matter particles into a zero-sized point.* But we don't have any means to verify this idea; this appears to be beyond the capacity of the mankind.

SIZE OF THE EVENT HORIZON

The sizes of the neutron stars generally range from 20 to 30 kilometers diameter wise, but even then they can be seen. This fact suggests that the size of the event horizon should be much smaller than this limit, but it is not possible to make any speculation about their exact sizes. However, the sizes of the event horizons, of the different black holes, must depend on the strength of their gravitational forces; more massive is a black hole bigger would be the size of its event horizon. In fact, gravitational force does not act only in two dimensions; it reaches out to the objects located in all the three dimensions. This means that this force acts or spreads out spherically in all the three dimensions, not only in two dimensions. Therefore, the intensity of the gravitational force of the black holes and other objects, at any fixed distance measured from the center of any celestial body, should decrease in the inverse ratio of the cube* of the distance, that is, in the proportion of the value of $1/d^3$, instead of the conventional value $1/d^2$, i.e., in the inverse ratio of the square of the distance. The mass of the black hole, that is, the total quantity of matter stored within its core, must bear a definite ratio with the size of its event horizon. Since black holes of different masses, capture light waves from different distances, the outer edges of the event horizon, of any black hole, should be formed at such a distance from its center, where the intensity of its gravitational force, that is, the value of the ratio m/d^3, shall be adequate to capture the light rays. Accordingly, sizes of the event horizons of different black holes, having different masses, would differ, but the intensities of the gravitational force, of all of the black holes shall always be equal at the outer edges of their respective event horizons.

---

*   See chapter-8, "Puzzle of Gravitation"

It may be envisaged on account of the above fact that if the mass of any black hole becomes double of its original value, then the size of its event horizon would increase by $2^{1/3}$ times, that is, 1.27 times of its original size. Similarly, size of its event horizon could only be doubled in size, when its mass increases by 8 times, that is, by 2^3 times of its original mass. It may thus be seen that only a ratio could be established between the mass of the black hole and in the size of its event horizon, it is, however, not possible to estimate the exact sizes, either of the event horizon, or that of the core of any black hole.

RELATION BETWEEN MASS OF THE GALAXIES AND THAT OF THE BLACK HOLES

Right from the creation of the universe to till to date, hundreds of billions of stars, after having run out of their fuel, might have turned into black holes. Therefore, besides the hard-to-see objects, such as white/black dwarfs and neutron stars, etc., the number of black holes, of different sizes and masses, might be greater than that of the visible stars. Therefore, total mass, of any galaxy, cannot be estimated merely on the basis of the total mass of the visible stars, as was done earlier in 1930s (Please see Chapter-14 "Dark Matter").

Almost 99% mass of the entire solar system is concentrated in the sun alone. All the planets, asteroids, comets and all other smaller bodies, etc., are orbiting the sun, because its mass is several thousand times more than the combined mass of all the other members of the solar system. Likewise, the disk of stars comprising any galaxy, orbits an invisible galactic center, which is in fact a "supermassive black hole." Analogous to the solar system, the mass of such galactic centers must invariably be many times greater than that of the combined mass of all the visible and invisible stars comprising different galaxies. This is necessary so that the gravitational force of the galactic center of any galaxy could compel all the stars of that galaxy, to form a whirling structure. Our milky way comprises about 200 billion stars, out of that a good-number of stars would be much more massive than our Sun. Cosmologists have estimated that the galactic center of our galaxy is only 4 million times massive as compared to the sun. This mass of the galactic center doesn't seem to be adequate to compel the entire lot of the stars to form a whirl, being far-below than the combined mass of all the stars going around it. This could be understood from the example of the sport of "hammer throw." A person can swing the hammer subject to the condition that his body weight and strength, both are greater than the weight of the hammer. The inverse of this is not possible; only the celestial bodies having lesser mass could orbit the heavier ones, heavier body can't orbit the lighter one. ***This fact suggests that the mass of the galactic center should be many times greater than the present estimation of the mass of the galactic center.*** Our present estimation of mass of the galactic centre is probably calculated on the basis of formula $F = G. M_1 M_2 / d^2$. In case the square of distance is replaced in the above formula by the cube of the distance, then the mass of the galactic center might work out to be many times greater than our existing estimate.

PRIMORDIAL BLACK HOLES

Scientists believe that the shock waves produced by the big bang would have compressed matter-particles to almost zero (0) size. This would have produced numerous low-mass black holes having a mass of few thousand million tons. Such ***hypothetical*** low mass black holes are known as "Primordial Black Holes." Said low mass black holes could have produced only when the explosion would have taken place either within the matter particles, or all around them. This could perhaps happen by massive explosions like hyper novae or hydrogen-bombs. Possibility of compression of the matter particles, by the big bang, doesn't seem realistic, because matter particles didn't exist when the big bang took place; matter particles are believed to have produced about 100 seconds thereafter. However, if low mass black holes could possibly be produced by such explosions, then their gravitational force won't be able to overcome the mutual repulsion of the subatomic particles, because their gravitational force would be very weak. For example, if a rubber ball is squeezed to minimum possible volume, and the applied pressure is removed thereafter, then the ball would bounce back to its original shape and size, likewise, every object could not possibly be turned into a black hole by simply squeezing it to zero size. In case the mass of a body is inadequate to maintain its own compactness against the mutual repulsion of its particles, then soon after the compressive force is removed, the same might bounce back to its original size. Black holes could possibly be formed when the compressive force, required to squeeze them to the last limit, remains active permanently. *Relativity* also envisages that the gravitational fields, of the "black holes," should be so strong that they could create infinite curvature in the space-time. A very large quantity of matter would be required to produce such a strong gravitational force. Thus, the formation of low mass black holes appears to be a very remote possibility.

However, if the primordial black holes were, in fact, created by the "big bang," then possibly, they won't be able to sustain their sizes and shape. The particles of such objects would repel each other, and thereby bounce back to their original state. Or alternatively, like other black holes, they would continually suck material from their surroundings and gradually grow bigger. The period of 13 billion years is more than sufficient, for such objects, to accomplish either of the two tasks. They won't be able to continue as primordial black holes for such a long period of time.

HYPOTHETICAL DEATH OF THE BLACK-HOLES

Stephen Hawking, one of the greatest physicists of this era, has proposed that black holes shall also emit some radiation from the regions lying just outside of their event horizons. This concept is based on the uncertainty principle of quantum mechanics. In brief, the Uncertainty Principle implies that there must always be some quantum fluctuations in the empty space - even outside of the black holes too. These fluctuations could be thought of as creation and destruction of pairs of the particles and their antiparticles; one of these particles would have positive energy, and the other one would have negative energy. It is also believed that any particle, lying close to a massive body, has less energy than those lying far away from that body (please see chapter-4 under "Positive and Negative Energy"). This assumption is based on the concept, that some work against gravity would have been done on the particles lying away from any black hole, to move them to their existing locations. When a black hole, due to its gravitational force, draws any particle closer to it, then energy of that particle would gradually decrease and might become even negative. Out of all the particles lying in the near vicinity of a black hole, the particles, having negative energy, would fall in the black hole, whereas, its partner, because of its positive energy, might escape the gravitational force and move away from the black hole. Therefore, on the one hand, it would appear to an observer from a distance that such particles are emitted from the black holes, and on the other hand, the inflow of negative energy would gradually reduce the mass of the black hole. As a result, the black hole would disappear in a few billion years, in a tremendous final burst of emission that would be equivalent to millions of hydrogen bombs exploding together.

According to the above prediction, the particles having positive energy would continuously be escaping from just outside of the event horizon of any black hole. In other words a shower of particles, having positive energy, or radiation of such particle, would appear to be emitted from just outside of the black holes. When focusing a telescope on the prospective location of a black hole, a very faint glow might appear to come from such a place. This radiation is known as "Hawking Radiation" to honor Hawking.

Scientists have also envisaged that smaller is the black hole shorter would be the distance from where the negative energy would be drawn within it. This would have two consequences: 1) smaller would be the black-hole more radiations would it emit & 2) quicker would it lose its mass due to ingress of more negative energy. This implies that smaller is the black hole hotter would its interior should become due to the annihilation of positive energy. Accordingly, it would lose more mass and the same would eventually evaporate; that would be its end. It has been estimated that by now the primordial black holes would have become so hot that they would be on the verge of being evaporated. Such black holes, at the time of their deaths, might emit a final burst of radiation. However, in spite of constant watch the scientists, so-far, couldn't see any such burst of radiation.

×   ×   ×

The hypothesis of decay of black holes is based on the idea that the particles, located closer to a black hole, have lesser energies, however, this idea contradicts the concept that "particles absorb energy from stronger energy fields." *Only one of these two assumptions can be correct, not both. Furthermore, contrary to the belief that gravity is negative energy, it never performs negative work; no object can move against the attraction of gravity, until a much stronger force compels it to do so. In fact, the particles, created after the "big-bang," were dragged closer to different gravity-centers, not driven-away from them; gravitational force of the "black holes" also drags the particles closer to it, for which work has to be performed. Therefore, particles located closer to the massive bodies must gain energies instead of losing it; no work was ever performed on the particles to drag them away from the black holes, therefore, they should not have gained more energy. Moreover, if any particle possesses negative energy, then the mass of such particle should also become negative, because mass is supposed to be the measure of energy of a particle or object.* Anyhow, in case the pairs of particles, having positive and negative energies, do really exist near the black holes, then the particles having negative energies should perform negative work and move in the opposite direction to the applied force, thereby they should be driven away. On the other hand, the particles having positive energies would move in the direction of the applied force, and be drawn within the black holes. Any particle, in order to escape the gravitational force of a black hole, should have energy, i.e. mass, greater than that of the black holes, which is impossible. *Had the particles with positive energy been capable to move away from the black holes, then formation of the stars would have become impossible; gas clouds would have been shattered away instead of collapsing* **within themselves.**

We know that the point sized cores of the black holes continually accumulate energy in the form of matter. This fact indicates that the temperature inside these cores should have increased infinitely. However, since their gravitational force never allows photons, or energy-carrier particles, to escape, they shouldn't emit any radiation from within. *Moreover, since the outward pressure, generated within the black holes, would always depend upon its gravitational force, such pressure would never be able to overcome the drag of the gravitational force. In view of the above fact, the possibility of death of the primordial black holes, by way of evaporation, doesn't seem to be feasible, at least to me.*

MAGNETIC FIELDS OF THE BLACK HOLES

Some scientists believe that the Earth's magnetic field is created by the flow of molten magma below the earth's crust, or due to the flow of charged particles around the earth, in the form of solar wind. This belief is, however, unable to explain the formation of magnetic fields of the compact celestial bodies like neutron stars, pulsars, magnetars and black holes, etc. A question therefore arises, that "how the magnetic force is generated in such compact bodies?" The fact that matter particles like atoms, electrons, protons and quarks, etc., are crushed and squeezed within the black holes to zero sized cores, attracts a question, "does gravitational collapse or compactness of the matter has any relation with the magnetism?" Whatsoever is the cause of this magnetism, it seems to me that the combination of infinite energy, pressure and temperature existing within the interiors of the black holes probably produces magnetism of a different kind. At such a high energy and temperature all the three nuclear forces, that is, strong, weak and electromagnetic forces probably unite with each other. This might be the reason that the black holes have such a strong magnetic force. However, the gravitational force maintains its separate identity from the rest of the natural forces. The very long reach of magnetic force indicates that the force carrier particles of the magnetism, i.e., the virtual photons, do not acquire any extra mass from the stronger energy fields of the black holes. Even though black holes are supposed to carve infinite curvature in the space-time, all around them, the magnetic force, or more accurately the force carrier virtual photons of magnetism, is surely capable to escape- even the most massive black hole, from both the poles, against their gravitational force. This fact poses a question, "how this becomes possible?" *Can the virtual photons propagate without the medium of space-time?*

The black holes regularly swallow as much gas and matter particles as is available in their surroundings; however, quantity of the infalling matter may vary from time to time. As the gas molecules move ahead toward the center of the black holes, the intensity of the energy field of the "black holes," goes on increasing. Aside from the kinetic energy, their heat energy also goes on increasing gradually, due to the persistent reduction in the volume. Scientists believe that that the in-falling gas heats up due to the mutual friction of the particles. Anyhow, as the temperature reaches the value of about 3,000°C and above, the gas molecules get iodized. This ionized gas, rushing toward the black hole, gradually acquires the speed of several thousand kilometers per second. The electrons while orbiting the nucleus that are moving with such a high speed, once move in the same direction in which the atomic nucleus is moving, whereas during the next half cycle, they move in the opposite direction, and at the same time they might also try to maintain the same distance with the nucleus. During the half cycle when any electron travels in the direction opposite of that of the nucleus, its speed would decrease due to a drag exerted by the nucleus, therefore, the same might retard. Even then, the electron would complete this half cycle in a shorter time period, because it would have to travel-through a shorter distance. In the next half cycle, when the electron and the nucleus, both move in the same direction, the nucleus would drag the electron and accelerate the same, but it would take longer time to complete this half-cycle, because it would have to cover a longer distance. The electrons therefore, would not orbit the nucleus in the way in which they orbit any stationary nucleus. Instead, they would probably move in the orbits similar to those as shown in the figures 9A, 9B and 9C. ***These orbital paths depicted in the aforementioned figures are only imaginative. I am not sure about the exact paths the electrons might adopt;*** however, the distances traveled by them, during each half cycle, would surely undergo periodic changes. This might result in the change of the rate of the accelerations of the electrons. In turn this would cause periodic changes in the rate of interaction between the electrical fields of the nucleus and that of the magnetic field of the electrons. Probably, this might be the reason, why the ionized gases, falling into the black holes, emit waves of different frequencies or photons of varying energies.

Probable path of the electron when the nucleus is moving at 1/2 the speed of the electron

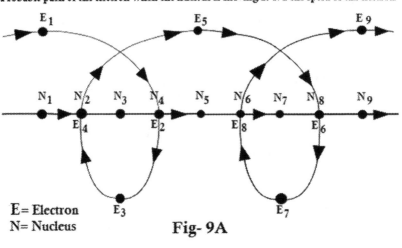

E= Electron
N= Nucleus

Fig- 9A

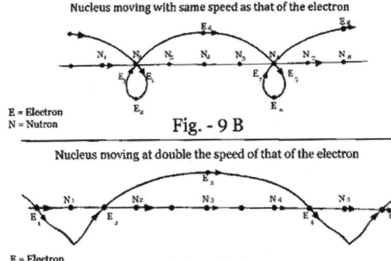

Nucleus moving with same speed as that of the electron

E = Electron
N = Nutron

Fig. - 9 B

Nucleus moving at double the speed of that of the electron

E = Electron
N = Nutron

Fig. - 9 C

When the gas atoms would reach closer to the black hole, say very near to the event horizon, the gravitational force acting on them would grow so strong that the electrons might not be able to return onto their orbital paths; they might break off from the nucleus and rush toward the black holes as independent units, the bare nucleus would also continue their voyages separately. The faint glow seen outside the black holes is probably caused by the splitting of the structure of the atoms. At distances, very close to the event horizon, the particle with negligible mass such as electrons and photons, etc., would also be arrested by the gravitational force, due to that these low mass particles, along with the bare nuclei, would also spiral into the black holes.

Since the magnetic field, created by the whirling ionized gas atoms, was not induced due to fluctuation of the magnetic field of the black hole, the same won't oppose the main magnetic field of the black hole instead both the magnetic fields would support each other. The magnetic axes of the electrons, after they are torn-off from their orbits, would be arranged by the magnetic field of the black hole, in such a way that the magnetic field created by the whirling of the electrons, would also add up to the pole strength of the black holes. This would mean that more is the quantity of gas that spirals into a black hole, stronger its magnetic poles would become. And in case the quantity of infalling matter varies then the pole strength, of the black holes, should also fluctuate accordingly.

The event horizon, of any black hole, is formed at a certain distance from its point sized core. This distance, depending on the mass of the black holes, would range from few hundred kilometers to a few hundred-thousand kilometers. In case the speed of the matter particles, on arriving at the event horizon, touches the speed of light, then immediately after the matter particles cross the event horizon, and move ahead toward the core of the black hole, their speeds might surpass the limit of the speed of light. And by the time they fall in the point core, their speeds would increase manifold. Trillions-of-trillion charged particles orbiting the core at such a high speed would further strengthen its existing magnetic field. At this speed, very strong centrifugal force would also be generated in the infalling particles that would keep them whirling for much longer time periods before falling into the core. In this case, a whirl or a cyclone of trillions of nano sized magnetic particles, i.e. electrons and protons, etc., would be created within the interiors of the event horizon. A very strong magnetic field, of the black hole, would also pass through this whirl of magnetic particles. This magnetic field, analogous to the experiment of magnetic trapping of light*, would trap any kind of energy waves, or their force carrying particles, within the said cyclone of these whirling nano-sized magnetic particles.

---

*   Please see "Some Least-known Properties of Light"

13: QUASARS

"Quasar" is a very hot and very bright disk of plasma or ionized gas that rotates around the central black hole of a galaxy. This disk emanates very powerful bipolar jets and radio signals from its centre, along both the ends of its rotational axis. Quasars are the most luminous, powerful and energetic astronomical objects, rather regions, known in this universe, which emit up to thousands times the energy output that an entire galaxy, comprising billions of stars, may emit. They are even more powerful than hundreds or even thousands hypernovae exploding simultaneously. The enormous amount of the energy that they generate is not a short-lived one like an explosion; it might continue to emit energy at such a very high rate for billions of years, subject to availability of adequate quantity of the gas. The radiation emitted by any quasar includes different kinds of radiations ranging from X-rays to far-infrared rays; they also emit ultraviolet, visible light, radio waves and even the gamma rays.

In the beginning of the decade of 1950s, astronomers discovered a radio source, for the first time, while they were looking for extra-terrestrial civilizations, supposed to be living on the exoplanets. Thereafter, by 1960, hundreds of such sources were discovered. During the year 1962-63, a source of radio waves was observed that was, in addition to radio-signals, emitting very faint red light too. First, it was thought that this very faint object must be a star located closer to the earth. However, its light spectrum was far different from that of the stars. This object was, therefore, called "Quasi-Stellar Radio Source." Such objects, as on today, are still known by the abbreviated-form of this name, that is, "Quasar." Very soon it was established that light coming from this source was redshifted to a great extent, and also that it was billions times energetic as compared to that of the stars. Scientists calculated that this object was located at a distance of about 15 billion light-years, and it was moving away from the earth at an amazing speed of 47,000 kilometers per second. By 1980, several quasars were observed, which are moving away from the earth at speeds even much greater than 100 thousand kilometers per second. This speed is only relative to the earth; their actual speed may be determined by adding Earth's absolute speed. Up till now about 1 million quasars have been found, but out of all of these quasars, as many as 90% quasars do not emit radio waves.

Though the nearest quasar is located in the Virgo Constellation, which is only 30 light-years away from us, most of the quasars are seen at the distance of about 12 to 15 billion light-years. Based on this fact, it is believed that the Quasars would have been created when the universe was very young, about only 1 billion years old. It is also believed that the quasars are formed in the galaxies where gas and dust are in abundance, and where new stars are being created at much faster rates. Such galaxies are called active galaxies. Activity of the galaxies increases manifold by merger or collision of two galaxies.

Scientists have found that quasars are always formed in the centers of very hot disks of gas, which rotate around supermassive black holes. These disks are called accretion disks, which are always associated with powerful bipolar jets comprising subatomic particles and energetic radiations. These jets spread out with almost the speed of light and they may extend up to far-off distances, measuring to several hundred-thousand light-years. Scientists have found that all the quasars are located in the centers of galaxies, but it is not necessary that all the galaxies should host quasars. It is believed that quasars are powered by supermassive black holes, which rotate with very high speeds. *Any supermassive black hole, irrespective of its mass, is capable to create a quasar, provided large quantities of gas and dust are available in its vicinity; the gases infalling into the black-hole would soon form a whirl, which, in turn, would be converted into a quasar.*

The luminosity of quasars never remains constant; it normally keeps varying and fluctuating. This might be caused by fluctuations in the quantity of the gases that fall into the black holes. On the basis of these fluctuations, scientists have concluded that in spite of the enormous amount of energy the quasars emit, their sizes are no bigger than any solar system. It is noted that in spite of being hundreds-of-thousands times smaller than their host galaxies, quasars can generate several hundred times more luminosity and energy, as compared to that an entire galaxy could produce. This fact suggests that the density of energy in a quasar should be enormous. In spite of generating energy at such a high rate, the quasars can produce energy for very long periods of millions of years; however, if the quantity of infalling gas falls below a certain level, than the quasars would cease to generate energy. However, when the central black hole of a galaxy is again infused with a fresh supply of matter and gases, the quasar might be reignited.

SOURCE OF ENERGY GENERATED IN THE QUASARS

Quasars rotate with unimaginable speeds, which is clear from the quasar hosted by the galaxy named M-84. Half the portion of the said quasar exhibits redshift and the other half of the same quasar exhibits blue-shift. This fact suggests that this quasar is not only rotating, its speed of rotation is even greater than the speed at which this galaxy is moving away from us, otherwise blue-shift, in one of its halves, could never be seen. Since the universe itself is expanding at very high speed, it could be imagined that how fast its accretion disk is rotating.

Since the gases within the accretion disks rush inward with very high speeds, great congestion is created all around the black holes, due to which a very high pressure and temperature is generated in the gases whirling within the accretion disks. Ignoring this fact, Scientists have envisaged that such enormous amount of energy at such a high rate is generated by the mutual friction of the gas-ions and dust particles. However, it seems to me that this explanation is not satisfactory because, *I feel that possibility of friction between the gas-ions, whirling at same speeds, is very remote.* Whatever be the cause of this energy generation, any supermassive black hole, in order to produce energy at such a high rate, should convert matter equivalent to hundreds to thousands of stars every year or 100 to 1000 earths every minute. This process of the energy generation is thought to be about 15 times more efficient than the process of nuclear-fusion that powers the stars.

CLASSIFICATION OF THE QUASARS

Different quasars, depending upon their energy and luminosity, are classified in different categories. Scientists, however, believe that all the quasars are of one and the same kind. All of them are like a flat rotating disk that emanates jets of energy and matter particles from their centers. However different Quasars might appear to be of different kinds because of the angles at which we observe them. Radio waves travel only in the direction of the jets, which can be seen only when their jets are directed straight towards the earth. This is the reason that only 10% quasars appear to emit radio waves. The quasars, at which we look in the direction of their jets, appear to be very energetic and luminous. The quasars, that we look at in the directions of the edges of their disks, appear to be very faint and weak, because a bigger part of their luminosity and energy is obstructed by the stars shrouding them. And those quasars, which are located at an angle in between the above two positions, appear to be more luminous and energetic in comparison to the former one; however, all of them are, in fact, of the same kind.

THE SECRET BEHIND FORMATION OF THE JECTS

Every quasar invariably emanates bipolar jets along their rotational axis. These jets travel almost with the speed of light. Apart from the jets, sometimes the infalling gas, while rushing towards the center, escapes from the poles of the quasars in large quantities. The speed of the gas escaping from the centers of different quasars that escapes against the gravitational force of the black holes is estimated to be just about 30,000 km per second. Such a vast difference in the speeds of these two kinds of emissions, escaping from almost the same place, suggests that both of these emissions must be caused by different reasons. However, no proper or satisfactory explanation is available for both of these emissions.

Scientists have predicted that when any black hole devours gas in excess of its capacity, then it vomits this excess gas through its poles. But the problem with this belief is that *"how nonliving object like a black hole, could know that it has swallowed gas in excess of its capacity and how much gas should it vomit?"* In fact, any black hole can suck only that much gas, which its gravitational force allows it to suck; *no excess gas, defying the laws, can fall all by itself in any black-hole. Neither any black hole can exert more force than its capacity nor can the gas falling into any black hole, speed up by itself until it is not acted upon by any force. Furthermore, neither gravitation can throw out anything against its own force nor the gas flowing in any particular direction can change its direction and flow out against the gravitational attraction of the black hole, without being acted upon by any external force.* Few other questions also arise on this belief that are, *"why any black-hole vomits the excess gas, only in the direction of its magnetic poles, why not in any other direction?"* And *"what is that force that acts in that particular direction, so that the gas is ejected only in this particular direction?"* These questions shall essentially be solved before we can understand that how and why these bipolar jets are formed.

Earlier, in Chapter-2 that describes some of the fundamental laws of science, we have learnt that strong magnets are capable to levitate carbonaceous objects - even living creatures too, against the force of gravity. This fact indicates that very strong magnetic force can act as anti-gravitational force for the non-magnetic materials. Yet another possibility was discussed in the previous chapter (Chapter- 12) that the strength of the magnetic poles of the black holes can increase due to increase in the speed or quantity of the ionized gases falling into the black hole. More would be the quantity of gas-ions falling into any black-hole more the strength of its magnetic poles would be enhanced. In case, above *speculation of mine* is correct, then the strength of the magnetic poles of the black holes would fluctuate due to variations in the quantity of these infalling ionized gases. Accordingly, whenever large quantities of gas falls in any black hole, then its pole strength might grow equal to the gravitational pull, or at times the strength of its magnetic force might surpass even the strength of the gravitational force. This would result in the creation of very small regions over both of its poles, where the strength of magnetic force, being comparatively stronger, would negate the gravitational force. As a result, gravitation might become ineffective in these point-sized zones, as if gravity-less windows have been opened at both of its poles. These point-sized regions would even repel the charged matter particles against gravity. *If creation of such windows is possible, then the extreme pressure generated within the interiors of the black holes, or more accurately, the force of the gravity itself, would eject the crushed matter particles in the space, in the form of powerful jets, through these windows.* The energy trapped within the black holes would also escape through these windows in the form of gamma rays and other kind of energy waves. The particles ejected as bipolar jets, would mostly contain protons, neutrons and atomic nuclei, etc., *that would be similar to the composition of the cosmic rays. The event horizon, because of these windows, might curve inwards at both the poles like a "toroid" or an apple, instead of being perfectly spherical. It might also have small windows, one each at each of the poles, through which these bipolar jets are ejected.*

The jets created just before the hyper-novae explosions, and during different stages of the star-formation, like the protostars and T. Tauri stars, etc., might also be created due to similar phenomenon; their magnetic poles might become stronger than the gravitational force due to the heavy inrush of the ionized gases.

THE SECRET OF EJECTION OF GAS

In any galaxy, the disk of stars is not as thin as a two-dimensional fabric; it might be as thick as 1000 light-years or even more. Likewise, the accretion disks of different quasars might have the same thickness. On the other hand, the black holes located in their centers, are only atom sized points. *Because of this vast difference in the sizes of the accretion disks and that of the black holes, the gas ions that start their journeys, from the top and bottom edges of the accretion disk, and rush towards the black hole at a very acute angle. Accordingly, the gas ions, while on their way, would surely encounter the repulsive force exerted by the magnetic poles of the black-holes. Any sudden gust of the infalling gas would enhance the pole strength of the black hole to such an extent that the gas infalling from the corners of the accretion disks, would either bend a little, toward the center, and would be sucked within the black hole, or as shown in Fig-10, it would take a 'U' turn and the same would be repelled back by the magnetic force.* The gas ions, so repelled, would be thrown out in the space, probably, with the same speed, with which, they started their inward journeys. The particles, so dispelled, would look like inverted rotating cones of plasma or flame, because of their spiral motions.

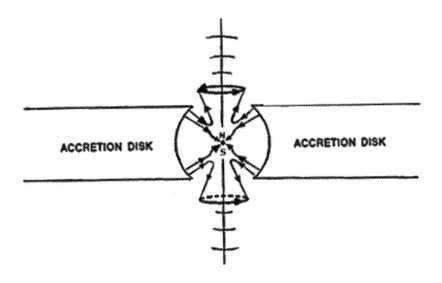

Fig- 10

The matter particles that fall into the black hole, would become the part of its point sized core, and whenever possible, would be ejected through the poles in the form of bipolar jets, with the speed of almost light. On the other hand, the particles, which were prevented from entering the black holes and were repelled-back into the space, from the accretion disk directly, would travel on their outward journey at much lower speeds as compared to that of the jets. According to the observations made by the astronomers, such rotating streams of plasma travel at about 10% the speed of the jets, that is, at the speed of about 30 thousand kilometers per second.

14: Dark Matter

In the year 1929, Edwin Hubble discovered that the universe is continually expanding. At that time, scientists believed that the mutual attraction acting between all the stars would one-day halt its expansion; thereafter, it would start contracting and eventually end up with a "Big crunch," into a small point. Later on, when the scientist tried to predict the mass of all the visible stars, they found that the combined mass, of all the galaxies taken together, must be about 1/100th times lesser than what is required to halt the expansion of the universe. Since then it is believed that the universe must contain a large amount of invisible matter, which is holding all the stars and all the galaxies together. However, in spite of the best efforts, presence of any such matter, couldn't be detected anywhere in the whole of the universe.

At that point in time, Swiss scientist Fritz Zwicky was conducting research to establish the relation between gravitational force and the formation of the galaxies. On the basis of the luminosity of galaxies and their rotational speeds, he mathematically calculated that the total mass of the galaxies is about 400 times more than the total mass of the luminous matter contained within it. It is also understood that during the period 1930 to 34, he made a computerized model of a galaxy and put the gravitational force in accordance with the mass of the luminous stars. However, instead of forming a galaxy, the stars, in that model, straggled away. Subsequently, he included some extra gravitational force in that model that resulted in the formation of a galaxy. On the basis of this model, it was concluded that all the galaxies must contain many times as much mass as is the total mass of the visible stars, so that they may produce adequate amount of gravitational force that is essentially required to bind them in the shape of a galaxy. Fritz tossed the name "Dark Matter," for this hypothetical invisible matter.

Above discovery also led to the conclusion that this invisible dark matter is the building block of the universe; had the dark matter not exist, all the stars would have scattered here and there in a disorderly manner. Accordingly, accumulation of stars in the early universe, over or around the dark matter, would have resulted in formation of the galaxies and clusters of stars. In view of the fact that many galaxies accumulate together around a bigger galaxy, and form local clusters of galaxies, it was inferred that more quantity of dark matter must be present between these galaxies. Similarly, more dark matter must be present between the super-clusters of the galaxies. *This idea, though, appears to be very convincing, it doesn't provide any clue about the fact that what force caused stars to accumulate over the dark matter, or how the stars started to form different whirling structures, that is, what force causes them to rotate in a particular direction and in a particular order?*

At the time when the hypothetical dark matter was conceptualized, that is, in the decade of 1930s, nobody considered the masses of the hard to see objects such as the white, brown and black dwarfs, neutron stars, pulsars and quark stars, etc. Although names like supernova and neutron stars were suggested by Zwicky himself, nobody was serious about them; most of the scientists considered them only hypothetical, not a reality; black hole was only a name at that time, nobody had any idea of their masses. Therefore, the mass of such objects that remained invisible at that time, and also the gravitational influence caused by them, would not have been included in any of the calculations. *When the exact data on the total number of such invisible objects and their combined mass, etc., was not available at that point in time, then how could the exact mass of the dark matter required for the formation of the galaxies could have been estimated?* Even as of today, we don't have any databank on the masses of such invisible objects.

These days, it has been unanimously accepted that a supermassive black hole compulsorily exists in the centers of almost all the galaxies; all the stars of any spiral galaxy rotate around this center. The mass of such a supermassive black hole alone should exceed billions of stars taken together. All the galaxies, besides the visible stars, also contain innumerable invisible celestial objects; white dwarfs and neutron stars alone might be many times massive as compared to our Sun. Besides these objects, hundreds of billions of small and medium sized black holes, of varying masses, might also exist in almost every galaxy. The mass of such black holes might range between tens to thousands times greater than our Sun. *Accordingly, the actual mass, of any galaxy, might be several hundred times more than that of the combined mass of all the visible stars contained in that galaxy.*

Since rules shall be the same for all the celestial bodies, it is necessary that analogous to the solar system, the bulk of the mass of any rotating galaxy shall be concentrated at its center, not anywhere else. Looking at the large number of the stars and invisible celestial objects orbiting the galactic centre of an average sized galaxy, it is presumed that the total mass of all the luminous stars alone, would be several hundred times greater than the combined mass of billions of Sun-sized stars. This estimate doesn't include the combined mass of all the invisible objects, including the supermassive black hole located in the center of the galaxies. Steady whirling motion in such a big collection of the stars, including numerous luminous and nonluminous objects, could be generated, when the mass of the galactic center of any galaxy may be many times greater than the combined mass of the whole collection of the stars and other objects that orbits it. Contrary to this fact, the mass of the supermassive black hole, located at the galactic center of our galaxy the Milky Way, is estimated to be only four million times greater than that of the sun. This mass doesn't seem to be adequate to produce whirling motion in the entire galaxy containing about 200 to 400 billion luminous stars. Since the celestial bodies like planets and their moons, etc., always orbit bigger bodies having many times greater mass than that of their own, it is necessary that the hypothetical dark matter must be located at the center of any rotating galaxy. If the quantity of the dark matter, needed for this purpose, is located elsewhere, then the stars would have been orbiting the center of mass, that is, the dark matter, instead of the galactic center. Based on the aforesaid fact, it could be inferred that, if the dark matter is holding all the stars together, then it must be located in the centers of different galaxies. This means that the centers of spiral galaxies are the best places where the dark matter is likely to be detected. Another possibility is that while estimating the mass of the supermassive black hole, some mistake* might have crept into our calculations. *In case the mass of a supermassive black hole is greater than the collective mass of all the stars contained in a galaxy, then dark matter would not be required to form any spiral galaxy; the galaxy would become self-sufficient, to form a rotating structure.*

We always depend on some kind of energy waves to see any object, or obtain information about that object, but the dark matter is invisible for all the kinds of energy waves or radiations. Neither any type of energy waves are reflected by the dark matter, and nor the dark matter absorbs any type of waves. Moreover, the dark matter itself doesn't emit any type of energy wave; it is, therefore, not possible to directly detect its presence. In spite of this fact, scientists have detected some places in the interstellar space where light rays are seen to deflect, as if they are bending under the effect of gravity lensing, however, no object could be detected at such locations. Scientists believe that this effect is caused by the curvature of space-time created by the invisible dark matter. Estimation, of the mass of such blocks of invisible dark matter, is done on the basis of the angle through which the light rays are found to bend. On the

---

*   See Chapter – 8, "The puzzle of Gravitation" & Chapter-12, "Black holes".

basis of the angle of the observed deflection of the light rays, astronomers have prepared different maps of the possible locations of the dark matter, and the prospective quantities of dark matter in such locations; such maps are available on the Internet. Large accumulations of stars are mostly found associated with such locations. However, negligible or very few stars could be observed at some of these locations. On the other hand, large gathering of stars was observed in some other places, where the effect of gravity lensing couldn't be observed. This fact indicates that the presence of dark matter is not necessary for any accumulation of stars; particularly when the effect of gravity lensing could be produced by any collection of black holes or even a single black hole.

In case the gravitational fields of dark matter causes the light rays to bend, then at least a few stars must also be found orbiting bigger blocks of the dark matter. Similarly, smaller blocks of dark matter should also orbit the bigger blocks of dark matter. In case some stars orbiting any block of dark matter, instead of any black hole, could be detected, only then the existence of the dark matter may be proved. In case dark matter is really the building block of the galaxies, then proof of its presence could be found in the center of any galaxy. The galactic center of our own galaxy is the nearest and most potent place where the dark matter could be located.

If the scientists fail to locate the dark-matter in the galactic center, then its existence would become doubtful. Non-detection of dark matter in the galactic center would mean that ignorance about the existence of the supermassive black holes, during the decade of 1930s, resulted in conceiving the concept, rather the misconception, of the dark matter.

15: GALAXIES- THEIR FORMATION AND CLASSIFICATION

Scientists have predicted that in the beginning, approximately within 500 million years after the "big bang," the first-generation stars were created, probably, one by one as single units; galaxies were formed much later. At that point of time the newborn stars were randomly scattered all around in a disorderly manner. Within the next few hundred millions of years, these stars would have gradually started to accumulate on/around the dark matter that would have resulted in the formation of the galaxies. Scientists also believe that the first black holes were created about 1 to 2 billion years after the formation of the galaxies. However, this concept of creation of the galaxies does not give any explanation that how these newly created galaxies start to rotate around their centers, especially when no direct proof of existence of the dark matter is available (please see the previous Chapter). In absence of any force no rotational motion of the galaxies can be generated.

The universe, in the beginning, was much compact and smaller as compared to its present day size, therefore, in that point of time, the newly created gas would have been many times compact and dense than what it is today. Scientists believe that more is the density of a molecular cloud, slower is the rate of star formation. However, I feel that contrary to this belief, stars in the early universe would have formed at a much higher rate. Probably, giant sized stars would have formed in the early universe because of the availability of dense gases in large quantities; these giant stars, due to their large masses, would have quickly run out of the fuel and became either neutron stars or even black holes directly. This is evident from the fact that heavier elements are also seen in very distant galaxies, which would have formed in the early universe. Supernovae or hypernovae explosions would have created these heavy elements in the early universe.

As discussed earlier (See Chapter-8 "The puzzle of Gravity," and Chapter-11, under the section "Alternative speculation on star formation"), in the early universe the new born protostars after acquiring adequate masses, would have gradually started to exert gravitational force on the other protostars, which would have been located in their close neighborhood. Bigger the protostars would have grown more the strength of the mutual attraction acting between them would have developed. Analogous to the whirlpool formed in the washbasins, the most massive protostar would have attracted smaller ones (with their protoplanetary disks) one by one, from its near vicinity, and as a result smaller protostars would have started to orbit the bigger ones. In such a configuration of the rotating protostars, different stars varying in masses between one to several solar masses, would have formed by the gravitational collapse of different pockets of gas. Protostars, so formed, would, in turn, orbit a nearby supergiant protostar. Each of the protostars, in due course of time, would have transformed into a regular star; each of them would have planetary systems of its own. Probably, smaller primitive galaxies rather, mini or dwarf galaxies, were born in the above manner. In the due course of time, the supergiant central star, after consuming its entire fuel, would have directly converted into a medium-sized black hole. Numerous mini-galaxies would have been created at different places in a big nebula, which would have been scattered all around, in a disorderly manner.

These mini or primitive galaxies, due to the formation of new stars, would have continued to grow in size. Their central black holes too would have continued to grow more massive by continuously devouring matter or even a whole star occasionally, from their close surroundings. Thus gravitational force of the central black holes of such mini galaxies, would have gradually gained more strength. Its gravitational field would gradually reach out to different central giant stars, or black holes of the other nearby mini galaxies. As a result, the smaller mini galaxies would have started to orbit that particular galaxy which possessed the most massive black-hole among all of them. In this way local groups or clusters of mini galaxies might also have been formed in the early stage of formation of the universe. Similarly, different bigger clusters of such mini-galaxies, scattered here and there in the early universe, would have caused the smaller clusters of mini-galaxies, to orbit the nearby bigger mini-cluster of galaxies, thereby bigger clusters of mini galaxies would also have formed. As the time passed on, such mini or dwarf galaxies, due to collisions and mergers with other galaxies, would have grown into still bigger galaxies; their central black holes, due to repeated mergers, would also have gradually grown into supermassive black holes. Such merger, of galaxies and their central black holes, is one of a normal activity of the universe; it had happened several times in the past and would be repeated several times in the future also. Almost all the bigger galaxies, including our own galaxy, have grown so big over past several billions of years, due to repeated collisions and subsequent mergers of the smaller galaxies.

Dark Matter in the Galactic Halo

The expansion of any galaxy, or its ambit, is not limited only to the outer edges of the disk of its luminous stars; a faint glow that surrounds the entire galaxy from all around is normally seen, this glow extends to a far bigger region. The said glowing region is an integral and extended component of any galaxy, which extends far beyond the main collection of the visible or luminous stars; its radius might be 3 to 6 times bigger than that of the galaxy itself. This sphere of the diffused light, or the said glowing region, is thought to be made of hot-ionized gases. These glowing regions, surrounding the galaxies, are known as "Halos" of the galaxies. Halos can be very distinctly seen in spiral galaxies, which are roughly spherical in shape. It was earlier believed that such halos contain an almost negligible quantity of gas due to that star formation is not possible in this region. Contrary to the aforesaid belief, which has now become outdated, the present day astronomers have predicted that this region contains very dense gas. They also believe that this accumulation of high-density gas deters the process of star formation. However, it appears to me that gas distribution just after the "big bang," would have been much denser; even then the high-density gases found in the early universe, would have surely facilitated the star-formation at a very high rate, instead of deterring it.

Scientists believe that galaxies were formed due to accumulation of the stars over larger blocks of the dark matter. *Relativity* envisages that the rotational motion in the stars contained in any galaxy is generated when they move in straight lines along the curvature of the indentation made in the space-time due to the mass of the dark matter. Einstein also believed that the rotational velocities of different stars should gradually decrease in the same pattern that is followed by all the planets of the solar system. Contrarily, as per the actual measurements taken by the astronomers, rotational velocities of stars are not found to decrease in the line with what was envisaged by Einstein. In fact, their rotational speeds flatten out when their distances from the galactic center increases; instead of decreasing, it rather increases gradually. This fact shows that the actual rotational speeds of the stars don't match with the assumptions of the *Relativity Theory*. This deviation is a matter of great concern for the astronomers. Astronomers, based on this fact, believe that such a behavior of the speed variation, in the rotational speeds of the stars, is resulted by additional gravitational force, which acts from somewhere else. Accordingly, scientists believe that some additional source of gravitational force must exist in the "halos" of these galaxies, which should be equally distributed in the halos, on both the sides of the disk of stars. In spite of best efforts, scientists could not find any additional source of gravitational force in the galactic-halos. Absence of any visible source of gravity, leads to the concept that dark matter in large quantities must exist in the halos, and which should be distributed equally on both the sides of the disks of stars. Scientists believe that the disk of the luminous stars must be embedded between the large quantities of dark matter. It is also believed that the density of this shroud of dark matter must be highest in the center and as the distance increases from the galactic center, density of dark matter gradually decreases. It is now believed that 95% of the galaxies are composed of dark matter. *However, in case the presence of dark matter in the halos of the galaxies, in such a large quantity, could not be established, then it would mean that the "Theory of Relativity, in regard to gravitation, is not correct and the same needs to be modified."*

Although, according to *relativity*, gravitation is not recognized as a force – even then it certainly attracts all the objects toward large masses of matter; otherwise speed of the falling objects would never accelerate. Now, if the invisible dark matter is really present in the halos of the galaxies, and the same is equally distributed on both the sides of the disks of stars, then both of these layers of the dark matter would either merge into each other due to their mutual attraction, or alternatively, they will try to pull the disk of stars toward each other, that is, in the opposite directions. Such a strong force, acting from both the sides, should tear the disk of stars apart, instead of producing whirling motion in this disk. This possibility is a big question mark on the presence of dark matter on both the sides of the disk of stars. *Moreover, if the disk of stars is really embedded by two separate layers of dark matter from both the sides, then these layers would either not at all warp the two-dimensional fabric of space-time around the disk of stars, which is embedded between them, or warp the said fabric in two opposite directions, which would, probably, not cause the stars to rotate. And if, at all, they start to rotate, even then their rotational speeds will go on reducing slowly that would not match with the actual pattern of their rotation.*

Similarity in the rotational patterns of any spiral galaxy, and that of the whirlpool formed in the wash basin, can easily be observed. As we go toward the center of both of these rotating structures, their rotational speeds decrease gradually. However, as we go closer to the center, the curvature of the paths of the orbiting stars, increases gradually, due to which value of the centrifugal force, produced in the stars, would go on increasing gradually. This is the reason, why these structures maintain a definite and stable shape while rotating. *The pattern of rotation of both the structures suggests that analogous to the water whirl, the stars in the spiral galaxies rotate due to the gravitational pull of the galactic center, not due to the curvature of space-time;* balance established between this pull and the centrifugal force produced in different stars, puts them in stable orbits.

CLASSIFICATION OF THE GALAXIES

Different galaxies differ from each other, in shapes and sizes. Some of the galaxies are so small that they are known as dwarf galaxies on the other hand, some of them are much bigger than our own galaxy, the Milky Way. The biggest galaxy seen so-far is almost 60,000 times bigger than our own galaxy. All these galaxies are not spiral in shapes like the Milky Way; the galaxies are, therefore, classified depending on their shapes not by their sizes. Apart from the spiral galaxies, the galaxies that appear to be perfectly spherical like a football, or elliptical like a rugby ball, are called "Elliptical Galaxies." Likewise, the galaxies, whose shapes resemble to the convex lenses, are called "Lenticular Galaxies," whereas, those galaxies, which don't have any particular or regular shapes, are called "Irregular Galaxies;" these out-of-shape galaxies, are probably formed due to the collision of two galaxies. Alternatively, a galaxy might be deformed by the gravitational force of any other nearby galaxy.

Astronomers believe that the galaxies formed in the early universe would have been elliptical in shapes. Later on, they might have flattened gradually due to the gravitational fields of the dark matter. As a result, such galaxies, in the next step of their developments, might have become lenticular in shapes. Later on, they would have become spiral in shapes, due to the continuation of the process of flattening. It is also believed that the elliptical galaxies were formed from such molecular clouds, which have been rotating at much slower rates, and the spiral galaxies would have been formed in those clouds that were rotating at much faster rates. However, no clarification, on the matter is available that "how and why this whirling motion was produced in different molecular clouds". Another question that remains un-answered is, "why different clouds were rotating with different speeds?" Rotation of gas-clouds was probably taken as granted. Nobody probably tried seriously to find out that how the clouds started to rotate and why different clouds started to rotate with different speeds? Since no explanation on the rotational speeds of different clouds is available, this hypothesis of the formation of different types of galaxies doesn't seem to be fully convincing, at least to me.

The scientists might have rightly predicted that numerous protostars (and their respective rotating disks of gas would have been born in the early universe as single independent units. However, as brought out earlier in Chapter-11, under the heading "Alternative Speculation on Star-Formation," since all these protostars were born due to a similar process, magnetic fields of all of them would have been pointing in the same direction. More mass these protostars would have accreted more strength their respective gravitational and magnetic forces would have acquired. As speculated in the aforesaid Chapter-11, all the smaller stars would rush toward the most massive protostar located within any local group of the newborn stars, but *the bigger one, because of the like magnetic polarity, would have repelled all of them, moreover, these smaller stars would also obstruct the inward movement of each other. Therefore, analogous to formation of the water-whirl, the inrushing protostars would have adopted spiral paths and would have started to orbit the massive one.* *The magnetic field, of the said most massive protostar, would have repelled the smaller protostars from both the sides, and compelled all of them to occupy the plane of the magnetic equator of the said massive protostar.* Scientists (astronomers) have observed that *whenever any moon of the planet "Saturn" passes through its rings then the ice lumps and particles that form these rings, instead of colliding give way to such a moon as if they are repelled, probably because of similar magnetic polarities of such moons and that of the particles forming these rings. If this speculation of mine, regarding formation of the galaxies is correct, then the mini galaxies, so created, should have adopted spiral shapes right from the beginning.* The fact, that most of the stars located in the spiral galaxies, are comparatively younger than the stars of other types of galaxies, may be a proof of the speculation that spiral galaxies are younger than all other types of galaxies.

It was also speculated in chapter-12, that the strength of the magnetic force of any black hole, depends on the quantity of the infalling matter. Therefore, if any of the black-holes is starved of gas, or the quantity of the matter falling into it decreases, then its magnetic strength would also decrease. In the above perspective, I feel that when a central black hole of any galaxy consumes almost all of the loose gas from its vicinity, then its pole strength would decrease gradually. Since the magnetic force that compels the stars to form flat disks, would attenuate gradually, the mutual repulsion acting between all the stars rotating around the said black hole might cause them to slowly and gradually move away from each other. As a result, such a galaxy might start to bulge. There may be yet another reason, in case the smaller companion of a binary pair of black-holes existing in the center of a galaxy, is thrown away by the primary black-hole, or snatched away by any other nearby galaxy, then the former galaxy would gradually bulge in the absence of adequate magnetic force; shape of that galaxy would start to fade away, and its stars would lose distinctive spiral structure. The spiral galaxies were, probably, transformed in this way into lenticular galaxies. Such galaxies after a long period would bulge further, and with time, would convert first into an elongated sphere, and thereafter, into a spheroid. Probably the elliptical galaxies were created in this manner.

16: THE DARK ENERGY
OR, THE DEATH WARRANT
OF THE UNIVERSE

Hubble discovered, in 1929, that the stars are moving away from each other. However, scientists were confident that one-day gravitational force would halt this expansion. Later in 1998, a very remote supernova was observed that revealed that in the remote past the universe was expanding with a much slower speed, slower than its existing speed. This fact indicates that instead of slowing down, the rate of expansion of the universe is continually increasing. As per the laws of science, speed of any moving thing can't increase all by itself, until and unless a force is acting on it. Scientists, in spite of persistent efforts, could not find out the reason for the increase in the rate of expansion, or any source of energy that is responsible for the same. Scientists have, therefore, predicted that an unknown force must be causing this increase in the rate of expansion at a gradually increasing speed. The said unknown force, or energy, supposed to be behind this expansion, is known as *"Dark Energy."* Looking at the speed of expansion, and the total mass of the universe, it is explicit that dark energy must be much stronger than the gravitational force. Scientists have estimated that only 4 to 5% of the total energy of the universe is in the form of normal matter that is contained in all the visible stars, and yet another 22 to 25% of the energy is in the form of Dark Matter. The rest of the 70 to 74% energy must be in the form of Dark Energy. In spite of the fact that the said dark energy is in abundance, it is so elusive that so-far we could not find even a trace of it.

Since no source of dark energy could be detected so-far, some of the scientists of the present era have predicted that the repulsive force acting between the matter and antimatter may be the cause of this expansion. Stars and galaxies are not distributed uniformly in this universe; some vast places in the known universe are almost devoid of stars. Some of the scientists believe that galaxies made of antimatter exist in these voids. They believe that the repulsive force, acting between the matter and antimatter, is acting like an anti-gravitational force. At times, it is heard that antimatter in small quantities exists even in the vicinity of our Earth, but it could not be authentically proved. Therefore, the presence of the antimatter in large enough quantities, adequate to form galaxies, seems only hypothetical and a postulate without proof. Scientists alone can tell what actually the fact is.

Scientists have predicted that the entire energy of the "big bang" was released instantaneously, and subsequently the entire matter was created by the energy so released. Creation of matter particles is supposed to have started after 1½ minutes after the big bang, and the same was completed in the next 1½ minutes or so. This means that all the matter particles were not produced at the same instant of time. If the period of one second could be divided into several billion fractions, then the matter particles would have been created gradually, part by part, in each of such fractions. Accordingly, gravitational force would also have gained its strength gradually, in billions of small steps. These particles, created in each of such steps, would have immediately started to move outward with the speed that was greater than the speed of light. On the other hand, gravitational force, in proportion to the number of particles created during each step, would have started to act between them with gradually increasing strength. As discussed in the chapter-10, under the "Big bang theory," the gravitational force would not have been able to halt this expansion due to very high energy and greater-than-light speeds of the particles so produced. In spite of this reason, the gravitational force might have resulted in slowing down the rate of expansion, at least to some extent. Perhaps, due to this reason, or some other unknown reason, the rate of expansion of the universe, at that time was slower than its present rate of expansion. On the other hand, the energy produced by the "big-bang," was only momentary, not continuous. Therefore, the said energy should not have produced any acceleration in the rate of expansion; an increase in the rate of expansion is not at all possible in the absence of any external force. Had no external force been active, gravitation was sure to retard this expansion, and thereafter, within a small fraction of the time, squeeze the entire universe back into a small point. This means that some force must have been continuously driving the stars away. But there is a problem with this idea that is, "such a powerful force couldn't be produced all by itself." This fact raises a question that when and wherefrom this so called "dark energy" was produced?

In case the dark energy is behind the expansion of the universe, then this force must be very powerful, because it is hurling all the celestial objects with the speed that is very close to the speed of light. On the other hand, the structure of the galaxies and the planetary systems of different stars including our own solar system, etc., does not seem to be distorted or affected, in any way, by the gradually increasing speed of this expansion. This fact indicates that this force, though very powerful, but at the same time it is not a violent or cataclysmic force, like that is supposed to be produced by a sudden explosion. Had this force been explosive in nature, then the structure of the galaxies should have shattered and destroyed completely; the stars would have scattered like splinters. In total contrast to the above possibility, this force is probably pushing all the galaxies and all the stars, etc., very gently, with a very soft hand to ensure not to disturb or damage their structures. *This force, since its inception, has been acting so delicately that no signs of its effect can be felt - even on the frail enclosure of the atmospheric air of our Earth.*

It is believed that the universe, in the present era, is expanding at an unbelievable speed, which is very close to that of the speed of light. In spite of such a high rate of expansion, the routine activities of the universe are going on as usual, without any hindrance. The molecular clouds, instead of expanding or shattering away under the influence of gravitational force, are still producing new stars. Similarly, the stars, after running out of their fuel, still collapse to form dense objects like neutron stars and black holes, etc. Dark energy being many times more powerful than the gravitational force, should be able to forcibly increase the sizes of all the gravitational structures such as the solar system and different galaxies, etc., with the same speed at which the universe is expanding; however, the size of our solar system doesn't appear to expand or distort – even by a bit. Likewise, shapes and sizes of all other similar structures such as local clusters of galaxies, etc., appear to be unaffected by this expansion. It seems from this fact that the dark energy is not able to increase the sizes of any object, or rotating structures, which are bound gravitationally, because the stars in such structures are located at comparatively closer proximities to each other. Only the super-clusters of the galaxies, because of very weak gravitational bonds among them, are perhaps, drifting away from each other. This fact signifies that the dark energy, within the close ranges, is not effective against the strong gravitational bonds. Similarly, nuclear forces too, which act within the range of the atomic radii, are probably, not affected by the dark energy. Could it be implied from this fact that the gravitation and nuclear forces, within the shorter distances, are stronger than the so called dark energy? Alternatively, does the dark energy act only on bigger structures? *How come the inanimate dark energy could select its targets, and also that at what time it shall attack any particular target; it must act equally on all the objects all the time.* These questions give rise to another question *"does any such energy exist at all?"* In order to find out the answer to these questions, let us analyze the following facts:

The strength of the gravitational force produced after the big bang, was sure to depend on the total quantity of matter produced. The amount of matter that was produced at that time is still available in the form of trillions of trillion stars and innumerable molecular clouds, etc. But the big question is "does the quantity of matter and the value of the gravitational force, both are still the same as it was in the beginning"? Out of all the astronomical objects, all the stars are burning a very big amount of their fuel every second that might amount to trillions of trillion of megatons; our own Sun is burning several hundred million tons of hydrogen every second. In the whole of the universe, matter in several trillions of megatons, is destroyed every second; the matter, so destroyed, is converted into mass-less energy. Moreover, a large quantity of the matter is also lost in the form of star wind. We are conversant with the fact that bigger is the star higher is the rate at which it burns its fuel; they consume more than two third of their stock of matter in less than one billion years. Besides the large number of stars, millions of quasars are also converting matter into energy with a much higher rate. It is very hard to imagine that what would be the total quantity of matter that has been lost during the last 13 to 14 billion years? What one could imagine is, *"the quantity of matter, which we started with, might have depleted by a great extent."* Although the amount of the matter, so last, is still available in the form of energy, but no other form of energy attracts and holds matter particles together; at least not from large distances. ***Thus the force that is responsible to prevent the expansion of the universe, is getting weaker, day-by-day, due to two reasons: 1) due to the gradual depletion of the mass of the matter we started with & 2) due to increasing distances between the celestial bodies.*** How this process depletes the strength of the gravitational force, is explained with the help of an example given hereunder:

Considering a scenario in which the distance between two celestial objects gets doubled in a certain time period. If, during the same time interval, both of them consume fuel equivalent to almost half of their initial masses, then the value of the gravitational force acting between them, would, as per the Newton's formula, work out to be $(m'/2).(m''/2) \div (2d)2 = 1/16 \, (m' .m'')/d2$. Or, in other words the force acting between these two objects would reduce by 16 times of its original value. Alternatively, if the value of gravitational force varies in the inverse proportion of the cube of the distance between different objects, that is, in proportion to $1/d^3$, then the value of the force acting between the said celestial bodies, in the time period under consideration, would be depleted by 32 times of its original value.

Continual attenuation of the strength of the gravitational force must be affecting the speed of expansion of the universe persistently. Had the entire energy, of the "big bang," been converted into the matter particles, then in the absence of any force causing the universe to expand, the mass of the matter produced within a short period of $1^1/_2$ minutes, should have eventually contracted back into a very small point, but nothing like this did happen. This means that only a small portion of the energy, released from the big bang, might have converted into matter. *This in turn means that the balance major portion of the total energy, released at that time, is probably causing the universe to expand.* As per Newton's second law of motion, acceleration of any object depends directly upon the force acting on it, and inversely upon the mass of that object. This could be represented by the equation $f = P/m$ or **P=mf**, where "P" means the value of the driving force, "f" means acceleration and "m" is the mass of the moving object. Thus, it could be seen, from the aforementioned equation that on the one hand, the force of gravity, which opposes the rate of expansion, is gradually depleting due to the reduction of mass of all the celestial bodies, and on the other hand, the force responsible for the expansion is probably constant in the absence of any resistance. *This is the reason that the force, causing the universe to expand is, day-by-day, getting an upper hand.* Now, since the mass of the stars and their density per unit area, both have consistently depleted, the rate of acceleration of the universe is bound to increase. Since the distance, between different super-clusters of galaxies, is far too large, the gravitational force acting on them does not seem to be adequate to prevent them from drifting freely. Even any weak force, if acting on them, may cause them to drift.

Another fact that needs to be necessarily considered is the **Gravitational Redshift.** *Special Relativity* predicts that as any light wave moves away from any strong gravitational field, it would gradually lose its energy, which in turn, would result in the gravitational redshift in the said wave. This gravitational redshift would be in addition to the redshift/blueshift caused by the speed of any moving object. In case this postulate is correct, then it would become difficult to assess the actual mass and speed of the source of such a wave. *Therefore, it appears that till such time, both of the above possibilities are not analyzed thoroughly, it might not be possible to ascertain the existence of the dark energy, and its strength.*

THE END OF THE UNIVERSE

It could not be ascertained that when the so-called dark energy became effective. However, if the dark energy really exists, then this force didn't interfere with the activities related to the creation of the universe, or any of its routine works. Creation of stars and galaxies, and their deaths as well, continued in the expanding universe. This resulted in the formation of different galaxies, stars, neutron stars and black holes, etc. In the meantime the Dark energy simply kept pushing different gravitational structures very gently; all the works of the nature related to both, creation and destruction, continued side by side. ***But how long this could continue?***

Scientists believe that one-day, this apparently quiet looking dark energy, would result in the end of the universe; even the universe is not exempted from the rule that "everything that was born shall die one-day". Based on the rate of expansion, which is very close to the speed of light, scientists have envisaged that all the galaxies would first move apart to such great distances that they couldn't be seen any more. Next, they would break the gravitational bonds, and wander alone here and there in an uncontrolled manner; the structure of the universe would be totally disrupted. After the stars would use-up all of their fuel, darkness would loom over everywhere. And thereafter, all the material objects, starting with the galaxies and eventually all the forms of matter, including the atoms, would disintegrate into unbound particles and radiation; they would shoot apart from each other. The universe would gradually become so sparse and thinned out that it would defuse into an endless void. Its existence would be completely terminated; nothing, except a vast emptiness or void, as the one that existed before the "big bang," would be left behind.

× × ×

Somehow, I feel that since the dark energy isn't a destructive force, it might not disintegrate the matter and its atoms. Accordingly, when all the stars would consume all of theirs fuels, no source of light and heat would be left. Only black holes of varying masses and sizes, ranging from supermassive ones to 3-4 solar masses, and the dense cores of dead-stars, of different sizes, would be left behind. However, even after such an end of the stars, gravitational force of their reminiscent cores would continue to act. In this scenario, the black holes and other dense objects, according to the masses of different objects and the mutual distances between them, would organize themselves in different families of the black holes, where the less massive ones would orbit more massive ones. In turn, these families of the black holes would start to orbit the different supermassive black holes. Different black holes, subject to the range of their gravity fields, would gradually devour the smaller ones from their vicinities; thereby they would keep growing gradually. Their mass and consequently their reach of gravitational force would also keep growing. Due to which they would start devouring smaller ones from even greater distances. In case all the black holes are not hurled off, by the dark energy, to very far off distances, then the black holes would continue to merge and grow bigger and yet bigger. *This would give rise to one possibility that all the supermassive black holes would merge into each other, as the last stage, to form only one single ultra-supermassive black hole, so massive that it would comprise all the matter of the universe. Thus, all the matter of the entire universe would accumulate in one small point. But what would be its consequences? Would this be the end of the universe? Or, alternatively, creation of immense pressure within the interior of such a supermassive black hole and simultaneously, due to concentration of all the kinetic energy at one small point, the said ultra-supermassive black hole would explode because it won't be able to handle the combined effect of the extreme pressure and centrifugal force so produced? This might result in an explosion similar to the "big-bang". If such an explosion could happen, then this might result in the creation of a new generation of the universe. This is probably the game of nature; the cycle of creation and destruction might be eternal and it might continue forever.*

On the basis of above prediction it could be said that even after the end of the universe, if at all it so happens, the vast void in which it was born, would not be destroyed, that is, the space would continue to exist; neither the space was born with the universe and nor would it end with the universe. And if the universe would reborn in the future, then time would also not end with the death of the present generation of the universe. Space and time, both, are non-materialistic entities which are immortal, totally free from the cycles of the births and deaths.

17: THE GREATEST MIRACLE-
ORIGIN AND EVOLUTION OF THE LIFE

Perhaps the most important question, out of all the unanswered primitive questions, is "what is life, and how did it come to existence?" Knowledge of biology, microbiology and genetics, etc. appears to be essentially required to find out the answer to this question. I, however, don't have any knowledge of these subjects. On the basis of the very limited information that I could gather from different sources, I am, in spite of my limited knowledge, trying to give below my own version of the answer, which is based partially on facts and partially on pure speculations.

It's a common belief among the human beings that the life and death, both, are controlled by the God; nature or the universe doesn't play any role in these matters. Of course, this might be the God's work indirectly, but the chemicals that are the building blocks of life, were created at the time of the deaths of different stars, which is a natural phenomenon. The nature, therefore, plays a direct role in the creation of life. It is also a common belief that *spirits*, or *souls*, are the base of life, which neither take births, and nor they ever die. *If this belief is true, then the number of living beings in this world should always be limited to the original population of the primitive living beings, or more accurately, equal to the total number of their spirits*. On the other hand, the total number of human beings alone has multiplied by billions of times when compared to the original population of those who were born at the time of inception of the human species. *In case, the total number of microorganisms and all other kinds of living beings is also considered, then it would be clear that the total number of souls, after creation of the life, has grown from zero to infinite in number. This fact raises a question "do the souls also multiply?"*

Microbes generally, reproduce by a process known as cell division, in which the parent cell first expands and then divides into two new living units of the same kind. This means that multiple creatures or more accurately multiple souls are created from a single soul. They, by cell division, multiply thousands fold within a very small time period. Besides microbes, there are some other creatures (amoeba) that do not die - even if their bodies are cut into several pieces, instead, each of such pieces grows into an independent body of the same creature. Everybody might be aware that several living copies of the same plant could be created by cloning; each, of them, lives independently. All these examples, in which a single living body is multiplied into several living individuals of the same kinds, point to the question, *"how a single soul could give life to all such living copies?" This question indicates that spirits might also take births with the newborn babies*; this fact, in turn, suggests that souls too, possibly, die after outliving their lives. Under this scenario, we cannot say that *spirits* are definitely free from aging, or the compulsion to die; probably they are neither immortal nor divine. *The fact that the souls might also take births, suggests a possibility that the life might have originated as a normal phenomenon of the nature, without being dependent on the souls.*

Probably, living bodies are merely electrochemical machines which are made up of elements like carbon, nitrogen, oxygen, hydrogen, silicon, iron, potassium, phosphorus, etc. and their different compounds. These machines are actually collection, rather a coalition of individual living cells; all such machines carry out their activities by electrical-signals. The living bodies differ from the man-made machines in the sense that living bodies are capable to generate their own electrical signals to fulfill their different needs; these signals are generated by these machines themselves, in their respective brains. Another point that is important is "in case of death, all the elements, which constitute the living body, don't undergo any change; only their brains cease to generate electrical signals." This clearly means that death is merely a failure of the brain, or in other words, *failure of the brain to produce required electric signals, results in death.* Even the death of the brain does not cause the entire body to die at once. *Death is, in fact, a slow and gradual process; different living cells (which might be several billions in number) die slowly and independent of each other, due to lack of oxygen and food. In fact a single body dies manifold deaths. Moreover, the old cells of the living- beings die regularly after completing their lives, and new cells are generated to replace the dead ones. Does this means that every individual cell of a body is a separate and independent soul? Or alternatively, can innumerable souls live simultaneously in one single body at the same time?* This being impossible, the very existence of the souls becomes questionable, rather unnecessary. *However, this fact fails to clarify that "what is the difference between the living and dead bodies?"* Moreover, the question *"how the life, in absence of souls, is infused in the collection of inanimate chemicals, "* makes the matter more complicated. These questions can confuse even wise of the wisest man; this fact indicates that *in case the souls do exist, then they must be far-different from our existing conception.*

Some of the apparent common features in the different kinds of living beings suggest that there might have been a creator who designed all of them. In case it is so, then at least following three possibilities might exist.

1) The creator, depending on his wishes, could have made the environment favorable and produced his best creation in the very first instant; nothing could compel him to go slow.

2) The designer was bound to abide by his own laws, that is, the laws of nature; he didn't want to take any freedom.

3) Alternatively, life might have evolved all by itself as a natural phenomenon. Since every particle is packed with intrinsic energy in the form of electric charge, the Nature, in totality, has ultimate powers; depending upon different environmental conditions, the Nature designed different life forms that were best suited for different environmental conditions.

It is evident from different fossils that the life didn't originate all of a sudden, like a stupefying miracle; it was instead a very slow and gradual process. This fact appears to be against the first alternate. However, aside from various common features in the living beings, everything in the universe follows a definite system. Nobody knows or understands that exactly what the mystery behind this orderliness is? However, as we have learned up till now that everything in the world is governed by the four fundamental forces of the nature. This fact raises an important question, answer to which seems to be beyond the capacity of the mankind; the question is, *"where from such a huge quantity of matter and energy did come into the existence, and how the properties of all the natural-forces were decided?"*

The oldest fossils have revealed that life did evolve after about 1 to 1½ billion years after creation of the earth. At that time, most hostile environmental conditions did prevail on the earth. That particular environment probably suited most, to the primitive life. Later on, those creatures that couldn't adapt to the subsequent changes in the environment, couldn't survive, and were abolished. This fact indicates that gradually changing conditions decided that which life-form would originate and flourish in what time and under what conditions.

It is difficult to understand how life would have originated from the lifeless chemicals, until and unless we find out that under what unfriendly and most difficult conditions can the life survive. Apart from the primitive ages, certain lifeforms, in the present era too, flourish even under the conditions which are thought to be most adverse rather fatal for the other life-forms that we normally see all around.

It is a common belief that oxygen and mild temperature, etc., are must for the thriving of life, and that the life is based on the energy we receive from the sun, and also that it is impossible for the life to survive in the absence of oxygen, water and temperature within a favorable range, etc. Contrary to this belief, some microbes found on the earth, can easily flourish in total absence of oxygen and most stringent environment that is considered unfavorable and even fatal for the life. All the life forms, normally known to the common man, are sure to die instantaneously if they are put under such harsh environment. In the long past, I read that a colony of some unknown microbes was found at the South Pole, beneath a half-mile thick layer of snow, where neither the sunlight had ever reached nor fresh air was available. Moreover, the temperature, at that place, was as low as minus 60-70 degrees or even less. On the other hand, the microbes are also found to thrive in hot rocks, at the depths of about 900 feet below the earth's crust, in total absence of oxygen, and where the temperature, as high as twice of that of the boiling water, exists. In the year 1966, new types of microbes were found in the water of the Grand Prismatic Spring, in the Yellowstone National Park, North America. Water of the said spring is extremely acidic and almost boiling hot. Besides Yellowstone Park, some species or micro-organisms have been found to thrive in even more extreme conditions found in the "Mono Lake" and geothermal area of mount Lassen (both in California). Microbes also thrive in Soda Lakes of Kenya and California. Similarly microbes also flourish in some lakes of very hot and hyper-saline or alkaline water found in volcanic areas of Iceland, New Zealand, Italy, the Kamchatka Peninsula of Russia, and also in South America. Highly acidic water of the River Rio Tinto (red river), of Spain, provides home to another kind of life. All such microbes, which thrive in the most extreme conditions, are known as "Extremophiles." Apart from extremophiles, extremely tiny creatures known as "Tardigrades", which have limbs similar to legs and hands, are also capable to survive most adverse conditions; they can survive extremely high and low temperatures, live without food and water for several years and even survive the absolute vacuum of the interstellar space, too.

One of the most primitive forms of the extremophiles, known as "Archaea," is found in the Atacama Desert of Northern Chile, which is the driest place on the earth. This microbe is said to eke out its living by chemo-synthesis of poisonous volcanic fumes containing Di-methyl-sulfide and

Carbon-mono-oxide. Similarly, some life forms are also found in the seabed, at the depth of about 2-3 kilometers below the sea-surface, where sunlight could never reach, moreover, temperature as high as 400 to 700°F is produced at some of these places due to volcanic activities. Creatures like Pompeii worm, and the microbes that live in hot alkaline water at the seabed, thrive on the poisonous chemicals like hydrogen sulfide, methane, hydrogen and carbon-di-oxide, etc. which are emitted through active hydrothermal vents. Microbes have been found even at the depth of 11 kilometers too, where pressure, capable to crush even an ordinary submarine, is produced; only specially designed submarines can survive such pressure. Recently a new kind of microbe was discovered that can eke out its living, by eating poisonous substance like Arsenic. Yet another microbe that lives in very deep gold and platinum mines of South Africa, thrives on the energy that is released by radioactive decay of old rocks.

Vast diversities in the conditions, under which extremophiles are found, and also in the food on which they thrive, suggests that an environmental condition, which might be adverse to us, supports any metabolic process, i.e., a process that provides energy to any form of life by splitting any complex molecule, to support its living, then that particular kind of microbe might evolve under that particular environment. In case the food, i.e., the chemicals that support metabolic process, become scarce, or any change in the environment ceases to support any such process, then that microbe would either die or go to sleep; energy is essentially required to sustain all kinds of life, and their activities. However, microorganisms are far more stubborn and unyielding than what we could imagine. Sometime back I read a news article that a bacterium was found in Alaska, which was completely frozen since last 32,000 years, and it, in spite of being completely covered by ice for such a long period of time, was alive; it became active after the ice melted. Microbes can survive, or even flourish, in impossible looking circumstances. Some of the microbes can survive without food and complete absence of water, for a very long period, and even tolerate massive doses of radiations up to 3000 times as high to kill a human being; they can even repair major damages to their DNA. Based on this fact, some scientists believe that life might have arrived on the earth through meteors, but no proof to support this belief is available. *If the life could have developed elsewhere, then there is no reason why it shouldn't have started independently on the earth too.*

Several scientists, since 1920 or even earlier, much before the discovery of the extremophiles, have been systematically studying the enigma of the origin and evolution of life. *In the year 1924, Oparin suggested that Oxygen-free or reducing atmosphere might have supported biochemical origin of life, and in 1929, Haldane too, proposed a similar idea independently. Later on, in 1952-53, Stanly Miller and Harold Urey, based on above idea, simulated the conditions of the Early- Earth, to test the chemical origin of life.* They heated the mixture of Methane, Ammonia, Carbon-di-oxide and water, to boiling temperature, and continually passed electrical spark through this mixture for few days. In this experiment about 20-25 types of amino acids, which are found in various proteins, were produced within a short period of about 2 weeks. However, nucleic acids could not be produced in this experiment, probably much longer time period is required for this purpose. In the beginning, complex molecules of the kind of Ribo Nucleic Acids (RNA) and Deoxyribo Nucleic Acids (DNA) would have formed in the Nature by the series of chemical reactions that would have continued for millions of years. As a result, the basic building-blocks of life, such as simple sugars, that is, the most basic hydrocarbons (monosaccharides) were formed by carbon and water, or more precisely, by carbon, hydrogen and oxygen. On the other hand, different *amino acids*, i.e., the building blocks of proteins, *glycerol* (the building block of fats) and different *nucleotides* (constituents of nucleic acids) might have formed separately.

Almost everybody might have heard the terms like "DNA," "RNA," "genes" and "chromosomes," etc. RNA (Ribo Nucleic Acid) and DNA, that is, "Deoxy-Ribo-Nucleic Acid", both are different kinds of complex molecules of nucleic acids, in which different kinds of nucleotides are attached to each other in different sequences. Both RNA and DNA are the basic and most primitive units of life; the DNA, which is found within nucleus of different cells, is capable of self-replicating, whereas, RNA (Ribo nucleic acid) is not. RNA can reproduce only in one condition, when it enters within a living cell; in this process it breaks the DNA of that cell and kills it. This means that the system of "hunter (parasite) and his pray" begun immediately with the beginning of life. Thenceforth, those who were not capable to fulfil their needs, started to snatch away the rights of others – even their lives too.

DNAs are the carriers of all the information that decide that how the next generation would look like and support their living. DNAs of different creatures differ from each other. The DNA of the simple creatures may carry very few instructions, whereas the DNA of complex and more developed animals may carry hundreds to thousands of instructions. Key to the information transfer lies in the molecular structure of the DNA that is a special arrangement, or pattern, made of four different kinds of the nucleotides. Each nucleotide consists of a kind of sugar, which is known as either *Ribose* or *Deoxyribose*;

these sugars are bound on one side to a **phosphate group,** and on the other side to a **nitrogenous base**.

A nitrogenous base (constituent of DNA) is an organic molecule containing one Nitrogen atom, which has the property of the base*. These bases are of 5 types those are "adenine" (A), "cytosine" (C), "guanine" (G), "thymine" (T) and "uracil" (U); these are known as nucleotides. DNA is made of Deoxy-Ribose sugar and four nucleotides A, G, C and T. The RNA molecule differs from DNA in the sense that the Ribose molecule, in RNA, replaces Deoxy-Ribose, and 'U' (uracil) replaces the nucleotide 'T' (thymine). Genetic information in DNA is stored in the form of different sequences or combinations of these 4 nucleotides, that is, the way covalent bonds are developed between phosphate group and two hydrocarbons comprising 5 carbon rings; such bonds are known as phospho-di-ester bonds. Enumerable possible combinations can be formed from the aforesaid 4 nucleotides (A, C, G & T) to form different strands within any DNA. Different pieces or strands of this chain of nucleotide bases that contains codes for producing a specific protein are called *genes, and a set of genes is called chromosome.* Chromosomes are found in the nuclei of both animal and plant cells. They are made of protein and one molecule of DNA. During the process of cell division the chromosomes ensure that the said nucleotides "A," "C," "G" and "T," always bind each other, *in a particular sequence so that the DNA is accurately replicated. It is this sequence that creates its own copy. The chromosomes are responsible for containing the instructions that make the offspring unique while still carrying traits from the parent.* Any alteration in any such sequence may result in some change in the next generation. Such changes are known as *"mutation."*

Since 1990 onward, scientists have been trying to synthesize complex molecules like Genes, RNA and DNA, etc., by joining their different constituents in different sequences. Time to time, news is received from here and there that scientists have even achieved some success in this work. During 2008 and 2010, I read the news that some scientists have achieved success in creating some structures similar to RNA of some virus; they have also created synthetic DNA or proto-cell like structures, which are though not living creatures, but are capable to make their own replica. *Looking at the efforts being made in these lines, specialists of this field are confident that synthetic life would probably be created in the next 10 years or so, i.e., the puzzle of*

---

* Bases are substances that, in aqueous solution, produce alkaline solutions that neutralize acids.

life would be solved very soon. Looking into these possibilities, it could be concluded that when even the mankind is on the verge of creating artificial life, then this work would have been easy for the nature too. However, the nature would have had to wait for the right time, under the gradually changing environmental conditions.

Scientists also observed in the year 2011, that the drops of oil (nitrobenzene) can perform many acts like living cells; these droplets can move through water at their will, can sense their fuel and absorb it from the surroundings. This fact indicates that the chemical reactions, which continued over very long time-periods, might have created the primitive life.

In order to understand that "how the spark of life was ignited," a broad outline of the environment that existed on the earth, at the time of its birth, and the changes that took place subsequently, is given below:

It is believed that around 5-6 billion years in the past, our sun was created out of the gas cover and the debris ejected by a dying star of probably the second-generation. Thereafter, Earth was also created approximately 4.7 billion years in the past, or a little earlier, along with other planets of the solar system. Initially, all the inner planets in the solar system were made of molten rocks and metals. Scientists have envisaged that these newborn planets lacked in the elements needed for creation of the life. However, different chemicals and water, in the form of stardust and ice, etc. were available in abundance at the furthest edges of the solar system, in the form of comets, asteroids and enumerable meteors. It's understood that conditions prevailing at that time were very violent and hostile. *The total number of the planets formed at that time, would have been far-more than what we see today. Total count of the planets would have been around a couple of hundreds or even more.* Due to this reason, the distances between these celestial bodies would have been much smaller than what exists today among the present day planets. In that era, the orbits of the different planets might have intercepted each other. This might have resulted in occasional collisions between most of them. Great upheaval was going on everywhere; planets, after such collisions, either merged into each other, or shattered into pieces. At that time the powerful gravitational force of the giant gas-planets, like Jupiter and Saturn, would have diverted the paths of different comets and asteroids, etc., toward the inner planets. As a result, a very heavy shower of comets and asteroids would have hit the earth and other planets. *Perhaps, this was the way in which the raw materials of life and water reached the earth and other planets. Alternatively, since all the planets, asteroids and comets, etc., were created out of the same gas-cloud, and by a similar process, therefore, the raw material of life should have been present on all the planets, since their inception.* But since the favorable conditions in that era didn't exist anywhere, life couldn't immediately originate on the earth, or any other planet. *Seeds of life would have been produced much later, when conditions became favorable to, at least, some primitive kinds of life.*

As the time passed on, the planets that could survive that upheaval, would have adopted stable orbits; other environmental conditions also started to change slowly. The Earth, in due course of time, cooled down a little due to which a thin crust would have developed over the molten lava. During that era, the inner heat of the earth would have created thousands of active volcanoes everywhere. Although shower of numerous comets might have brought the bulk quantity of water on the primitive Earth, active volcanoes would also have been emitting large quantities of water vapor. Besides water vapor, volcanoes also would have continually emitted columns of volcanic ash, different gases and poisonous fumes, etc., which might have formed the first atmosphere of the earth. The atmosphere in that era was much different from what it is today; it was made up of poisonous volcanic gases like Sulfur-oxide, Hydrogen-sulfide, Carbon-mono-oxide, Methane, Carbon-di-oxide, Nitrogen and its different oxides, etc. and, of course, the water vapor. At that point in time, the "Ionosphere" that gives protection from the harmful radiation, had not yet formed. Therefore, powerful radiations would have been reaching the earth unobstructed. This radiation might have facilitated the formation of some chemicals that were impossible to form in a radiation-free environment. This could be understood by the process known as photosynthesis, which takes place only in the presence of light that is also a sort of radiation. Besides radiation, repeated discharge of lightening was also responsible for the production of different types of new chemicals such as different carbonates, hydro-oxides, oxides and nitrates, etc. At that point in time the chemicals, such as Arsenic, Phosphorous etc., and the different compounds of these compounds, were in abundance, but free Oxygen was almost absent. Creation of life and living beings, in apparently such an unfavorable condition, is a very complicated process. Even the nature too, might have to wait for the conditions to become favorable.

Condensation of water vapor in the upper layers of the atmosphere would have caused repeated rains, but the Earth's surface was so hot that drops of the rain would have evaporated even before reaching the earth's crest. This process must have helped to take away some of the atmospheric heat. Within next 200 to 300 million years or so, when the temperature of Earth's surface dropped down to about 100°C, a sea of boiling water would have formed, which covered almost the entire Earth's surface; continents might not have formed by that time. Volcanic gases and fumes, emitted by different active underwater volcanoes and thermal vents, would have dissolved in the water of that boiling sea. As a result, the entire seawater would have been converted into a soup or broth of the primitive chemicals. This broth was necessary for the origin of the life. On the other hand, ice caps might have formed over both of the geographic poles. At that point in time different types of acids were also produced by dissolving different oxides of phosphorus, sulfur, carbon and nitrogen, etc. in water, and on the other hand, elements like Sodium, Potassium, Calcium and Lithium, etc., would have been forming different alkalis by reacting with the water. This in turn would have produced some new chemicals. *Russian scientist, Alexander Oparin, envisaged in 1924, that the atmospheric oxygen prevents synthesis of certain organic compounds that are the necessary building blocks of life. This fact implies that the oxygen-free or reducing atmosphere formed in that era, would have helped synthesis of the building blocks of the life, especially when chemical activities of all the substances did increase a lot, due to high-temperature and excessive-radiation.*

As brought out earlier, a sea of boiling hot primitive soup was formed around 4.4 to 4.5 billion years in the past, which at both the poles would have become ice cold. This temperature difference would also have helped the formation of some different kinds of chemicals. Boiling water is essentially required for synthesis of some of the constituents of the DNA such as Cytosine, and also that of Uracil which is a constituent of RNA. Whereas, freezing temperature is necessary for the synthesis of Adenine and Guanine. This means that different constituents of different nucleic acids would have been formed at far-off distances from each other. However, the natural sea-currents formed in the oceans, probably due to the temperature difference, would have washed them off from their places of origin, due to which they could have come in contact with each other. As a result of the above phenomenon, and a long chain of different chemical reactions, pre-cell like structures of nonliving chemicals would have been created about 4.2 to 4.1 billion years ago or so, in the said boiling sea of the primitive soup.

DNA was not produced all of a sudden or by any miracle, instead, a long time period of several million years was required for this process. Different proteins, phosphates and nitrogenous compounds would have formed as a first step. Lack of oxygen would have facilitated the formation of different kinds of hydrocarbons and sugar molecules. In the beginning, a chain of different chemical reactions would have resulted in the formation of numerous simple molecules, which would have been based on carbon, hydrogen and nitrogen. Later on, different types of base chemicals, similar to the amino acids and nucleotides, would also have been formed. Numerous different permutations of chemical reactions would have resulted in the formation of different combinations of these building blocks. In the beginning, some nonliving chemicals that were precursor to living cells, such as different combinations of amino acids and hydrocarbons, etc., would probably, have formed around the underwater active hydrothermal vents. Subsequently, as a result of long chains of chemical reactions, different kinds of nucleotides that formed earlier, would have combined together to form different sequences, or chains like structures. In due course of time, molecules similar to nucleic acids but, simpler in constructions, would also have formed. Such chains would have combined together in numerous different permissible ways. As the time passed on, development of more complex molecules would have continued. Gradually some lifeless, pre-cell like molecules, and various structures resembling to the RNA would have been created, which would have been much simpler in construction in comparison to the RNAs and DNAs. How did life induce in those lifeless chemicals, is not known; this fact appears to be beyond the man's perception. ***The solution of the mystery of origin of life is probably hidden in the intrinsic properties of the matter-particles, which are given below:***

We know that matter, whether living or inanimate, consists of electrons orbiting the positively charged nucleus, that is, the flow of electrical energy is intrinsic to all kinds of matter - even including the living beings too. Electrons always move in a specific and prefixed order within different atoms or molecules, that is, every substance, in accordance with the nature's law, comprises a specific circuit of electricity that is typical to only that particular substance. When any chemical reaction takes place, then the electrons of the final produce share the orbits of more than one atomic nucleus, thereby electrons adopt different but definite prefixed and more complex paths. Regardless of the quantities of chemicals put together, molecules of different chemicals would always combine in a prefixed order that would be decided by the properties and molecular structure of those chemicals, and also the prevailing conditions of pressure and temperature, etc. During such reactions, the paths of electrons, in the different molecules of the end-product, would be automatically reorganized in a prefixed order. Each of the molecules of these chemicals, so formed, would also have a fixed order of the flow of the electrons that is specific to that particular chemical only. It is believed that when the electrons, orbiting any nucleus, undergo change of direction, then they emit different types of waves, therefore, specific paths of electrons might play an important role; every substance, probably for this reason, has its own unique spectrum.

We may get another clue to the riddle of life from the single-celled microorganisms. Scientists have observed that whenever a unicellular organism known as Amoeba, senses food, it reaches out to the food, engulfs it and eject out the waste. ***From this fact, it could be inferred that the body of all the single-celled microbes must be capable to perform all the functions of different limbs too, which are required for moving, eating (as the mouth), sensory organ like eyes or any other sensory organ to sense the availability of food, and of course, they act as the brain too.*** Every unicellular creature too, might possess similar abilities. Primitive microbes also should have the senses to find out food and favorable conditions for their living. This fact gives rise to a question that ***"how do they do this?"*** In order to understand the enigma that how the life would have infused in the lifeless chemicals, we need to understand how the microbes can sense the exact direction in which they have to move to find their food, rather, ***how their brains do function?***

We have already seen in the preceding paragraphs that the electrons, in different molecules, orbit their nuclei in different, but definite ways, each one of them, therefore, may emit a definite electromagnetic signal. Any DNA comprises numerous genes, all of which contain different, but definite sequences of nucleotides. Each gene probably produces definite electromagnetic signals. We also know that all the electromagnetic fields and radiations of different frequencies, affect the orbital paths of electrons orbiting in different molecules in a definite manner; intensities of these fields/radiations vary with distances. It, therefore, might be possible that the electromagnetic signals emitted by different substances or from the sources of different radiations, which come from any distant object, might affect the paths of the electrons within the different constituents of the genetic sequencing of the microorganisms. These signals might alter the paths of the electrons, or probably divide various orbitals into the hyperfine structures[*]; each signal might produce a definite reaction in accordance with the laws of the nature. Microorganisms, because of the above reason, might cognize these signals and react accordingly; they might have learned to use these alterations to differentiate between different substances, and make an accurate estimation of the directions and distances of these substances. Human-skin and eyes are also capable to sense such alterations caused by infrared radiations and light waves, etc. Our sensory organs are connected to the brain through a chain of interconnected nervous tissues or neurons. When we touch, hear or see any object, then an electrical impulse or

---

[*]   Kindly see Chaptar-7, under "Ticking speed of Time"

signal is generated in the first nerve-tissue. This signal produces some chemicals, called neurotransmitters, between two interconnected tissues, which in turn generate similar electrical signal within the next tissue. In this way the signal reaches the brain. *Single cells or microbes too, might be using a similar electrochemical process to transmit or decode various information; they may even communicate with each other by electrochemical signals.* This fact indicates that *a particular electromagnetic signal is capable to assemble particular chemicals found within the cytoplasm, that is, the fluid found inside the living cells, and then converts them into neurotransmitters.*

Now, based on the above inference, it may be imagined that under the gradually changing conditions, which prevailed at about 4 to 4.2 billion years in the past, different chemicals might have combined together due to continued chemical reactions, and thereby different inanimate sequences of nucleotides were formed. Since the electrons always orbit the nucleus of different atoms at some definite energy levels, therefore, the electric fields created by different constituents of such a sequence, would fluctuate with a definite frequency. Based on the capability of the electric signals to create Neuro-chemicals within the neurons, it could be imagined that different constituents of the said sequence of chemicals, would have produced a specific electric field. This electric field might have interacted with the electric fields of different chemicals dissolved in that hot primitive soup and thereby broken down a complex molecule into two or more simpler molecules. The energy waves, so released, might have synchronized with the field strength of the said sequence. Resonance (increase in amplitude of the wave due to frequency matching) created among these two frequencies might have intensified their strengths. The aforesaid field might have attracted identical constituents of the said sequence, from that hot primitive soup, and assembled them in that particular sequence to create exact but inanimate replicas of the parent molecule. What actually happened thereafter is beyond imagination; *probably at a particular environmental condition, the electrons of the different constituents of the said sequence, might occupy such energy levels that the waves emitted by them, would have bestowed the capability to gain continual energy by metabolizing the chemicals available in their near vicinity. This capability might have infused life in those inanimate replicas.* Consequently, primitive forms of life might have created later on, as a natural phenomenon, under some favorable environment. Different chemicals created during the deaths of stars are probably capable to create life in due course of time, only under a particular environmental condition. Such a possibility indicates that life can be created artificially under the appropriate environmental conditions, by arranging different chemicals in a correct sequence; both, ***appropriate conditions and particular sequence of nucleotides are perhaps equally important for the creation of life.***

The fossils of earliest Archaea and Cyanobacteria (blue-green algae) found so far, are though only about 3.5 to 3.8 billion years old, but life on the earth might have evolved a little earlier than that, that is, within first ½ billion years, or so, after the creation of the earth. ***The primitive environment that appears to be very harsh to us would have been the most favorable one for the different types of living beings that evolved under that particular environment.*** The life forms (Archaea), which developed at seabed, were able to generate energy for their living and multiplying, by breaking the molecules of Hydrogen-sulfide which were in abundance in that environment. During the same era, another kind of life, that is, the Cyanobacteria would have evolved on the surface of the sea, where sunshine and carbon-di-oxide would have supported life by photosynthesis, which is the process that breaks the molecules of Carbon-di-oxide into Carbon and Oxygen. Likewise, depending upon the acidity, alkalinity and different temperatures, etc. that prevail in different places, different kinds of life forms, which might have been well adapted to the environmental conditions of that particular place, would have evolved in that place, as if they were especially made for that particular environment, and to eat that particular food. In other words, if a particular kind of microscopic life form is capable to support its living in any specific environmental condition, by metabolizing any particular substance or food, then a microbe of that very kind would evolve in that particular environment. A particular environment and specific kind of food, both are necessary for the origin and evolution of any particular kind of the life-form.

Initially, under that primitive environment, food was probably available in abundance in the close vicinity to the colonies of newly evolved life forms. Therefore, mobility would not have been necessary for them. However, favorable conditions can't prevail forever at any place. Probably, closing down of a thermo-vent would have created scarcity of food, which might have forced the living beings to either change their ways of metabolism by eating dead or living ones, or develop ability to move toward the place where food was available. The law of Nature ***"Might is Right"*** came into force during such a calamity. The life forms that evolved during such an eventuality of acute scarcity of food were unable to generate energy for their living, supply line having been cut-off. They were forced to adapted to the new circumstances and started to eke out their living by snatching away food from others or even devouring them. Even as on today, almost all the lifeforms, excepting a few most primitive ones like Archean bacteria, Cyanobacteria and Plants etc., depend on enzymes driven from living ones or their dead bodies; they cannot generate energy from non-living chemicals like Carbon, Hydrogen, Nitrogen, Oxygen etc. Those who failed to change their food habits, or could not develop the ability to move, would have perished or become inactive. Microorganisms are capable to change themselves or mutate their genetic codes according to the needs, to enable them to cope up with almost any situation. This is evident from the fact that bacteria, within a very short period, are capable to develop resistance or immunity toward antibiotics.

Almost for the next one billion years, the environment continued to change, and the temperature continued to fall gradually. During this period, different microbes continued to produce "Oxygen" as a biogenic waste, which was probably harmful to the microbes that evolved in the Oxygen-free environment. As a result, some genes of some of the microbes would have become inactive, whereas, other genes mutated their codes to adapt to the changing conditions. Within another billion years or so, different life forms would have adapted themselves to survive the new conditions. Excess of oxygen probably brought such changes in some of the microbes that their offspring, after the division of the cells, couldn't move away from each other; instead, they got stuck up together. Probably multicellular creatures would have emerged-out due to such changes. Besides such mutation, different kind of microbes would have developed the skill of living together to avoid extinction under new conditions; such relations are known as symbiotic relations, in which both the partners depend on each other for their survival; they gather food independently from different sources, and they share the energy obtained from metabolizing different foods in different ways. In due course of time such a relationship would have paved the way for development of complex and improved life-forms.

A good number of examples of such relationships can be seen in the nature. One of the best examples, out of the lot, is that of hundreds or even thousands of species of gut bacteria living within the intestines and all over the bodies of different animals including ourselves. In such a relationship these gut bacteria get a safe home to live in; in addition they get regular supply of free food as a bonus. In return, they break down the food of the host into useful nutritious components and simple glucose, etc., which provides energy to the host to live. Gut bacteria also protect the host from harmful microbes; they also train his immune system to fight with the harmful microbes. Unbalance in the number of different types of these gust bacteria may cause insulin resistance, obesity, asthma in the host and even cancer too. Absence of proper type of gut bacteria may also affect our learning process, motor control, etc., and even our genes too, which eventually paves the way of mutation in our genes.

It is a general belief that the brain of any creature is the organ in-charge, but its functioning also depends on our gut flora. The brains of all the hosts, whether human or other animals, are directly connected to their stomach and intestines; brain sends signals to our guests, and the gut bacteria also communicate information to our brains. This is the reason that mental-stress affects our digestion system or the food we eat affects our mood and even the way of our thinking too.

The story doesn't end here; the host animal eats only that food which these guests can digest. Different body parts of the host are also shaped according to the food they need to eat. Carnivorous animals have different types of teeth and claws, whereas, cattle are very much different from them in body construction and also in their nature; all this is the magic of the electrochemical communication between the brains of the host and the guest gut-bacteria.

Although different types of gut bacteria live within the intestines of different species of animals, but different individuals of even the same specie don't have all the gut bacteria of the same type. Probably this is the reason that all the individuals are different from each other in nature and behavior.

It is manifest from the above description that the gut bacteria are the natural partners of different creatures including ourselves; they are essential for our living. Contradicting this fact, I have seen an advertisement on the net that suggests remedial action for getting rid of millions of harmful gut-bacteria living within our intestines. I understand that in the same lines some researchers/doctors are planning to develop different types of drugs that would target the suspected culprit. *I, somehow, feel that such a line of treatment might further increase the unbalance in the number of different types of gut bacteria; this may even result in serious side effects, because unbalance in the number of different types of these gust bacteria may cause insulin resistance, obesity, asthma, rheumatoid arthritis, ulcers, etc. in the host animal and even cancer too. This is evident from a very simple fact that antibiotics upset our digestive system. In view of this possibility, I feel that instead of killing the suspected gut-bacteria, efforts shall be made to restore the balance by way of gut-bacteria transplant or by food supplements rich in the type of gut-bacteria that are lacking in number.*

ARE WE ALONE IN THE UNIVERSE?

Normally it is believed that in the absence of favorable conditions, life doesn't exist elsewhere, except on the earth. However, three such places exist in our own Solar System where life can flourish in one or other form, one of them is "Europa" the moon of Jupiter, and remaining two are the moons of Saturn, which are "Titan" and "Enceladus." Water is in abundance and active volcanoes are present on Europa and Enceladus, on the other hand, some other forms of life based on liquid methane can flourish on Titan, because volcanic activities are going on, on this satellite too. The scientists are, therefore, hopeful that life in the form of microorganism might possibly flourish on these moons too. Of late, the scientists have also found several proofs that about 4 billion years in the past, water in the liquid form was available in plenty on the planet Mars. It also did have thick atmospheric air and a magnetosphere, which was capable to protect different life forms. Later on, due to some unknown reason, Mars lost its magnetic field and subsequently the atmospheric air was blown away by the solar winds. About 10,000 years in the past* liquid water too completely vanished from that planet. Both, Earth and Mars, had come into existence almost at the same time, but Mars, being much smaller in size, must have cooled down much earlier. Since similar environmental conditions might have prevailed in the beginning on both, Earth and Mars, there are strong possibilities that life might have evolved on Mars earlier than it did on the earth. This prediction is supported by a meteor known as "Martian Meteorite ALH 84001" that was found in December, 1984, in the South Pole. This meteor is believed to have dislodged from the Mars, about 4.5 billion years in the past, and fell on the earth some 13000 years ago. Researchers have found organic carbon compounds and also biogenic crystals of magnetite in this meteor, which many microbes and animals produce to detect Earth's magnetic polarity. The carbonaceous matter found in the said meteor has some resemblance with a microbe known as GFAJ-1, which was found in the Lake Mono. Thus, there is a very remote possibility that the aforesaid compounds, found in this Meteorite, might be the fossil remains of some microorganism. If some life forms were, in fact, developed on Mars, about 4.5 billion years in the past, then there is a remote possibility that their fossil-remains might be found on Mars, in the future. Even as of today, methane gas has been seen coming

---

*   Civilization suddenly evolved on the Earth at the same time period almost or a little earlier.

out of some of the areas of this planet. The presence of methane suggests that either some volcanic activities, or alternatively, some biogenic activities are still going on under the surface of the planet Mars.

Since extremophiles can originate and thrive in the most adverse conditions, it is most likely that at least some of them could still flourish under the conditions prevailing on the planet Mars or at least on the moons of Jupiter or Saturn, etc. Recently a new kind of microbe has been discovered in the upper layers of the atmosphere where the air is very thin and extremely cold; this variety of extremophiles could survive in the atmosphere of Mars. Similarly the microbes, found in different lakes of hyper-acidic or hyper-alkaline water, or those thrive around the hydro-vents found at the bottom of the sea, might also survive on the moons of Jupiter or Saturn. One of the most primitive forms of life, an "Archaea" found 2-3 meters below the surface of Atacama Desert, could probably also survive on Mars, 2-3 meter below its surface. NASA scientists had, some time back, discovered a microbe known as GFAJ-1, which thrives on Arsenic. This creature is entirely different from other varieties of microorganism found on the earth; Phosphorus in its DNA has been replaced by Arsenic. Although other scientists couldn't find any such microbe, anywhere, but in case such a creature does really exist, then this is a very important discovery. If life could also be made by the combination of entirely different chemicals, then such an entirely different life-form might thrive in the most unfriendly and unimaginable, rather alien environments, those might exist on exoplanets.

If life can prosper in our solar system, then there are all the chances that it could also evolve in other galaxies too, which are several hundred billions in number. Astronomers believe that at least 17% stars in our own galaxy, the Milky Way, possess their own planetary systems. In case life is thriving only on 1% of these planets - even then life, similar to that known to us, or in some other form, would be thriving on several hundred million planets in our own galaxy alone. This means that very strong possibility exists that we are not alone in this vast universe. No wonder, civilizations more advanced than us might be living on some of the exoplanets of - even our own Milky Way. The count of such planets, in the whole of the universe, might reach up to a few billions.

EPILOGUE

18: CLOSING REMARKS

In short, long back in the prehistoric ages, the curiosity of the mankind put him on a long journey of discoveries and inventions; the nature had, perhaps, made him for this purpose only. Defying some undeclared prohibitions that would have been ruling in those days, some curious and crazy people started their endeavor to find out the reasons behind various natural phenomena. Perhaps since then the paths of the religion and science diverged from each other. Science started its onward march staggeringly, on an endless path, with the help of the crutches of bare speculations and imaginations.

Mother Nature had provided food to all the living beings, but conferred them only that much of wisdom as was necessary for maintaining their existence. Mankind too, was not different from the others; it was not wise enough to unveil any mystery in its very first attempt. The journey of science was, therefore, not easy and smooth going; in fact it was a blind journey. In the absence of any means, guidance, or any definite strategy, they had to proceed with the help of speculations and imaginations only. In the beginning, the power of imagination of our ancestors was, unfortunately, very blunt; they didn't have any prior-knowledge of the laws of the nature. Non-directional efforts of the mankind led him to innumerable misconceptions, but somehow he muddled through. The mankind started its journey in the search of the "truth," but since the very beginning, he kept divagating and aberrating from one direction to the other; the "true knowledge" remained as elusive as it was before.

Afterward, the philosophers and scientists like Aristotle, Galileo and Newton, etc., gave new directions, in their own ways, to the growth of science. Scholars and scientists, of every era, had tried their level best to explain the unknown, but the theories made by them were soon either had to be revised or abandoned. Even the modern theories, which replaced the old ones, couldn't give clarifications to some of the problems. Search for a more comprehensive theory is, therefore, still going on. Science has thus reached to its present stature, swerving from one direction to the other.

It is true that during the last couple of hundreds of years, the science has surged ahead with a very fast pace. But, in view of different doubts raised in this book, we can't rule out the likelihood that at some unknown point

263

in time, we might have gone off-track. However, it is not easy to realize this fact, because it is not possible to ascertain that the knowledge we have earned during all these years, is absolutely pure in all respects. This doubt of mine is based on the question that *"have we acquired all the possible knowledge prior to formulating new theories in our effort to explore the unknown or to unveil the absolute truth?"* What I mean to stress upon is, *"whether our theories are based on complete facts and the true knowledge, or we have yet to discover some more facts that may give new direction to these theories?"* Or, alternatively, *"have we established correct root cause of the puzzling problems that we are trying to solve?"* If not, then how it could be ascertained that the theories developed in the recent past, are absolutely perfect in all respects, or any further improvement is not needed in these theories?

As was brought out in the story of "Two Professors" (chapter-1), it is necessary that the root cause of any puzzling problem should be established first, before making any effort to solve any of such problems. Similarly, the story of "Elephant and the Blind students," tells that incomplete knowledge, miss-estimations and wrong inputs, etc., might lead to misconceptions, wrong conclusions and even blind-faith. Of course, above conditions don't necessarily lead to wrong findings always. For example, about 2000 years ago, when the mankind didn't know anything about the internal structure of the atom or about charged particles - even then he learned to generate electricity by rubbing two dissimilar materials. Likewise, in 1660, in spite of our total ignorance about the electrons, we succeeded in making machines to generate static electricity. It could be inferred from these facts that at times inventions could be made by chance, for which absolute and pure knowledge is not at all necessary. However, proper knowledge is absolutely necessary to unveil the truth and thoroughly understand the true cause of any deep mystery; incomplete knowledge leads to misconceptions.

As we know, the truth is always hidden behind the multilayered veils, therefore, it is not necessary that the conclusions we have arrived at till to date, are absolutely correct and ultimate. We, therefore, should never be satisfied with the achievements we have made till to date, because deeper and unimaginable mysteries might still be waiting their turn to be unveiled, the matter might not be as simple as we had assumed; it might be far-more complicated than what we could even imagine. Our efforts should, therefore, go on to identify shortcomings in our theories, if any, so that such shortcomings could be sorted out and removed at the earliest.

In the above context, it may be seen that most of the important scientific theories of the modern era have grown almost 100 to 200 years old. Several new discoveries have been made after the formulation of these theories, due to which our knowledge has grown manifold, but no change has been made in these theories. We probably, believe firmly that these theories are absolutely perfect; we are, therefore, carrying-on our research work only on the basis of these theories, with full faith in them. The students of science, from the very beginning, inculcate these theories by heart, and with great respect; their minds are shaped according to these theories, they probably can't think on any other lines. Our scientists have spent their whole lives working with these theories without any doubt whatsoever, about the correctness of these theories. Nobody, perhaps, ever doubted that some deficit might exist in these theories, or these theories also need to be reviewed, modified or even abandoned. One thing could be noted very explicitly that our modern theories were developed on the basis of one or other unproved postulate. These theories were developed at different times, on the basis of the result obtained from a particular experiment or a particular school of thought. Therefore, it is possible that some shortcoming might have crept-in, into these theories at some unknown time, but somehow we could not take any notice of the same.

For an example, in 1864-65, when James Clerk Maxwell established the wave-nature of light, knowledge of the mankind was very limited; we had no clear idea about photons or any other subatomic particle. Therefore, at that point in time, it was, probably, not possible to establish the correct reason, if any such reason really does exist, other than what Maxwell established to explain the wave nature of light and a host of other radiations. This fact indicates that the "Wave Theory" was, probably, formulated on the basis of *incomplete-knowledge and partial-truth.* That might be the reason why we have no explanation of how *"radiated energy has properties of both, particles and waves."* During the subsequent period of 150 years, the knowledge bank of the mankind has increased manifold, but the aforesaid theory has not been modified even by a bit. The same is also true for all other theories which were developed subsequently. At that point in time, mankind had very limited knowledge, therefore, it can be said that in case any unidentified shortcoming exists in the wave-theory, due to lack of comprehensive knowledge in some particular field, then such shortcoming might have been carried over into the subsequent theories as well.

The common man, by nature, thinks that he simply has to blindly follow the thoughts of the renowned persons; he need not take any initiative of his own. Probably our social structure has shaped our thinking like this. Our thoughts are still governed, unknowingly, by some conceptions that were conceived by the prehistoric man. I feel that this propensity also prevails in the fields of science and philosophy, as well; since long past, the scientists of the new generations have been following the theories formed by their predecessors. It means that once we conceive a conception, then we take it for granted that the same is an ultimate truth. We normally avoid deviating from such concepts; probably our belief prevents us from doing so. This tendency is, however, detrimental in the path of the development.

For example, it is still believed on the basis of the ***Michelson and Morley's Experiment,*** which was performed as early as 1887, that *light maintains its normal speed even in the reference frame of the moving objects too, or, it doesn't have any relative speed when viewed from the moving objects, it moves past the moving objects with its normal speed; even relative to such moving objects too.* In order to justify this belief, it was also imagined that the time dilates and distance contract at the speed of light. Similarly the light from the most distant stars though takes an unimaginable time period, of 13.2 billions of years, to reach us, it is still believed in *Relativity* that time totally stops at the speed of the light. However, had the time really come to a standstill, then either light shouldn't have taken any time to reach us, or alternatively, light couldn't reach us, at all, because no event can happen in the frozen time, that is, nothing would be able to move in the still time. This fact indicates that the information of that instant, at which light was emitted from its source, travels with light, whereas, time doesn't stop even for the light; it continues to lapse at its normal rate. Accordingly, while light rays move past one end of the sun to its other end, that is, these rays cover a distance of about 1,500,000 kilometers, the sun, moving with the speed of 250 kilometers/second, also moves through a distance of almost 1250 kilometers. Light, in order to travel through this extra distance, would take an extra time of about 0.00416 seconds. The aforesaid fact not only defies the prevailing belief, it very clearly reveals that even at the speed of light neither the distances contract nor the time dilates. This fact could also have been inferred from the Sagnac's experiment, but this experiment too, is thought to be a proof of relativity. Now, in the existing era, we can measure time more accurately than it was possible in the year 1887, when Michelson-Morley's experiment was performed. We are, therefore, in a better position to find the truth out, whether *a unidirectional light beam (not a beam moving both ways) takes equal time to travel through equal distances in the direction of Earth's motion as well as in the direction opposite of it.* Even an ordinary man like me, can establish this fact by a very simple experiment, provided expensive equipment required to perform the experiment are sponsored by someone. If this could be done, then the humankind would be able to establish the fact whether the conventional belief is correct that light, in the reference frame of the moving objects, moves with its normal speed, or this conception being incorrect violates the ***reality***.

In fact, in order to counter the Newtonian concept of gravity, i.e., the apparent infinite speed of gravity, it was proposed in the *General Relativity theory* that gravitation is merely a consequence of the curvature of space-time. Although we don't have any direct proof to establish the fact that whether any fabric of space-time do really exist, we have accepted both of the aforesaid ideas, that is, the existence of the said fabric, and also that an apparent effect of the gravitational force is really produced by warping this fabric. However, the speeds of distant stars don't seem to follow this theory, because the measured rotational speeds of the stars rotating in any galaxy, doesn't match with the speed that is calculated by the *general relativity.* Based on this observation, we are trying to explore the existence of dark matter in the galactic halos, but so far we have not made any effort to review above concept of gravitation. In fact, if the theory of Relativity is correct, and the fabric of the space-time really does exist, then the coin should be able to orbit any massive object floating in the space, all by itself. Einstein's concept of gravitation could be verified very easily by sending the equipment as shown in Fig-4B, to a space station, and by rolling a coin along its curved surface. ***In case the coin fails to go round along the curved surface of the said equipment, then it would be proved that the concept of fabric of space-time is not correct.***

Both, quantum theory and string theory were devised in conformity to the Relativity Theory. Like Relativity, The Quantum Theory and The String are both are based on the continuum of Space-Time. Matter particles, internal construction of the atom and strings, etc., are based on the hypothesis of space-time. On the other hand, at many places of this book, it is logically proved that no such object like space-time does exist. In case, if space-time does not exist in reality, then all of these three theories would have to be reviewed.

Further, Quantum Theory envisages that pairs of positive and negative energies are created and destroyed in the vacuum, but no direct proof of the same is available. ***There is no explanation in this theory that 1) how the pairs of particles and antiparticles are created out of nothing. 2) How these particles move apart from each other against their mutual attraction.*** Both of these assumptions are against the laws of science. On the other hand, the fact that has not been given any importance in the quantum theory is, "both, the subatomic particles and celestial bodies orbit only the objects having more mass than their own." It is clear from this fact that mass must also have a direct role in the construction of the atoms too; however, the Standard Model of Particle Physics doesn't give much weightage to this fact.

Of course we have made numerous discoveries on the basis of our modern scientific theories, but we still don't have any answer to a few important questions. We have discovered that light has duel properties of waves and particles, but we don't know the reason behind this duality. Similarly, we don't know that how light-waves would vibrate while expanding spherically in three dimensions? *Ignoring the fact that subatomic particles, when observed by the most powerful microscopes, appear to be point like objects, and their photographs can also be taken, and furthermore, they cast shadows too - even then all sorts of particles, such as atoms and electrons, etc., are, since 1920 onward, thought to be matter waves, vibrating strings, or disturbances in some sort of energy field.* However, our theories are unable to explain that *1) if particles are disturbances in the energy fields, then wherefrom these energy fields are created? And 2) why particles behave like waves? 3) Why these particles or waves have property of spin?* All above facts indicate that our theories are not perfect; they need to be reviewed and improved further.

I have no idea that what our scientists think about such unresolved problems, or what actions they are planning to resolve them. However, in the absence of any new theory, they are probably dealing with such unresolved problems on the basis of the same theories which are in vogue. Some of the probable shortcomings, in these theories, have been brought out at different places in this book. In case, any of these theories really do have any shortcoming, even then nobody would, probably, trust a layman like me. The fact that the points brought forth in this book are totally against the widely accepted conventions or many of the existing theories, gives rise to a possibility that the specialist scientists, and the common men, both without any differentiation, might reject these points in a similar manner; the strength of this book is its weakness too. Any new thought that is inconsistent with the prevailing ideology, is normally totally disapproved. In 1912, Alfred Wegener's theory, of continental drift, was adjudged ridiculous and was rejected for the above reason. There are strong chances that this book might meet a similar fate, but this possibility cannot stop me to present my viewpoint – even if whole of the world makes a mockery of me; I am ready to pay this price also.

What I feel that the entire world respects the existing theories like "Bible," "Quran" or "Gita"; everybody has full faith that these theories are absolutely correct and perfect in all respects. Under this scenario, in spite of some inconspicuous proofs that have been found from time to time, we might have deliberately ignored some of the facts, which would have gone against our theories. As enthusiastic supporters of our theories, we interpret such findings in such a way that the correctness of the existing theories could anyhow be established; the facts going against these theories were deliberately negated. Till such time we will continue to give preference to our theories and their founders, over such unexplored truths, it would not be possible to unveil the deep mysteries. Our habits, to stick to our earlier achievements (?) and worship our heroes blindly, are the obstacles in the path of proper development of the science; we will have to get rid of these tendencies and examine the existing theories thoroughly, so that they could be revised if necessary. No conclusion should be deduced by neglecting even an apparently trivial fact, otherwise we would never be able to unveil the complete truth.

In spite of very grim chances of meeting public approval, I have written this book because I simply want to push general awareness among people, toward the probable shortcomings in our existing theories; this is my main purpose. Up till the time any doubt won't bother our heads that our modern scientific theories too, may have some flaws, nobody would try to examine them with the alternate angle discussed in this book. I earnestly want that in spite of the best efforts by the humankind to find faults, as pointed out by me, not even a slightest fault might be found in these theories. However, if any flaw really exists in any of these theories, then the same should be identified and eliminated at the earliest possible opportunity. If necessary, we should modify these theories, or discard old ones and formulate new theories, which might explain the puzzles remaining unresolved hitherto. The earlier this could be achieved, better it will be for the mankind and for the smooth development of the science too.

Although strong possibilities exist that the points brought forth in this book would be ignored in a likewise manner by the specialist and commoners both, but I am still hopeful, rather I have a firm belief that someday, may be after 100 years or so, someone would seriously examine these points with an open mind, without any prejudice or bias toward the existing theories and critically analyze the logic behind each point raised by me. I can't say what would be the outcome of any such scrutiny, if, at all, one is conducted, but I would have the satisfaction that in the capacity of a common man having no standing in any of the fields, I have done the best at my level to achieve this goal of spreading awareness toward the probable shortcomings in our existing theories. Anyhow, the chances of my success in achieving my goal, depends on the fact that how seriously you people, especially the curious younger lot, will take this book.